Art Bondage: The Black Book

BY
B T Richards

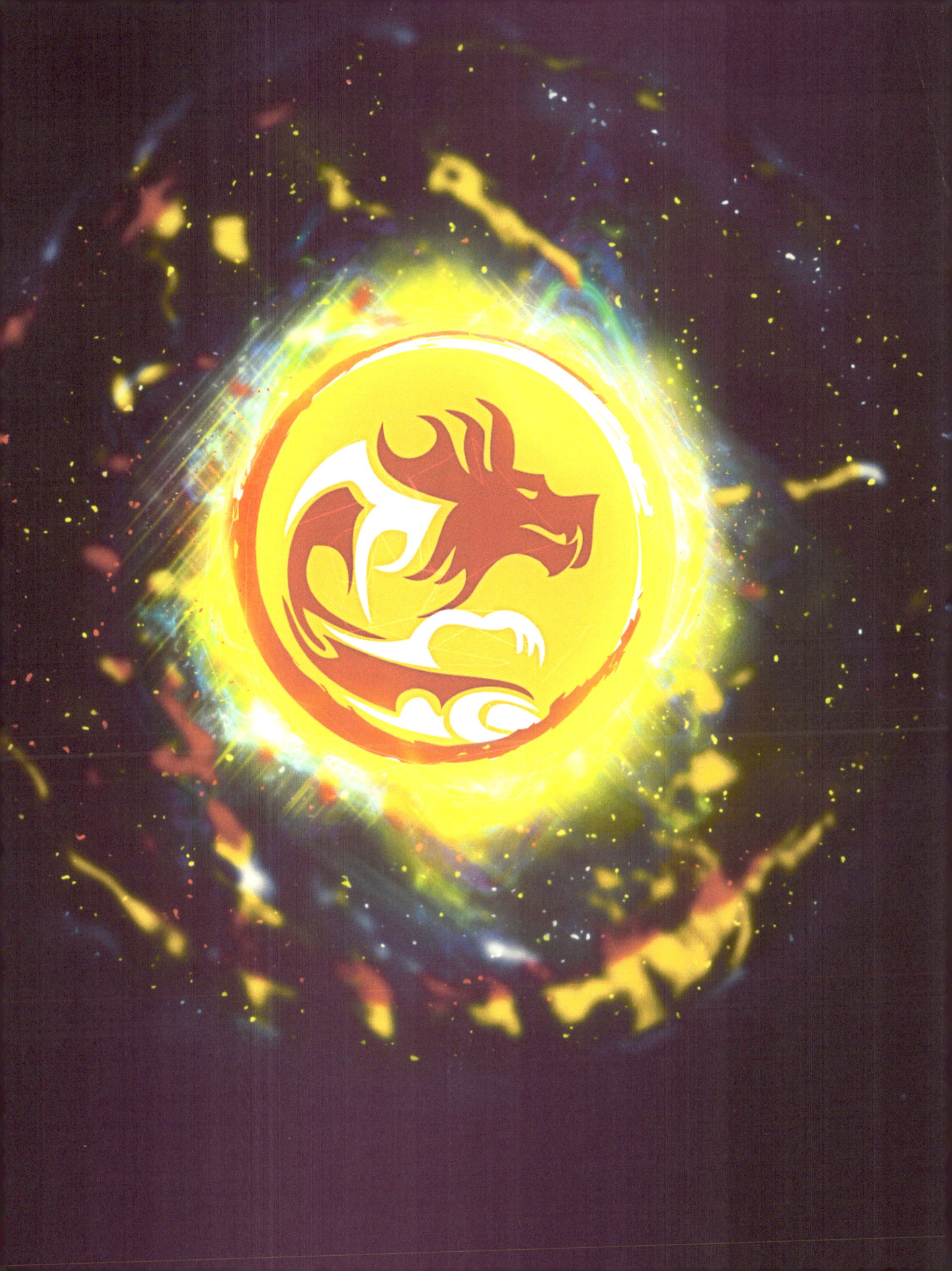

To my wife, my love and my partner in all things, Krystal
Without your support and trust this book would never have happened. I love you.
Always.

To the people who where with me and believed in me from the very beginning when I
had no idea what I was doing, Cheyenne and Meagan
Even when you didn't agree with the content of what I was shooting you still supported
me and helped in ways too numerous to even list. You are both my sisters from another
mister.

To every model listed in this book, I love each and every one of you for the trust and
support you providing during this project. Many of you had to step out of your comfort
zones to be in this book and I am profoundly grateful that you did this for me.

Finally,
To everyone at my largest bondage panel in April of 2016,
This book is all your fault. You just had to cheer me on.
Thank you!

Acknowledgments

There have been so many people that have helped with this that I felt just a dedication page wasn't enough. So here is where I am going to tell all the awesome people in my life just how awesome they are.

I'd like to start with my wife. You have no idea how many times she has let me practice design ideas, lighting changes, camera setups and just generally made herself available as a stand-in any time I needed it. The level of trust she has in me is incredible. There are not too many wives that would be okay with their husband tying up nude women for living. You should all be so lucky to have someone who loves and trusts you the way she loves and trusts me.

In the beginning, many many years ago, I had this wacky idea that I could become a photographer if I had the right equipment. Unfortunately my ideas where bigger than my bank account. Michael stepped in and believed in my idea and believed in me enough to fund my start up. Without his belief in me this all would have ended before it even started.

Family is important. One thing I have learned being on my own most of my life, is that family isn't about who is related to you. People who share no blood with you can often become your closest family members. Cheyenne is my sister from another mister. She was with me from day one and is with me to this day. She has always been my number one fan and has always been there in ways I'm not sure she even knows about. She was the first person I ever took a professional picture of. A real trooper, standing in 40 degree weather, covered in paint, wearing a little black dress. I offered to postpone the shoot but she wouldn't have it. That's her in a nutshell; never gives up, never backs down from a challenge. Her determination inspires me on a daily basis.

Some people come into your life and then leave. Others come into your life and you just know from the beginning they will be apart of your life forever. Meagan is the latter. I've watched her grow into a bright adorable young lady to an amazingly beautiful and driven woman. They say the eyes are the windows to the soul. Meagan's soul is pure and compassionate and cannot be hidden. It shines from her eyes with a light you cannot imagine. They say that you cannot stare a person in the eyes for more than 6 minutes without falling for that person. Meagan proves this is true.

To me trust is a big deal. It's one of the biggest compliments I can get when someone tells me they trust me. Kristen was one of the very first models to let me shoot fetish with. She came from many states away and trusted me with taking some very risqué pictures of her. Her personality was infectious and she showed me that shooting fetish was okay. That it was possible to make art out of what most people would consider trashy. She encouraged me to not be afraid to approach people with my ideas.

I moved from Kentucky to Tennessee and while I was still new to the area I got to shoot with the most attractive Elvira I've ever seen. Her name was Sydney. We just clicked right away. We went out to eat that first night and talked for hours and hours. You should have seen the looks people gave us; me and this beautiful Mistress of the Dark on my arm. She has always trusted me and has put herself in my care on more than one bondage adventure. She's a doll, for sure.

It's really hard when you actually want to know if what you are doing is any good. Strangers will probably nitpick and find something wrong with what you are doing for the sake of "constructive criticism". Friends will often tell you that you are amazing even if they don't think so. When you have classes and panels you don't even hear peoples opinions of what you do. Unless it's bad. The people who don't like are usually the only ones to speak up. Steven, Gena, Billy and Corrine where the first people who actually seemed sincere when they came to one of my panels and praised my skill afterwards. They may not even know it but they where the final piece of the puzzle that convinced me to actually do this book.

I had done many small classes before April of 2016. That month was special because it was the first time I was going to do a panel in front of a large crowd and I mean large. Not only was it a much larger group than I was used to but it was the very first time I was doing this with a group that wasn't entirely made up of people from the fetish community. A mixed crowd, what would they think? I was a bit nervous. Out of no where came this adorable girl. Emma, a perfect kitten. I don't know if she since my nervousness or not but she helped me get through that class with her magic fingers and offers to help in anyway she could. She's still the most adorable kitten you could ever meet.

From the fetish part of things I'd like to acknowledge the absolute creeps I met in the beginning. Before I even knew what the BDSM community was all about, because of you, I already knew what I DIDN'T want be. As we journey through life I feel that none of us really stop to think about the way negativity can change us in positive ways. You may not even recognize bad habits in yourself if you never see them in others.

I'd like to acknowledge everyone who has been brave enough to post the activities in the fetish world online. Where I started from, what little community there was, wasn't a good one. I learned more from people I chatted with on various forums. Thanks to people who aren't afraid to be out and open there is a wealth of knowledge out there to be absorbed. Thanks to them there is no reason why anyone can't safely learned all there is to know about BDSM.

Lastly, you. Yes you reading this right now. Thank you for supporting me!

Contents

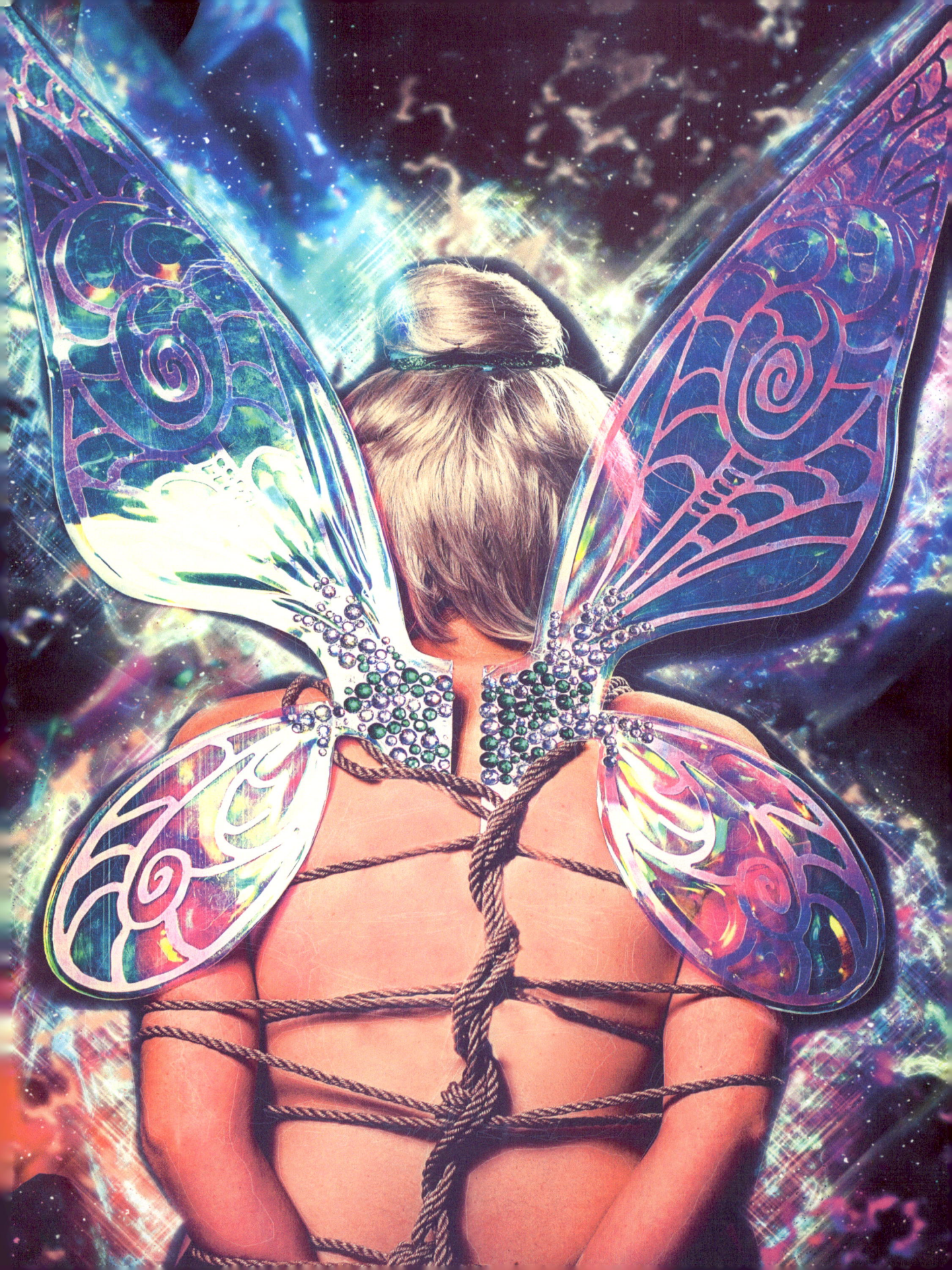

What is Bondage?

Technically bondage is any act in which a person is bound. Typically when you speak of bondage in a BDSM context the styles of Shibari and Kinbaku come to mind though.

Shibari vs Kinbaku. This is an argument you will hear over and over in the BDSM community. Which one is better? Where did they come from? Is there any difference in them? Even after 10 plus years in the community I still cannot claim to be an expert in this but I will tell you what I have learned over the years. Shibari is the term most people are familiar with. The main argument around this term is that it doesn't actually mean bondage. It means "the act of tying". You can use this term to mean tying up a package, tying some twine around a pot, or anything that involves tying with rope. Many bondage terms coming from Japan include the word "Shibari" but it is more like the use of "knot" in phrases like "Square Knot". However at this point, at least in the west, it has become synonymous with bondage and is perfectly acceptable to use.

Kinbaku means "Tightly Bind". Again here you'll notice that there is nothing in the definition that has anything to do with bondage in a fetish since. Those that favor the word Kinbaku like to say that it also means to be tied to someone emotionally. Referring to more intense emotional levels of bondage. There is another term that fits more closely to the idea of tying someone up for sexual and erotic purposes and that's Kinbaku-bi. It means "The beauty of tightly binding".

Either way they came from the practice of tying up prisoners in Japan called Hojojutsu. Different people came up with different ways to tie up a person in a way that would keep them restrained while not causing them any harm. Over time the style become more and more elaborate and then it started crossing over into peoples bedrooms. From there it traveled to the US where we have it as it is today. Now I know this doesn't give you a lot of detail. The reason is if you really want to know more about the history of bondage there are many much better resources out there. Please explore them. Learn all you can. You can know every term, every Japanese phrase out there and it won't make you any better at tying someone up. In the end, it doesn't matter what you call it. All that matters is that you enjoy yourself, that you are safe, and that you are happy with your results. Don't let anyone tell you that you are doing it wrong or that their way is the only right way. Your journey into the world of bondage should be as personal as any other art form. Learn what you can from others then make it your own.

Ropes and Bunnies and Macramé Oh my!

So where do you get started? A bit later in this book I'll cover resources on where you kind find out more information and where to purchase supplies. Here I'd like to talk about what to do after you've purchased your first set of rope.

You'll need to find someone who'd let you tie them up. The person you choose will really depend on your intent with the bondage. If your intent is sexual then it would need to be someone who is willing to be sexual with you. I know this seems obvious but I have seen people get excited about doing bondage and forget to tell the person they are tying up that they wanted to touch them in a sexual way. If your intent is to just practice then it broadens who you can ask. Anyone who can just stand there will work. They don't even have to remove their cloths for you to practice. So ask a friend, a neighbor, someone you met at your local gathering. If you are up front and honest with the person and make sure they know that you just want to practice and nothing more, you'll be surprised how many will say yes. Also if you are just practicing you can ask people of any gender because since it isn't sexual it shouldn't matter who you would be sexually attracted to. I highly encourage this actually. It lets you concentrate on your rope work and not get distracted by the person you are tying up.

Once you have practiced and you feel more confident you can move on into the art of bondage. The things you see in this book. If you've been to my class or panels you will have heard me say many times that none of this is as complicated as it looks. You master just a few ties and you're there. Many people will try to make it out as if this is something exceptionally difficult to do. That you have to learn under a Master. Some even say you need to travel all the way to Japan to learn about bondage. It really isn't that hard. Not to say those people aren't good at what they do and that they, and you, wouldn't benefit from learning from a Master. What I am saying is that you don't have to do that. You can have plenty of fun and make for some beautiful rope art from day one.

So you've found someone to tie up. There are many names people like to call the person getting tied up; bottom, submissive and my personal favorite, bunny. There is a little bit of a difference in these terms however. A bottom is generally anyone who is the person receiving what ever is happening. They aren't always submissive themselves. They can even be Doms who just want to experience something new. I always advocate a Dom experiencing something first hand before trying it on someone else so if they are doing this then that makes them the bottom for that particular moment.

A submissive is someone who identifies as the submissive person in BDSM relationship. This general means that they end up being the bottom in scenes but is not always the case. Finally, the bunny. To be honest I don't even remember the first time I heard someone refer to the bottom in a bondage scene as a bunny but it stuck with me. I really liked it. As you can tell from this book and if you've met me in class I don't get hung up on labels and terms. I've been doing this for a long time and I've found that no one is 100% any one thing. No Dom is 100% dominant. No sub is 100% submissive. That's perfectly okay. You don't have to be one or the other or any of the above. Be you. That's why I like bunny. It has no real meaning, it gives an easy way to refer to the person being tied up that is short and sweet. Also bunnies are cute and fierce. Have you owned a bunny? They can be sweet and nice but can also bite when they want, and bite hard. I feel that covers most anyone willing to be tied up. Cute and sweet but will bite you if you upset them. So don't upset them.

Why macramé? mac·ra·mé noun : "the art of knotting cord or string in patterns to make decorative articles." Honestly I feel this more closely describes the style of bondage I do even more so than Shibari or Kinbaku. It's also a great place to get ideas. If you decide you want to step into being artistic with your bondage and not just be able to tie someone to their bed you'll want to start getting ideas from places outside the fetish and erotic realm. Macramé for one. Celtic knot work, survival guides, maritime knots...even Boyscout manuals. Be as creative with your resources as you are with the final product. I draw inspiration from things around me all the time. You ever see those fancy flower pots with the intricate rope work done in twine around them? I've bought one just to take it apart and see how they did it. There is no lack of inspiration out there. Books, manuals, photos, even other bondage photographers and riggers. If you have a patient bunny you can even just wing it and try random patterns until you find one that you like. I've said this before and I'll say it many more times: All that matters is that you are safe and are having fun.

Safety

I keep bringing up safety but how do you be safe? Start with being prepared. Know the rope you are using, know any limitations your bunny has. These could be physical limitations such as injuries, sensitive areas, even fresh tattoos. Anything you, as the rigger, may want to avoid. You don't want to make anything worse. After all if you break your toys you can't play with them again. Your bunny can also have personal limits and these are just as important as physical limitations and you should respect those. Examples of these could be that maybe they don't want to be fully nude, or maybe they don't want to have any rope go between their legs. Not only are knowing these things important because you want to respect your bunny's limits but also because it may mean that you have to adjust what you had originally planned on doing.

Take care of your bunny. Make sure they are comfortable. Not too hot, not too cold. Have water for them to drink. Some of the sessions I have done last 2 to 5 hours. They may not even realize they haven't had anything to drink in the last 4 hours. Offer breaks. If they aren't used to staying on their feet for hours they may need to sit or have a soft mat to stand on. In my experience bunnies won't tell you when they are uncomfortable so it is up to you to keep an eye on them and watch their body language. If they are looking pale and you offer them something and they refuse, insist. Have it handy so you can be handing them that bottle of water even before they have finished saying they don't need it. Keep in mind that as the rigger you are probably dressed while your bunny may not be. Even if the room temperature is comfortable for you it may not be for your bunny. It is better that you are a little too warm or too cold than your bunny so make sure they are comfortable.

As the bunny there is just one real safety concern. Speak up! If you are uncomfortable for any reason, be it you're too cold, the rope is too tight, your thirsty or the rigger is being a creep then speak up. Say something. The sooner you say something the sooner the situation can be fixed. If you are letting someone you don't know tie you up check them out first. Bring a friend, ask around. Be sure you are safe and know what you are getting into.

Be prepared to handle emergencies. Have a safe way to remove the rope in a hurry. Do not use a knife. A knife could cut the bunny, especially in an emergency situation where you are in a hurry. Have a set of EMT shears on hand. They are cheap, just a few bucks and they will cut through just about anything without cutting the bunny. Have a first aid kit handy too. Lastly, if there is a real emergency, such as your bunny passes out and won't come to, call 911. Don't worry about being embarrassed or having to explain what was going on. The EMTs only want to help and trust me, they've seen it before. Even if you have some explaining to do, isn't a few minutes of your time worth the life of your bunny? If you have someone you tie up often and they have a medical condition then take it upon yourself to learn about it so you know what to do should it become a problem. A good example is if your regular bunny is diabetic do you know what to do if they go into hypoglycemic shock? Maybe they have seizures, do you know what to do should they have a seizure while they are tied up? Sit down and talk with them about it. Come up with a plan. Make sure you have everything you need to handle it within reach. Lastly communicate. Talk, ask questions. Keep making sure everything is okay and never just assume it is okay.

All the Ropes

There are many kinds of rope out there. Each has their own pros and cons. Here I try to go over the more popular options.

Hemp and Jute: These can be very rough in texture when you first get them. They have to be treated to get them comfortable to use. Although some people like it rough. This type of rope is very popular for several reasons. It has a good grip. Due to the texture of the rope it doesn't slide much. It tends to stay put, not only on your model but also on itself. Knots hold well and the rope is easy to work with. There isn't a lot of stretch in these ropes. That means that however tight the rope was when you tied is how tight it will stay. They both have a unique natural smell and hold oils (used for treating) well. You can dye them in many different colors and for those that are vegan it is an all natural fiber that is easy to obtain untreated so you know exactly what goes into it. Some of the downsides to this type of rope is that it is rough when you get it raw. It has to be treated which takes time and effort. When you use it there will be fibers that fall off. You will get fiber on you and your cloths.

Cotton: This has a bit more stretch and slips easier than Jute and Hemp but is sometimes easier to obtain and can be cheaper. Cotton tends to be significantly softer than Jute and Hemp and doesn't need to be treated. It comes in a large variety of sizes and can be found in different colors but white is the most common. If it is pure white then it may have been bleached which can irritate skin but isn't usually a problem. I think most everyone I know, myself included, started with cotton rope. One thing to keep in mind with cotton is that knots tend to shrink. Ever tie a knot in your shoe laces by accident? Remember how hard it was to get undone? Just be aware of what you are doing and if you are using cotton just keep an eye on your knots and be ready to cut them if needed.

Silk: We aren't talking the kind of silk that lingerie or silk sheets are generally made out of. This is raw silk and feels and looks very much like cotton. It's so close to the look and feel of cotton you have to be careful on who you buy it from as they could just sell you a cotton rope and you wouldn't know. Silk carries less friction than cotton and is overall, a higher quality rope. That also means it costs more. Can come in a variety of colors and can also be dyed. Depending on the diameter of the rope it can be a challenge to work with but the bunnies like it because it's nice and soft on their skin. Since it has less friction, less "teeth", it can slip and move so it can become a bit difficult the more of it you have in a single length.

Bamboo: Bamboo can be expensive but it has many good qualities. It gives you the benefits of natural fibers but it can be made to shine like synthetic. It has less grip than other natural fibers but carries antibacterial propriety so stands up to more uses with less cleaning. Like most other natural fibers this can be obtained in a variety of colors and if you can't find the color you like you can always dye it. Bamboo also has a unique smell that many people enjoy.

Synthetic: Many people will tell you to stay away from it. I fall into that same category. What they won't tell you is that we've all used it. Usually though, that's why we say to stay away from it. Now don't get me wrong. It does have some good qualities. For one, it's cheap and you can get it just about anywhere. There is a huge variety of lengths, colors and types. You can get it as thin as thread and thicker than your arm. There are a few reasons to stay away though. Synthetic isn't as durable as natural fibers. It breaks easier and more suddenly. While there are soft varieties, for example there is a synthetic hemp, these ropes tend to be stiffer and harder to use friction based ties with. If you have any sort of flame near by for your play, then don't use this rope. It will melt.

All that information is all things you can gather from other books and Google search. Let me tell you my personal experience with each kind:

Hemp and jute are my personal favorites. It's cheap and although it takes some work to get to a workable texture I enjoy it. I feel like when I am tying someone up with these ropes that it contains a part of me. The whole "blood, sweat and tears" feeling you get when you use a tool you hand crafted yourself. I also like that I know what is in it, what oils specifically. I like the smell it has. This natural grassy kind of smell that mixes well with the oil I like to use. Knots hold well but don't lock down so they are easy enough to undo if needed. You can dye it just about any color you want. It can b retreated as you use it, giving it lots of life. For the amount of rope I use this is a huge benefit, and if something happens to a piece if rope, like it gets something on it I can't get off it's easy enough to replace.

I've use both cotton and silk. Cotton was a great way to start out. It was easily obtainable. I think I bought my first rope meant for bondage from Wal-Mart actually. So please don't feel bad if it's all you have. I've had people come up to me before my hands on classes and ask me in an embarrassed way, if it was okay for them to use the cotton rope they had bought at the store. I always tell them that it's just fine, and it is. If that is what you have then use it. Silk is better of course but honestly, in my opinion, there isn't enough of a difference in silk vs. cotton to justify the difference in price so it becomes a personal choice. Maybe you feel the quality difference is worth it.

I haven't used bamboo personally though I've been at events where it was used and had a chance to gets hands on some of it. It has an interesting texture and feels very natural. It had a bit of a crackle to it and was a shiny. I'm sure with just like any thing else there are different qualities so I can't speak on what quality rope I had seen.

As I said before we've all used synthetic rope. I personally don't like it a will probably never use it again. It's just too stiff for my taste. I've seen some amazing work from people using these ropes that have removed the core of it so it lays flat and it looks really cool. Just not something I've had any luck with. I also just don't enjoy the look of synthetic rope as much as I like the look of natural fibers.

Treating Your Rope

There are as many ways to treat rope as there are types of rope. This is just one way to do it. What I have found works best for me. I sort of, combined a few different techniques after trying each one and not getting exactly the result I wanted.

When you get your rope tie knots in each end if you haven't already. If you bought it in bulk at a large length go ahead and cut it to length then tie knots in the end. This is to keep it from unraveling later. You can also go ahead and lash or whip the ends now if you like. If you don't know how it's easy and easy to find instructional videos online.

- If your rope is dyed you'll want to soak it in vinegar, salt and water. For each gallon of water add 1/4 cup salt and one cup white vinegar. Make sure the rope is fully submerged and let it soak for 24 hours. This will help to set the dye. Now this doesn't keep it from bleeding but what it does is helps the rope soak in more of the dye and helps lock in what's there. You can also get dye fixative that will work as well.
- After you have soaked the rope or if your rope wasn't dyed the next step is to boil the rope. This is for several reasons. First being that manufactured jute is treated with Jute Batching Oil. This is derived from crude oil and can be toxic. Boiling it with just a little bit of detergent will help get rid of this if present. This

will also help loosen the fibers. I boil mine, well more like simmer, for about an hour. You'll want to hang it to dry. Try to keep the rope under tension while it is drying. You can hang a weight from them to accomplish this.

- This next step is a step that I added. Many articles I read said to do this OR boil but it wasn't necessary to do both. I didn't like the result of I got from doing one or the other so I did both. Wash your ropes in your washing machine. I find it helps to uselaundry bags so the rope doesn't get hung around the center spool of your washer. If you have a washer that you can pull that out or one that doesn't have one you can just throw it in but using the bags also helps keep the rope from getting tangled. Was in cool water without soap. This does a few things; it rinses out anything left from boiling and "beats" the fabric. Loosening it and making it softer.

- Now toss it in your dryer. Be for warned this will fill your lint trap up quickly so if you are doing several batches make sure you are checking the trap.

- Once it's dry you'll need to scrap it. Find something with a hard edge, like a square fence post, and rub the full length of the rope against it. Like you're trying to saw the post in half with the rope.

- At this point you'll have a very rough rope. Now repeat these steps: Boil, dry, wash, dryer and scrap. I do this twice you can do it as much as you like until the rope feels better.

- Now to burn off the loose fibers. I've seen people do it with a candle but I personally use a small blowtorch. Works much faster and more thoroughly. You just have to be careful because it is very hot and can quickly burn your rope if you leave it in one place too long. I use brood sweeping motions to keep it moving. Kind of like painting with an air brush. This will produce smoke so probably best to do outside or take down your smoke detector. Just make sure you put the smoke detector back when you are done.

- After that I rinse out the soot in cold water and hang to dry.

- If the rope is still too rough just start from the beginning and repeat until you like it. Keep in mind, as you oil it and use it it will get softer so at this stage you'll want the rope to still be a little rough but close to what you want.

- Now to oil the rope. There are many kinds of oils you can use. I personally use Jojoba oil. It's cheap, doesn't go rancid, has a nice natural smell and it's hypoallergenic. You can use whatever oil you like just keep in mind that cooking oils tend to go bad. So probably steer away from vegetable oil, canola oil and the like. I'd also stay away from anything with a really strong smell. You may enjoy an over powering scent of patchouli oil but your bunnies may not. Use a clean cloth to rub the oil into the rope.

- Now bake the rope in the oven at 200 degrees for 2 hours. Warning: Depending on what oil you used it may smoke. It helps if you know the smoke point of the oil you are using. That's the temp at which the oil begins to smoke.   For example Jojoba smoke point is around 195 degrees. It is also a good idea to know what the flash point of your oil is. This is the point at which it will catch fire. Jojoba flash point is 295 degrees.
- Oil it again until you are satisfied with how it feels. As you use your rope you'll want to retreat in whole or in part as needed. The llonger you can go without retreating it the longer your rope will last so when you do have to do it only do exactly what you need. If it's feeling a little dry add a bit of oil. If it's getting frayed or "hairy" run a quick flame over it. If it ever gets so bad you think you have to start all over again it may just be easier to get a new peace.

A bit on length of rope. The standard that you'll find is 8-10 meters. These work out great most of the time but it is handy to have a few shorter peaces for tying hands and feet. If you are trying to save money and buy in bulk the longer the peace you buy the cheaper it is generally. So you'll save money by cutting your on lengths. As with all things, do what works best for you.

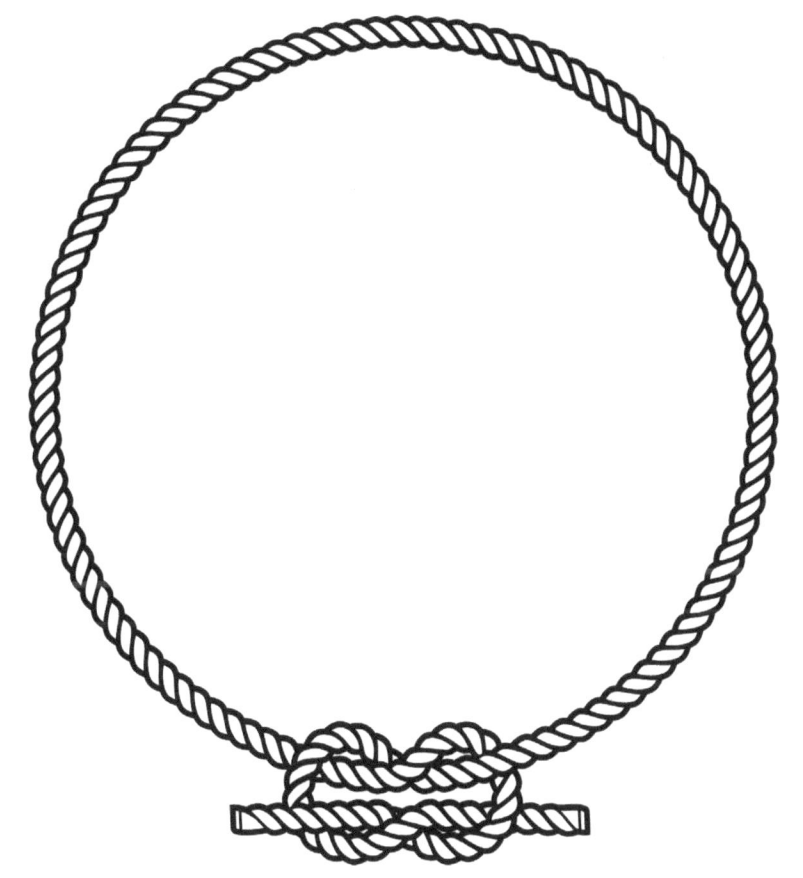

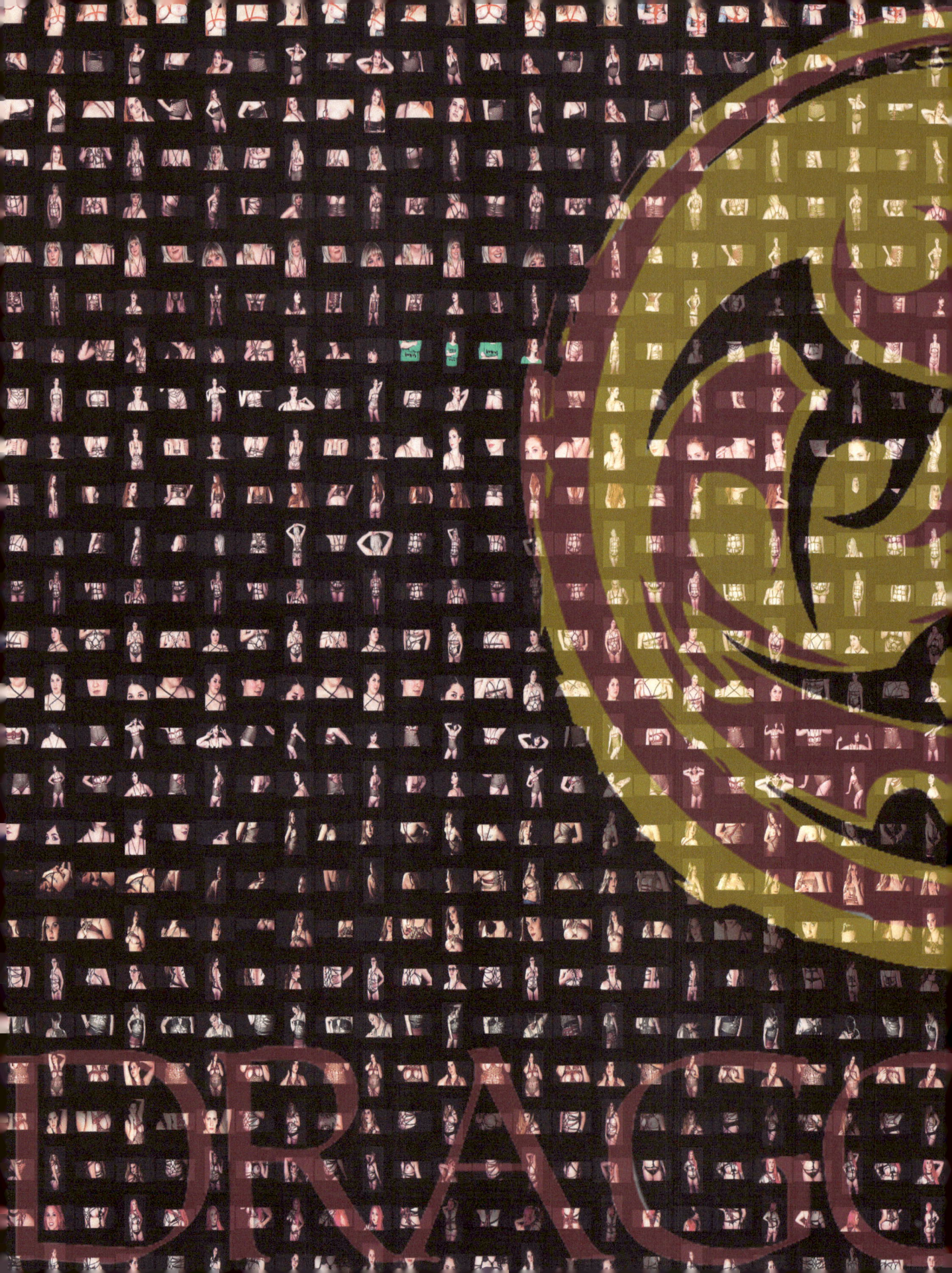

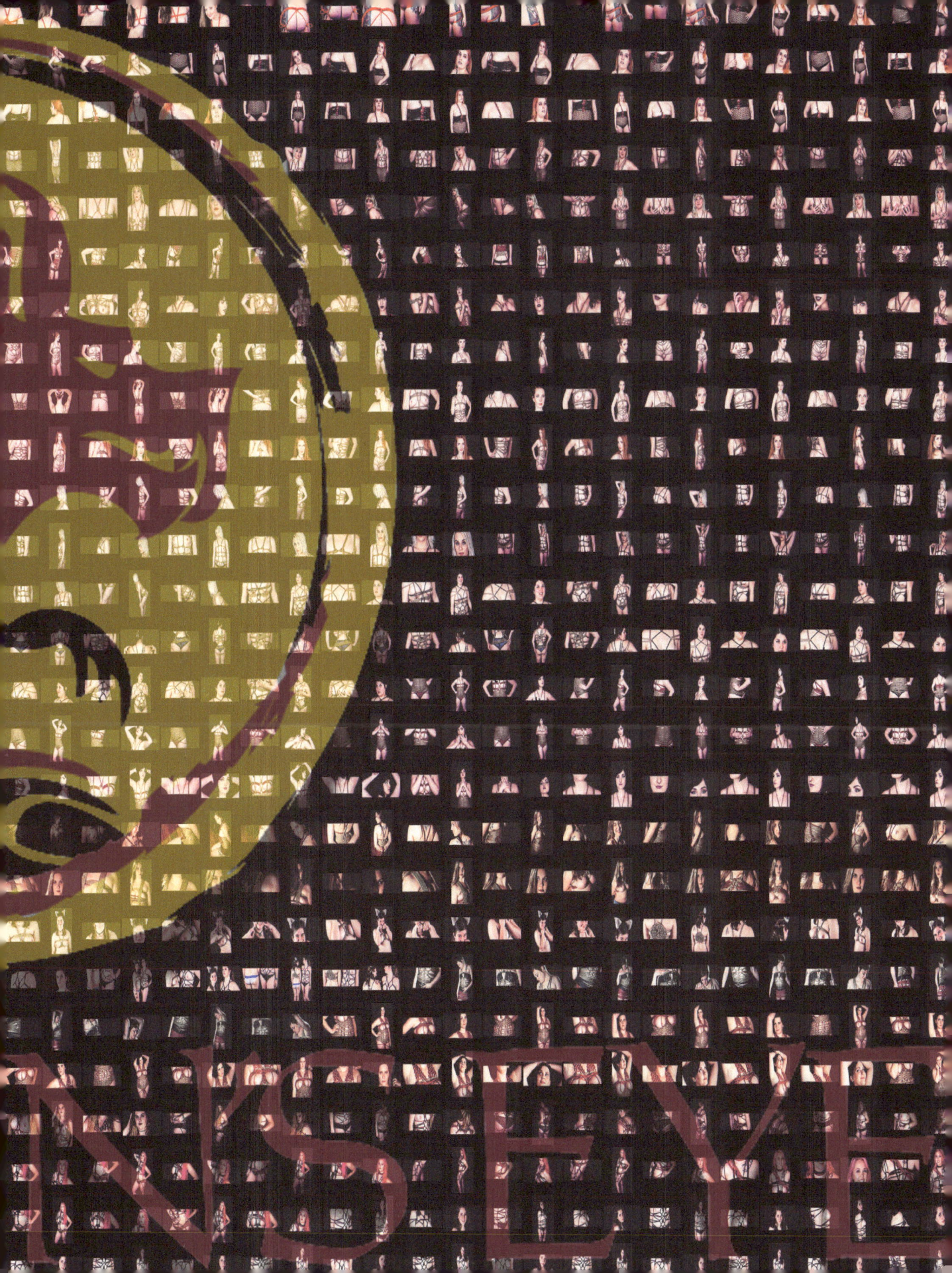

Emma & Dani

Sometimes the most fun happens in the moment. Both of these wonderful women where in one of my classes and where inspired to model on the spot, together!

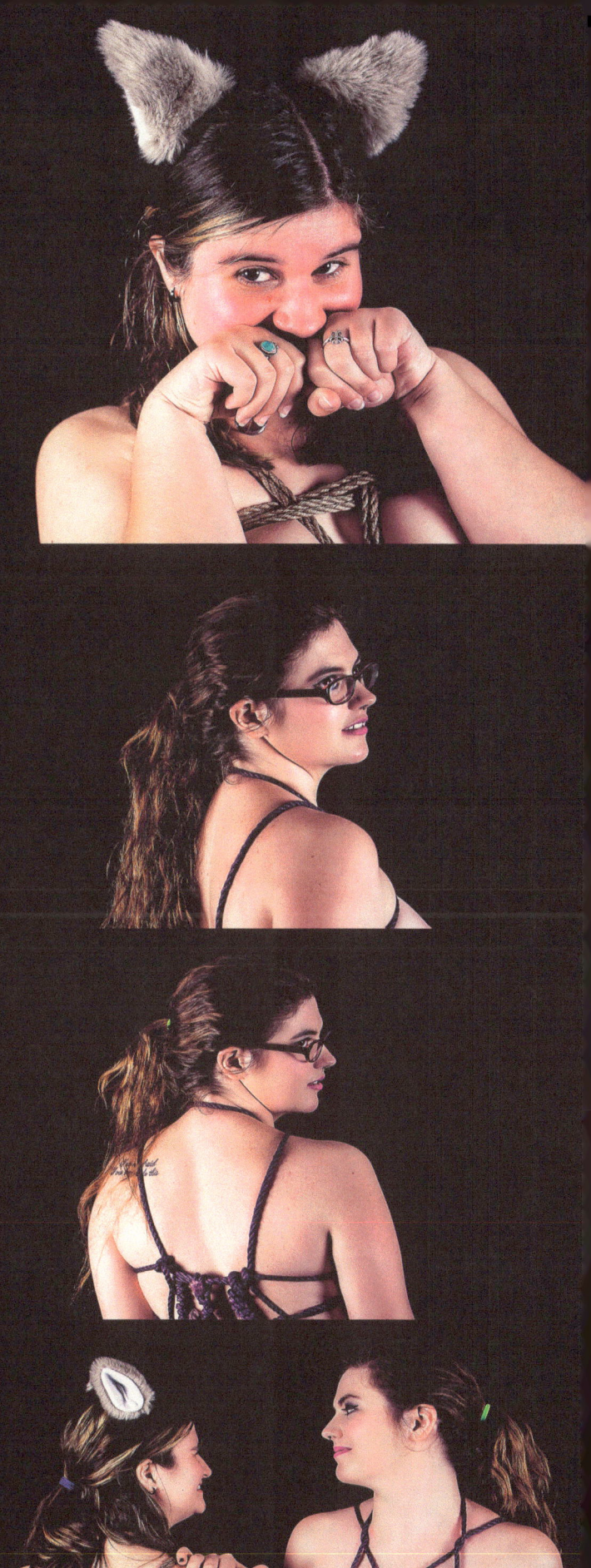

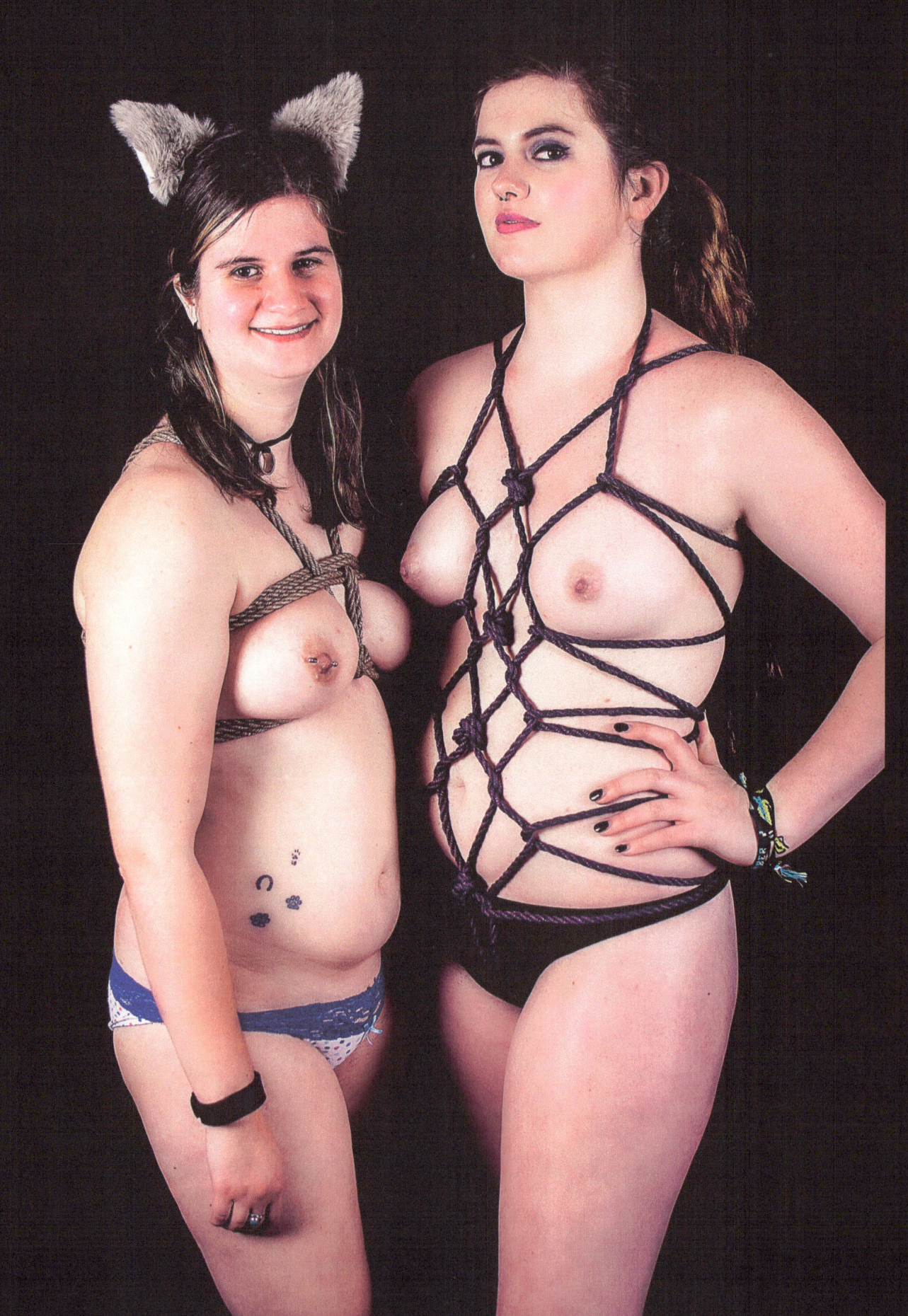

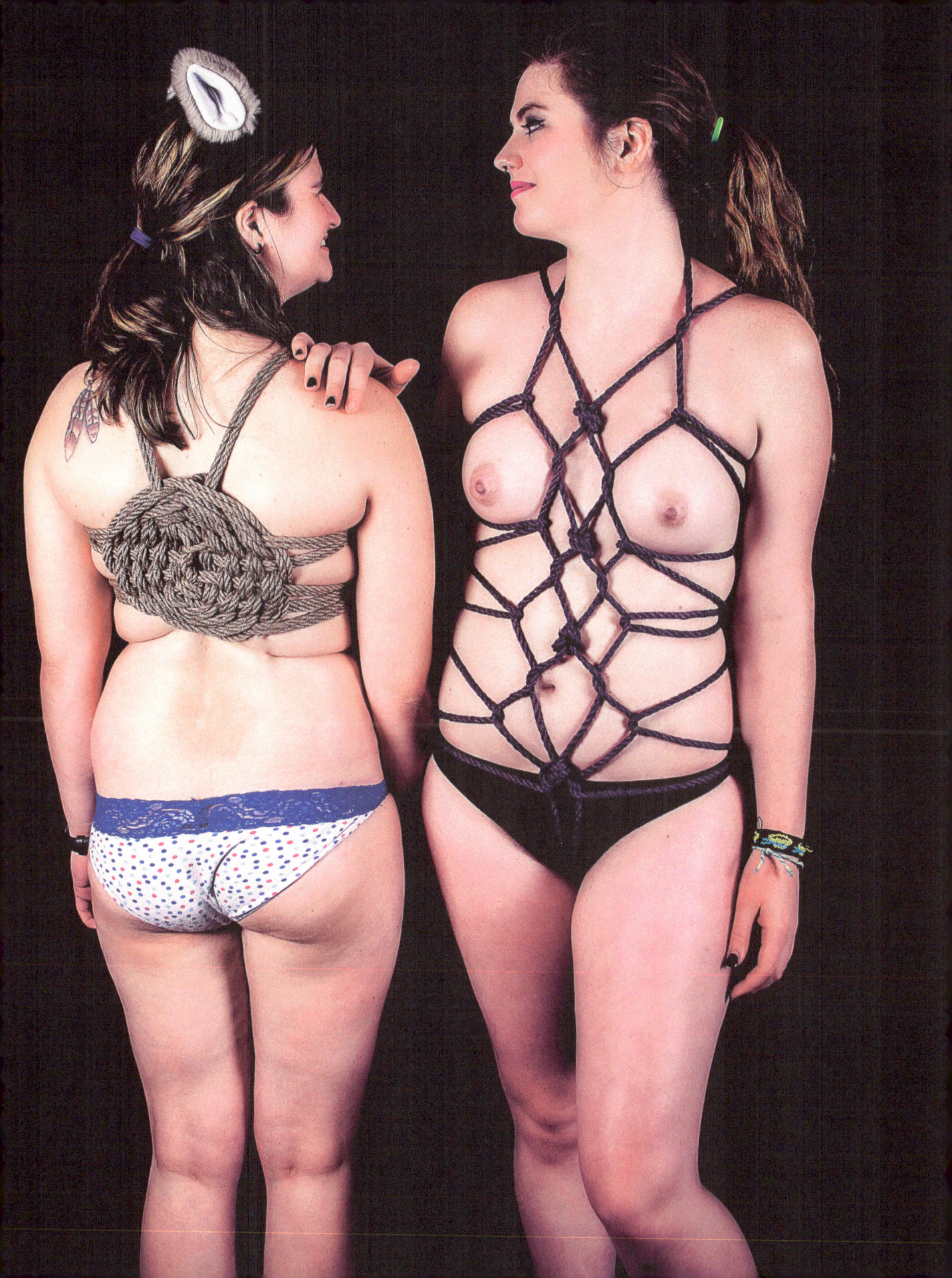

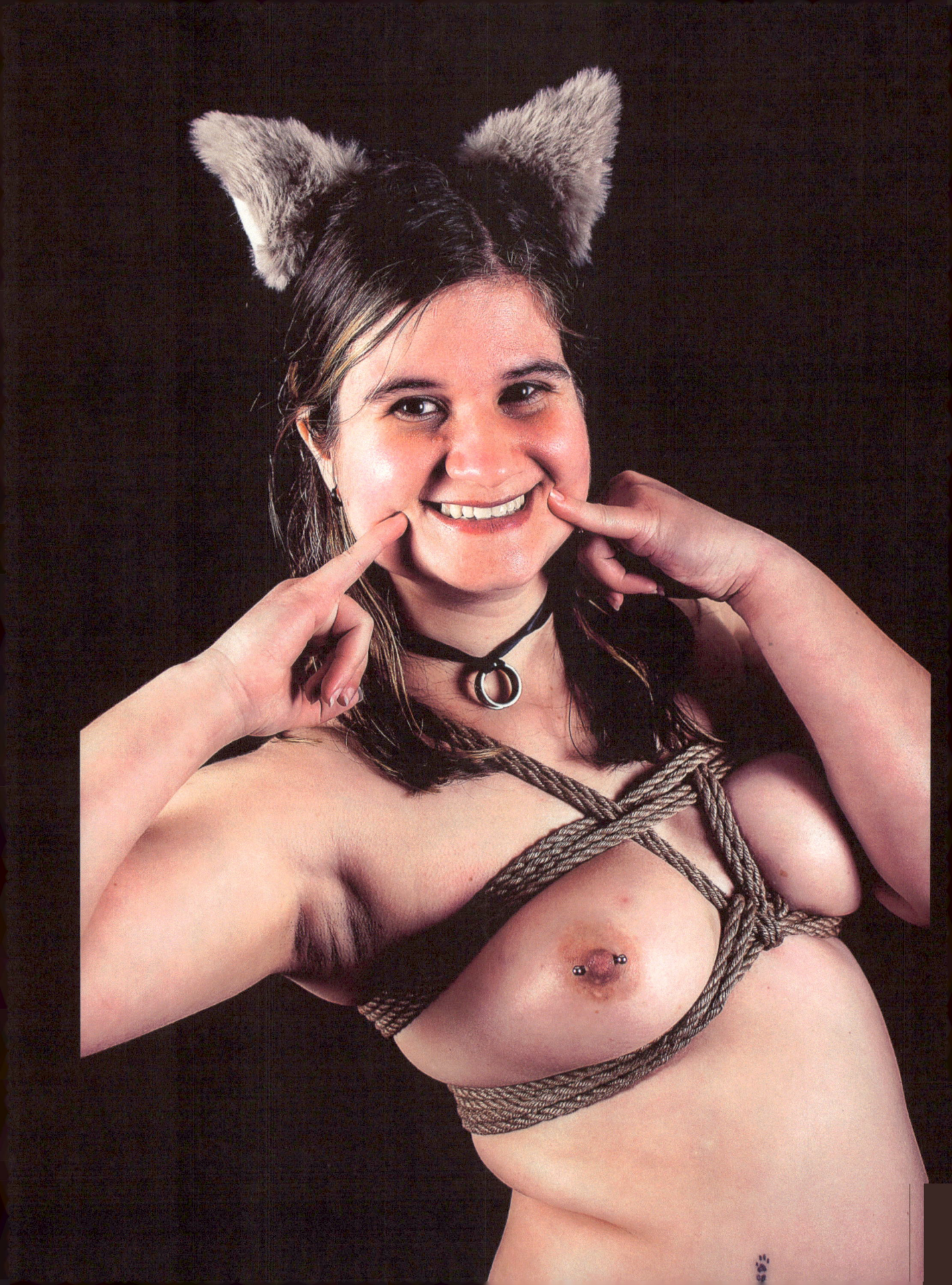

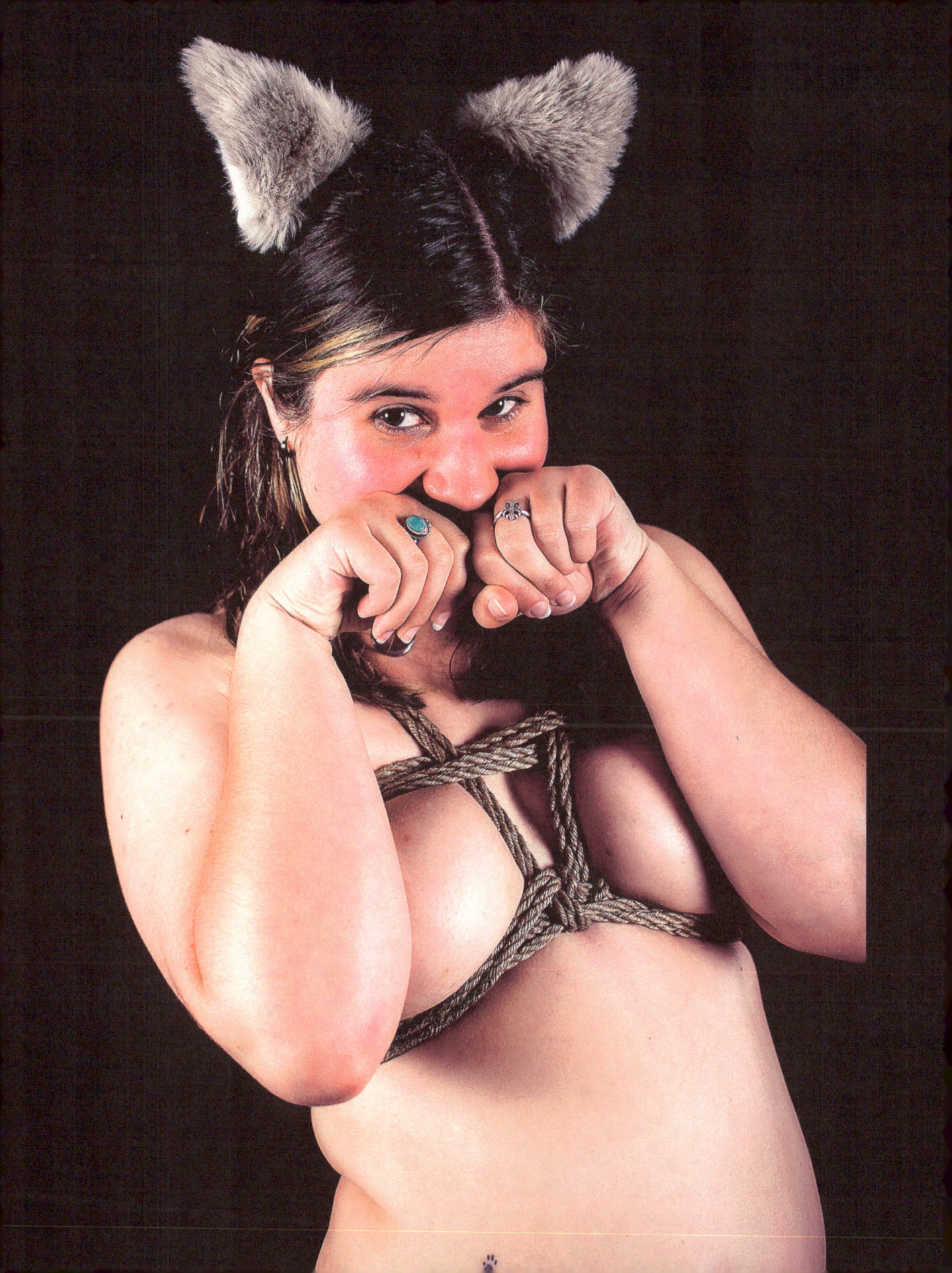

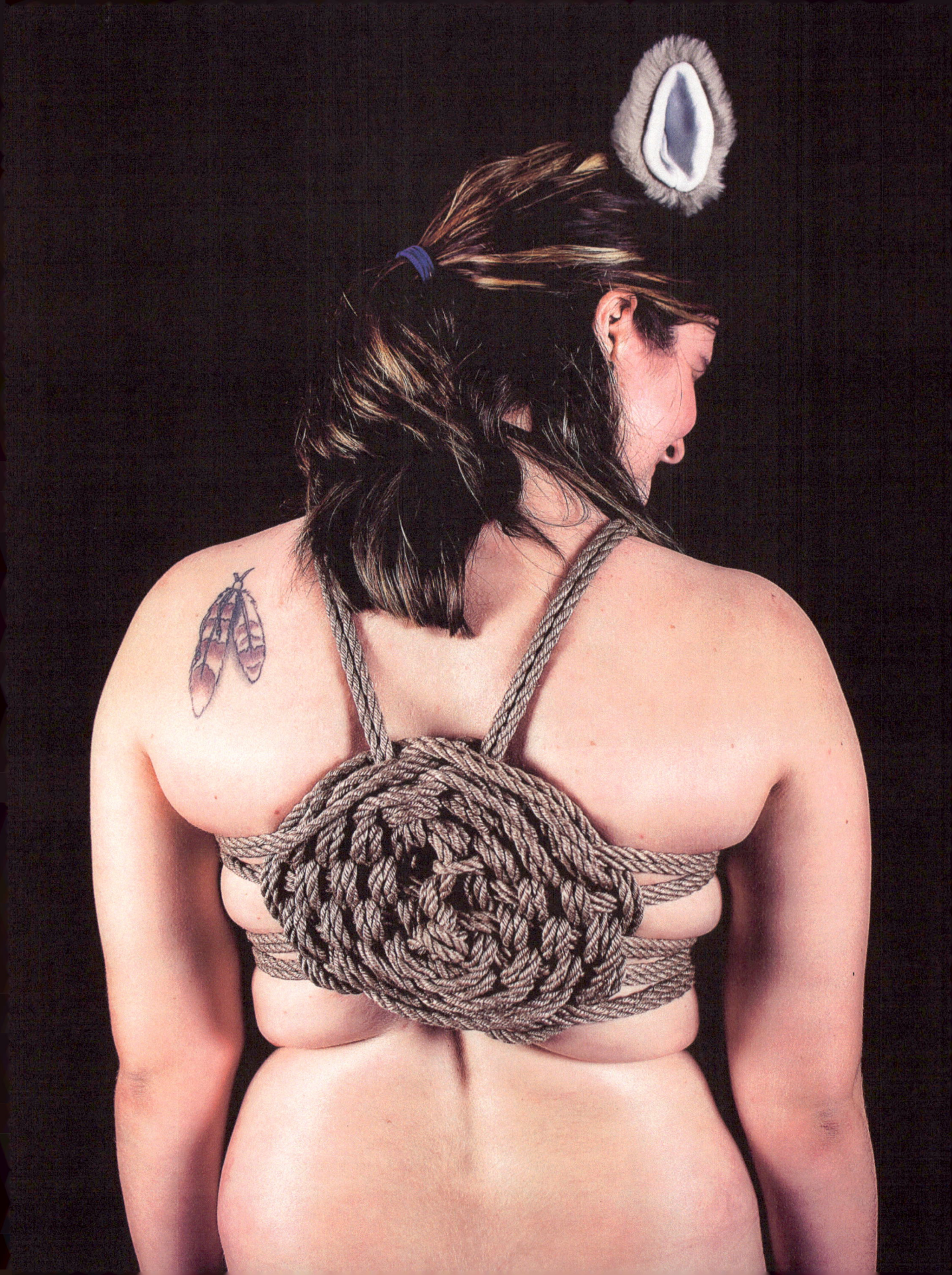

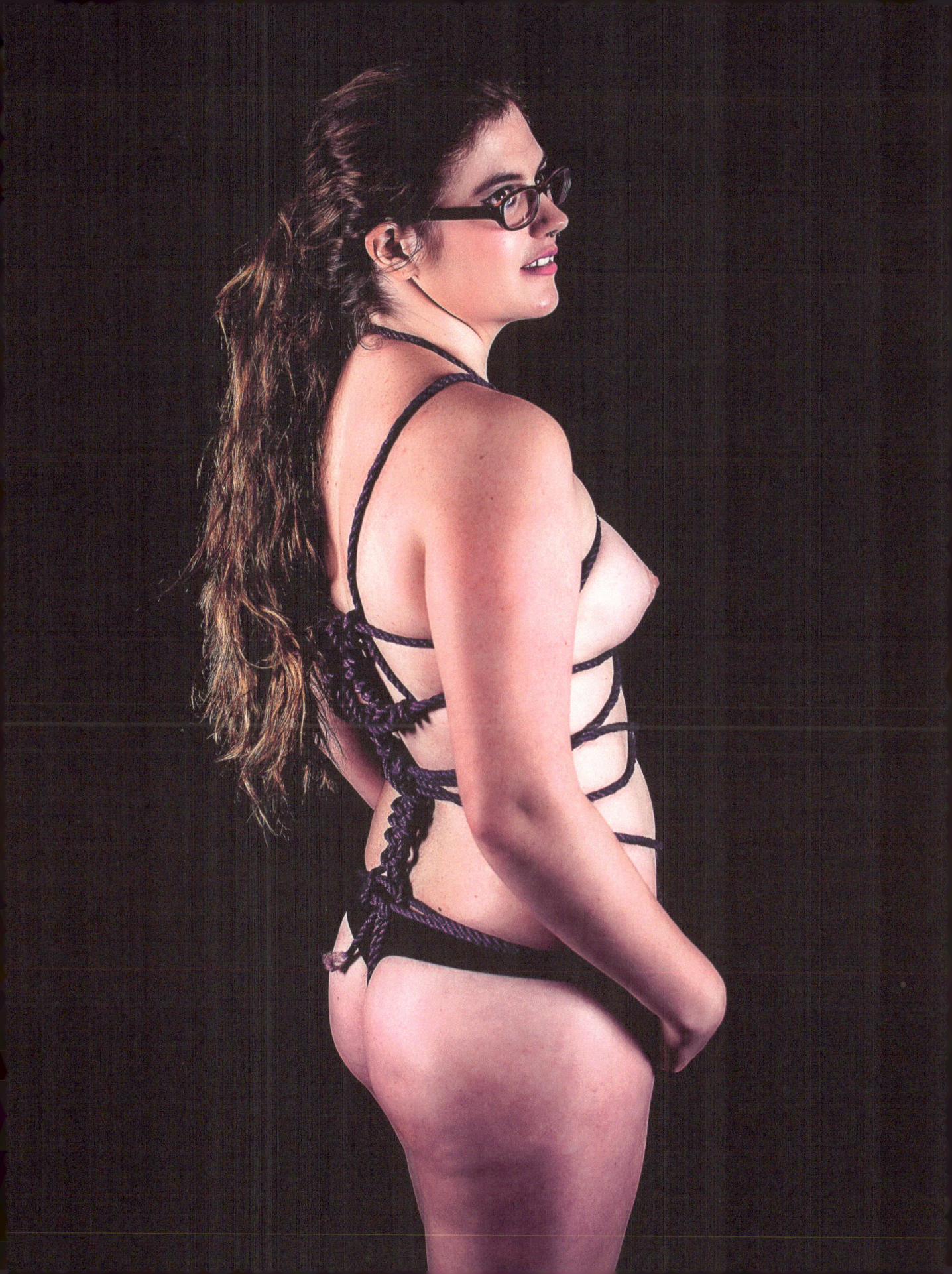

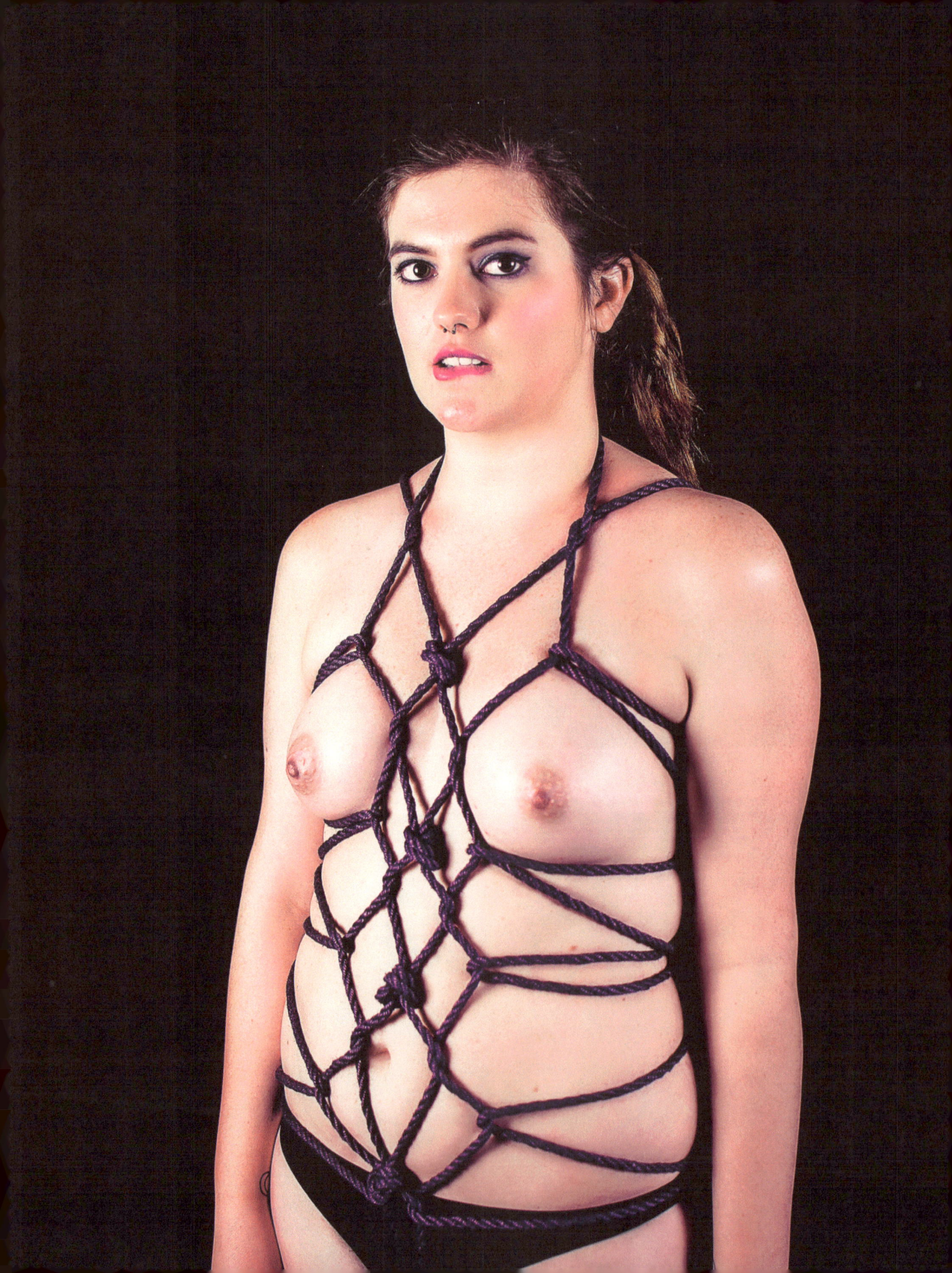

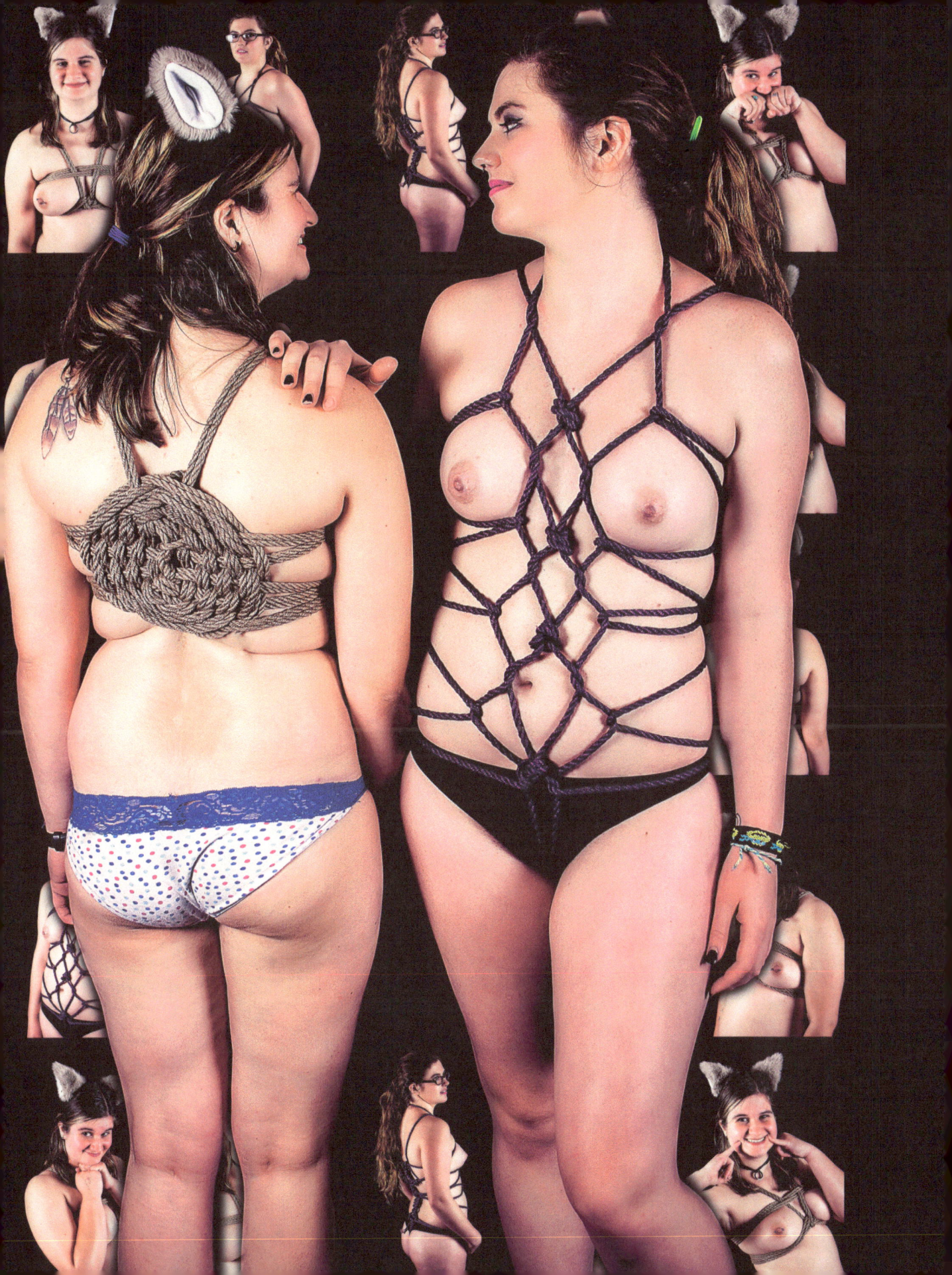

Arista

Sometimes you don't have to look far for models to shoot. Ask your friends, you never know who already has bondage experience.

Q: What was your experience with bondage before this?
A: Extensive in both art and the bedroom

Q: What did you think of this experience?
A: Loved every minute of it!

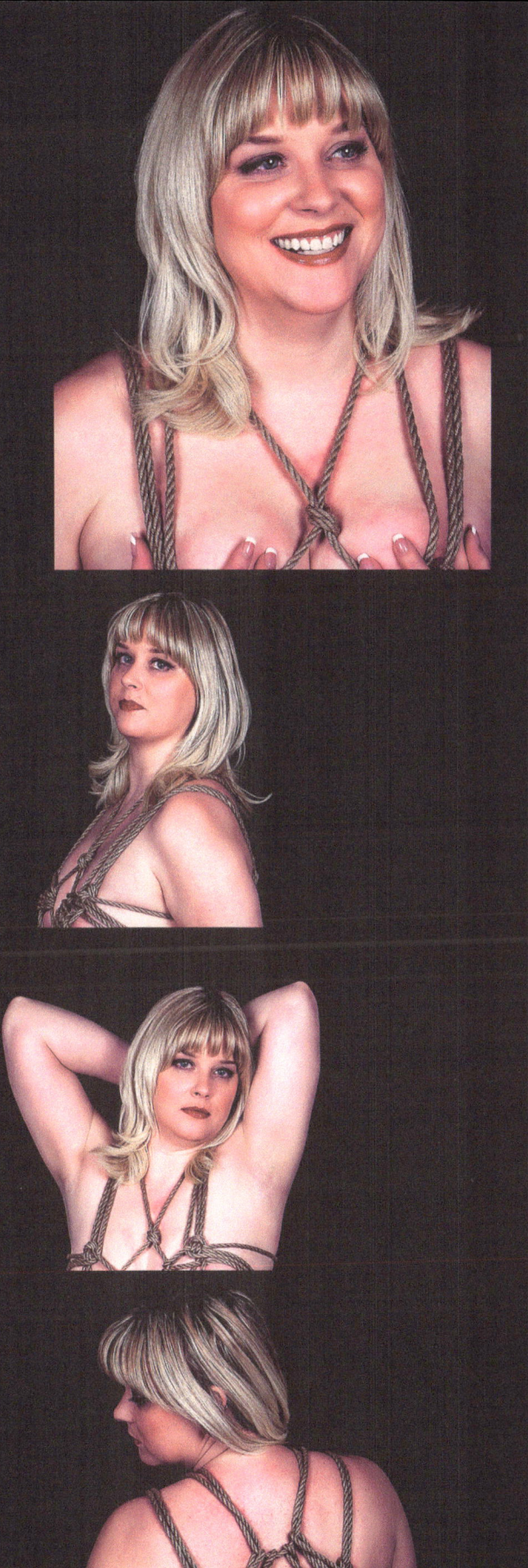

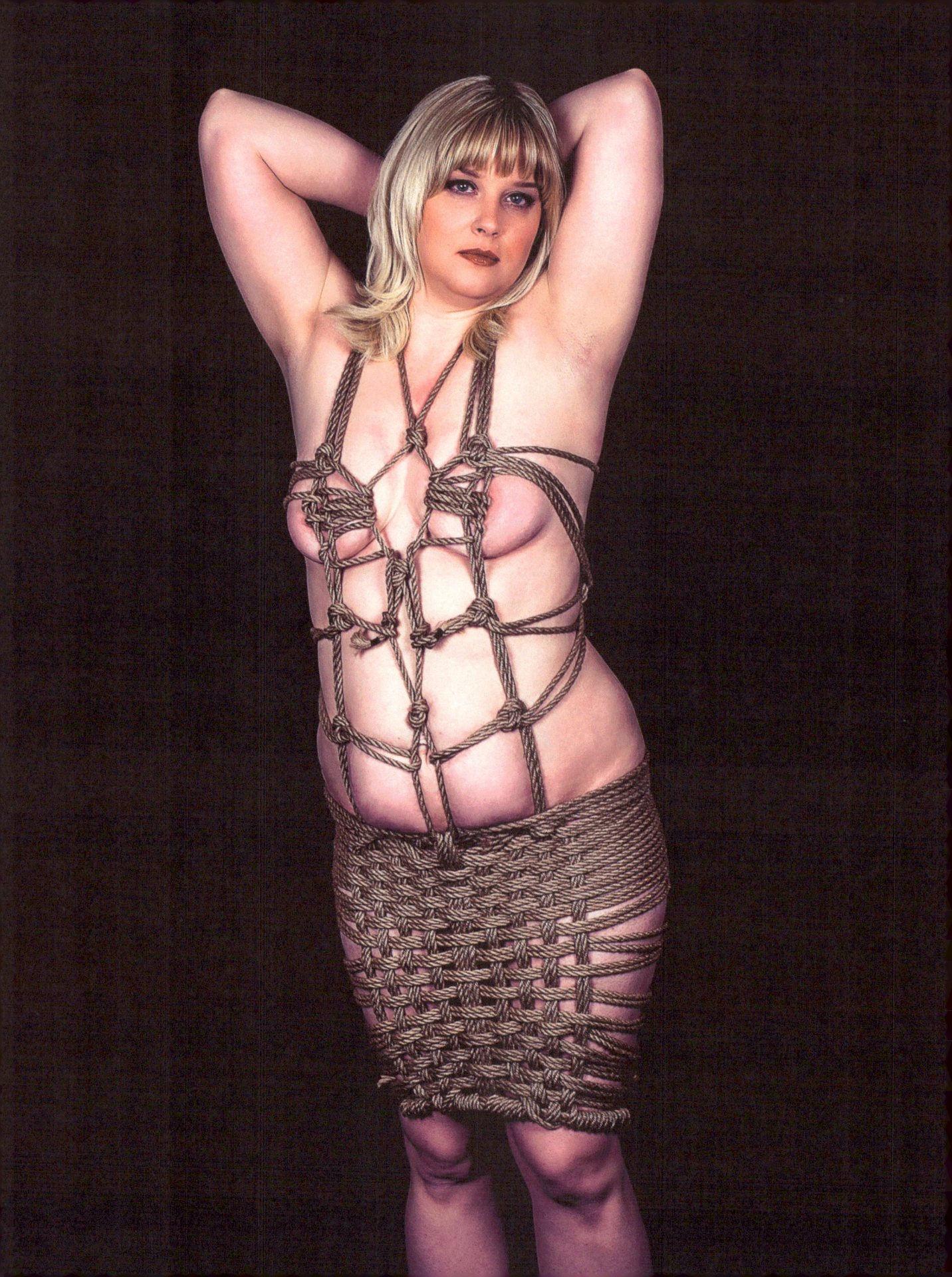

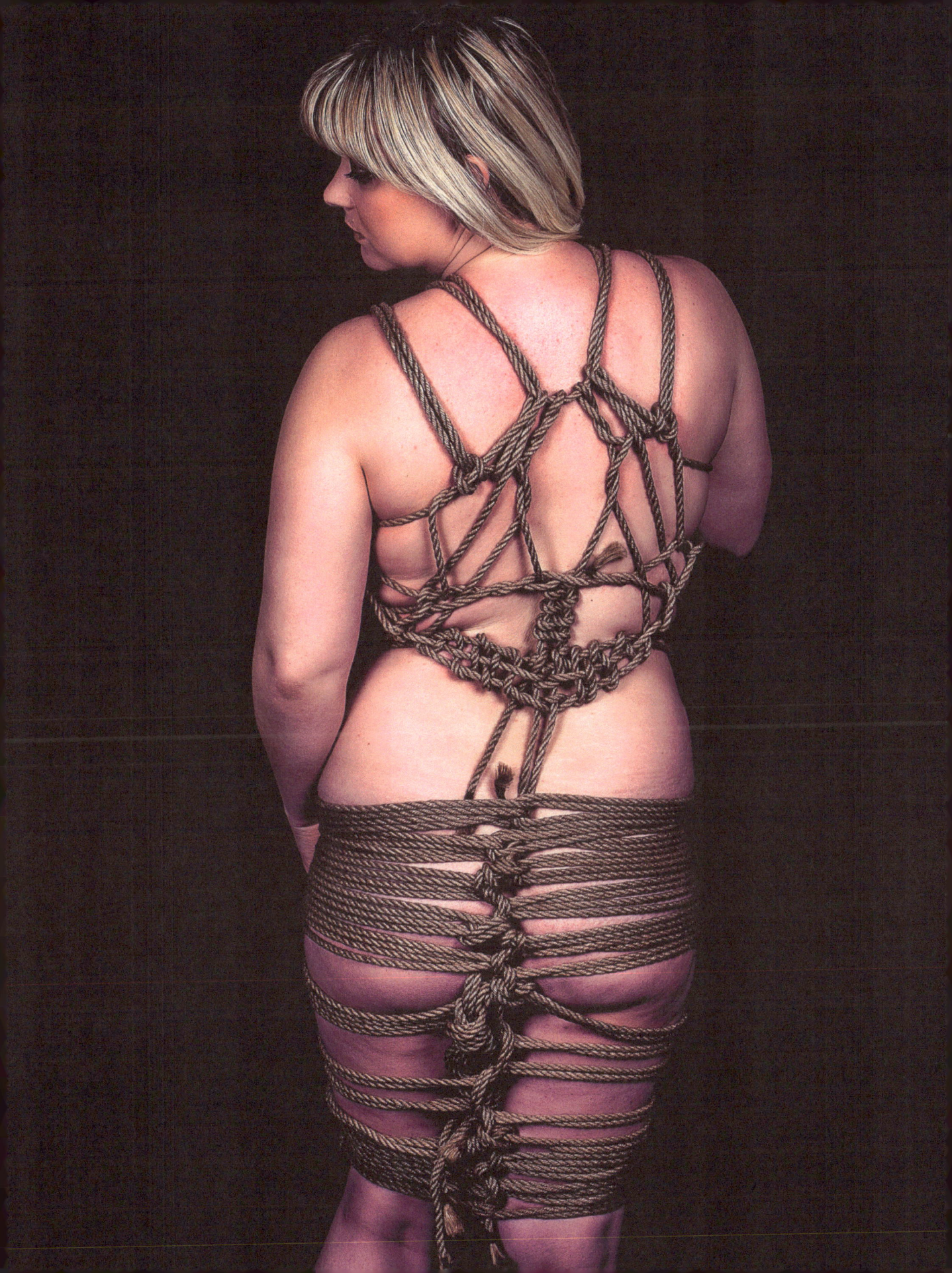

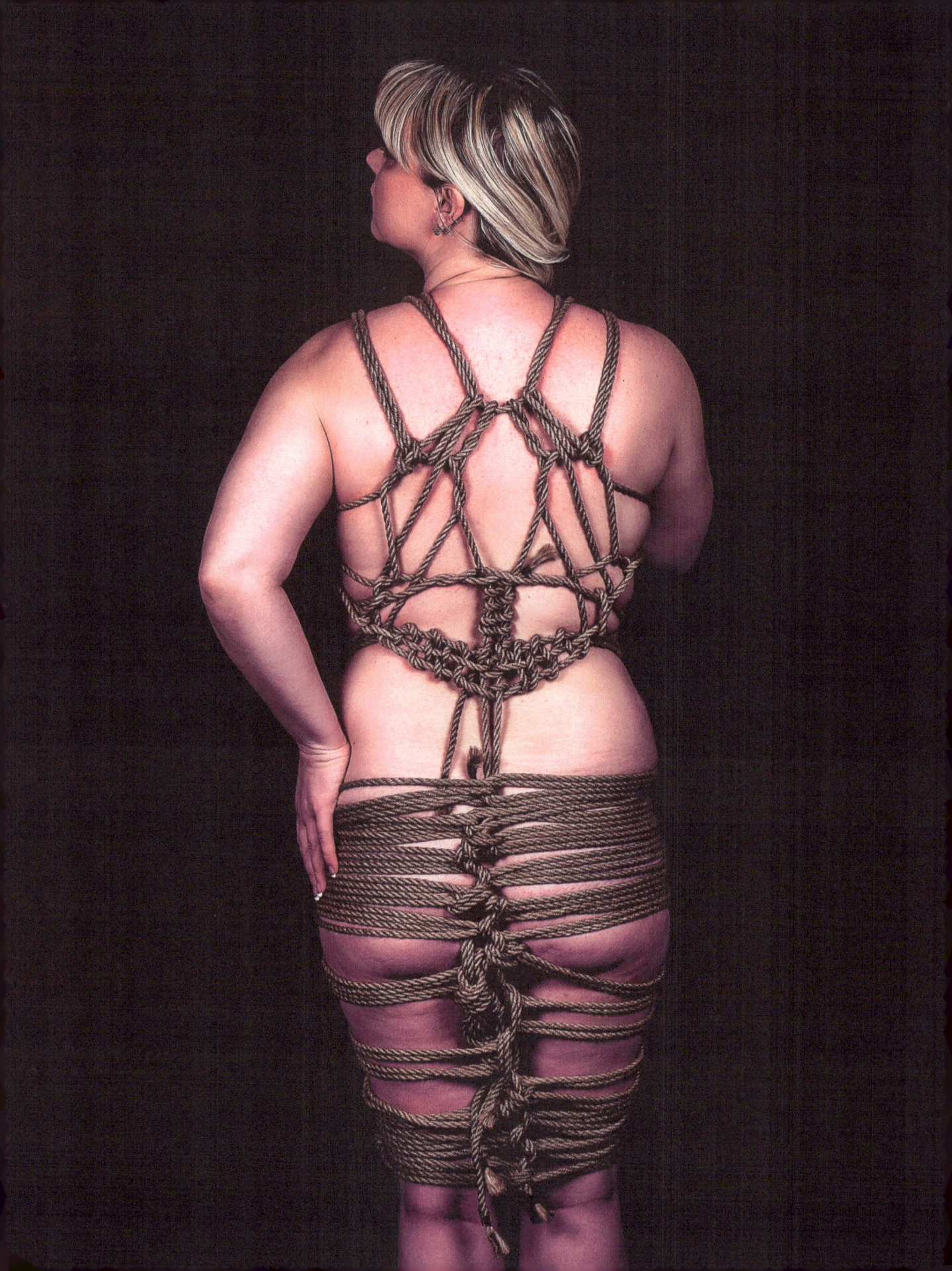

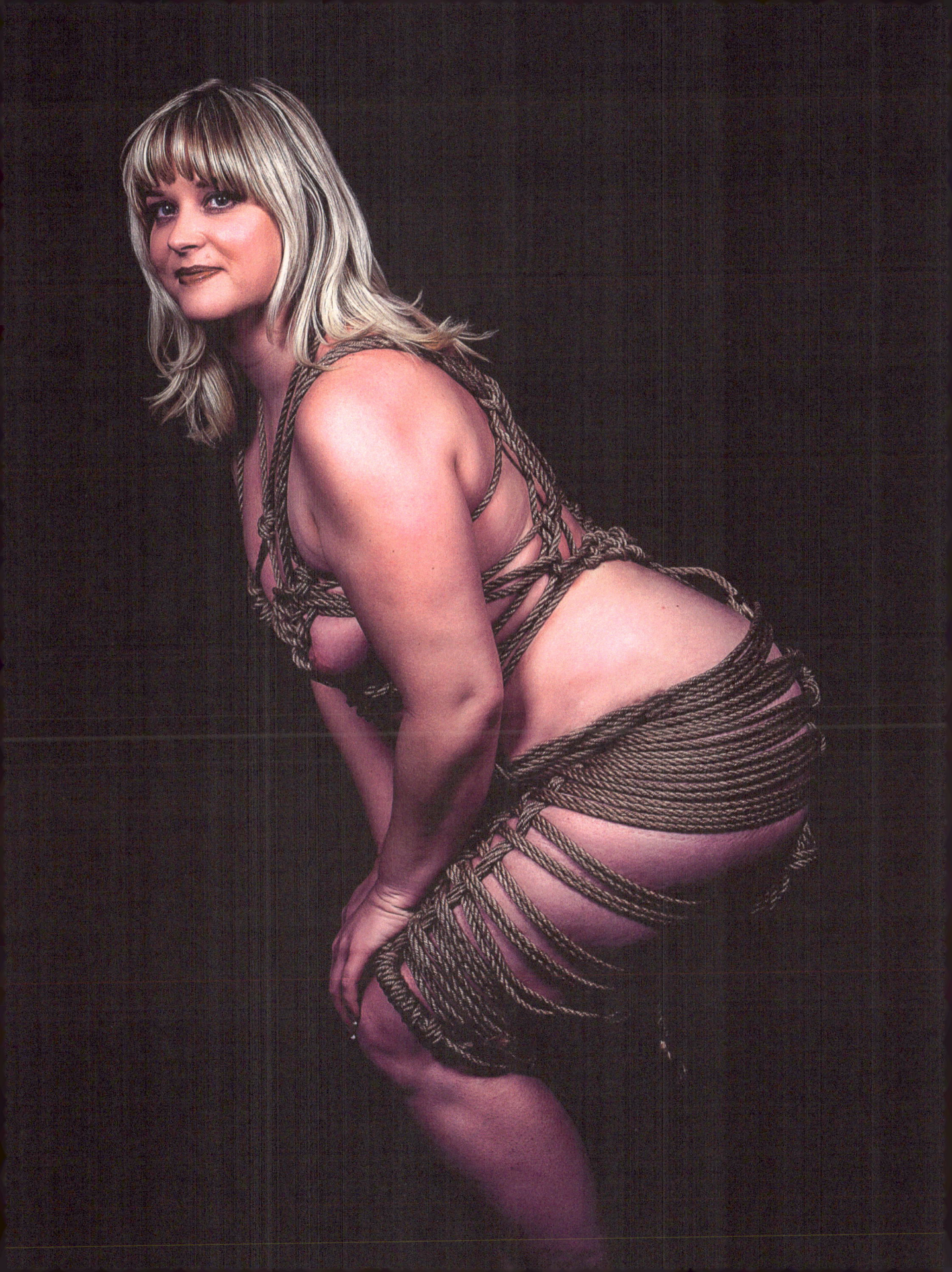

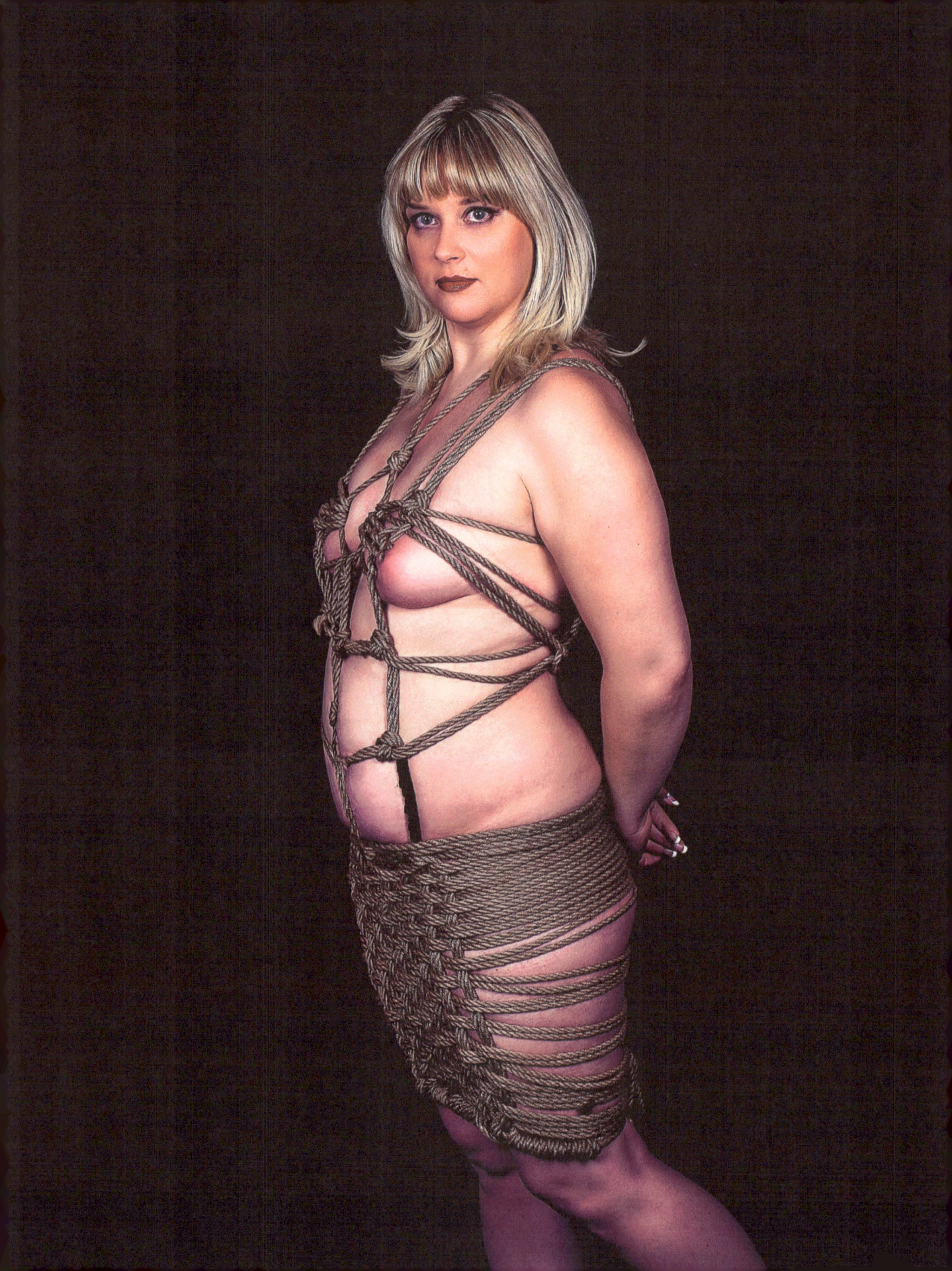

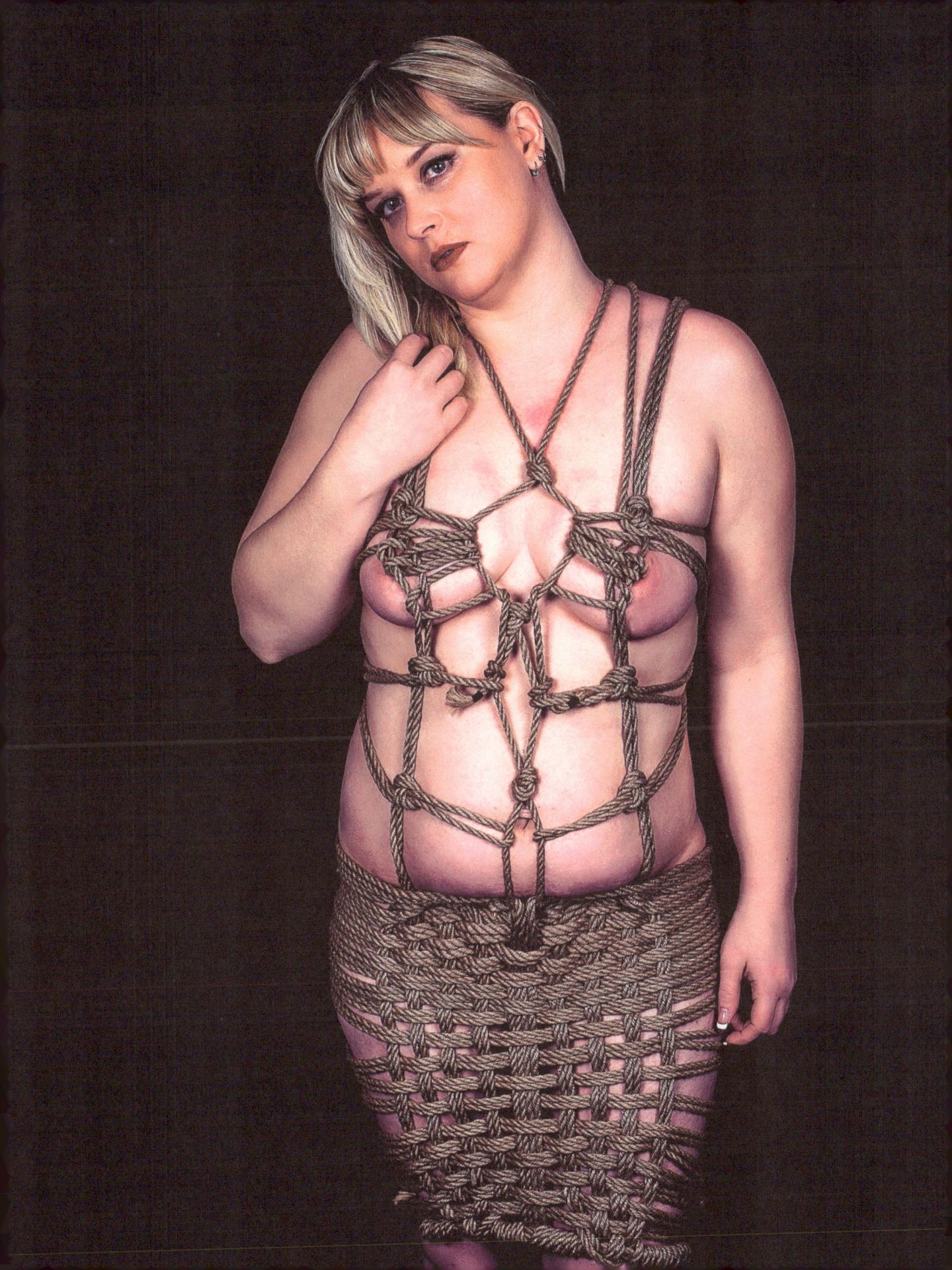

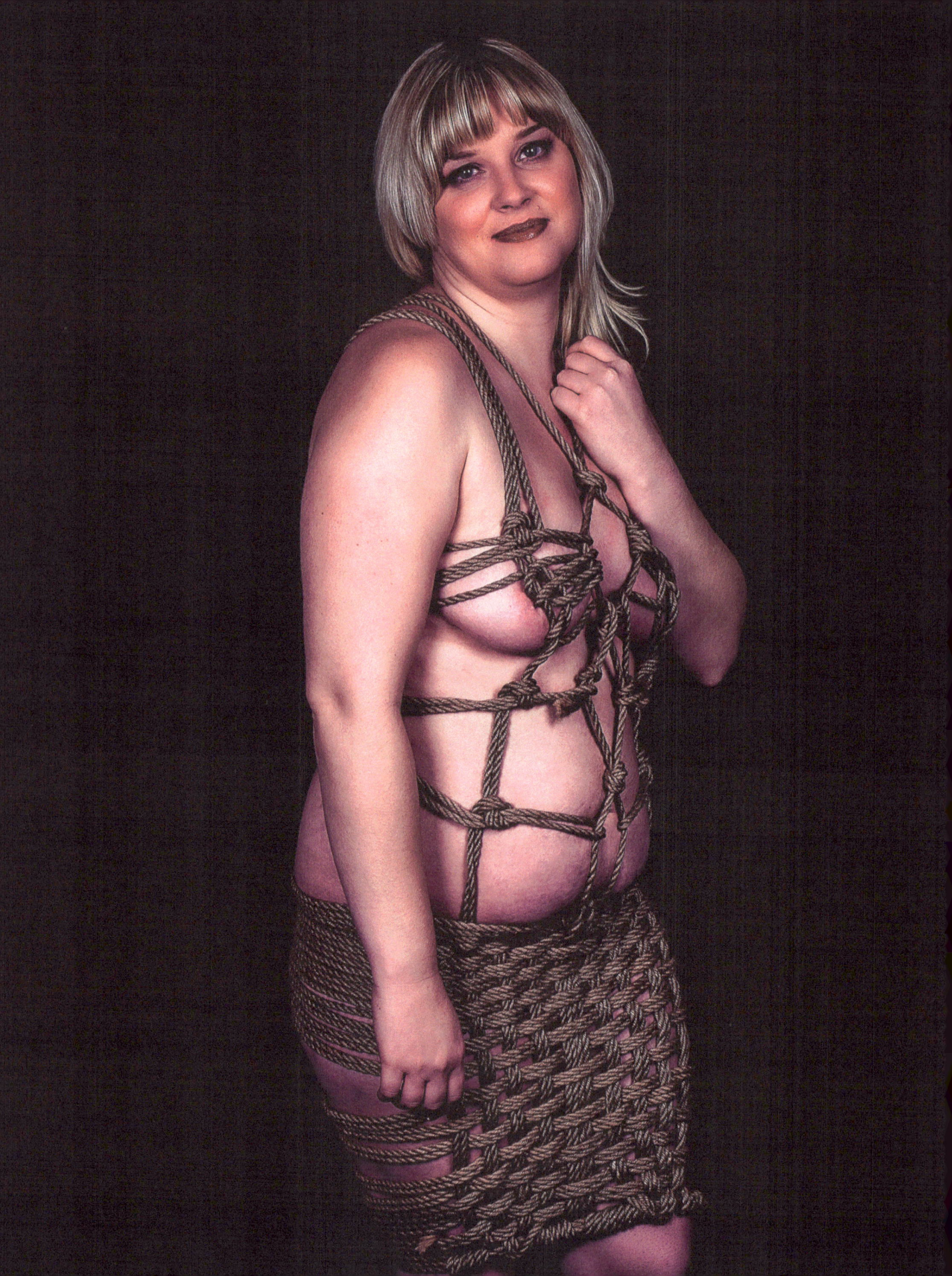

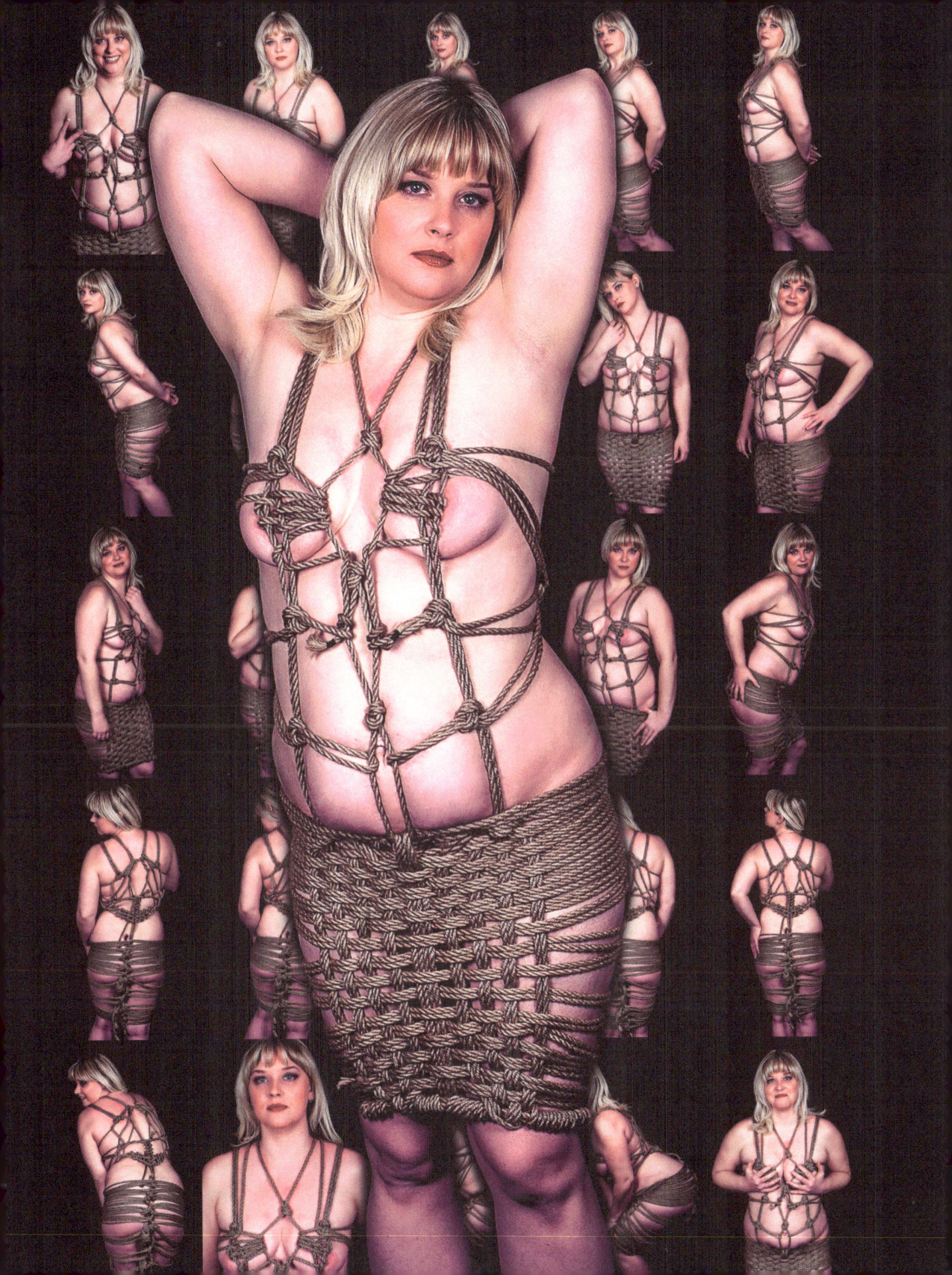

Allie Angel

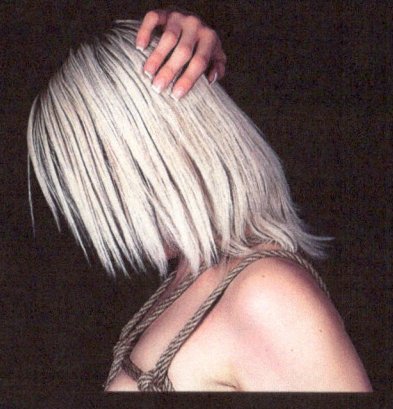

Even simple designs can hold great beauty.

Q: What was your experience with bondage before this?
A: None

Q: What did you think of this experience?
A: Awesome!

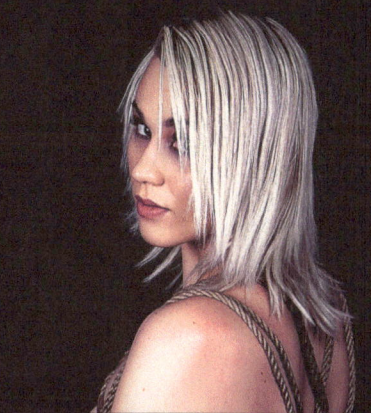

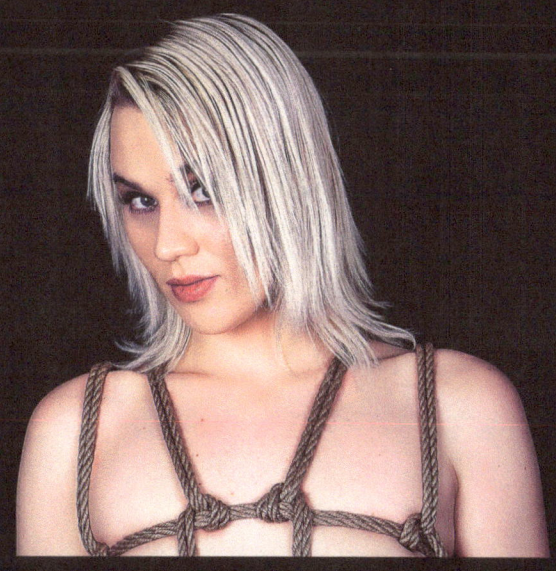

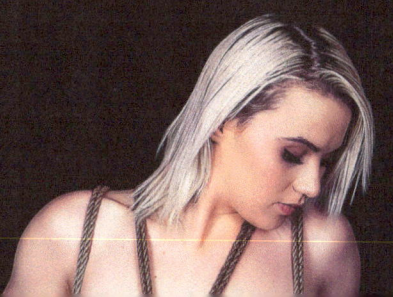

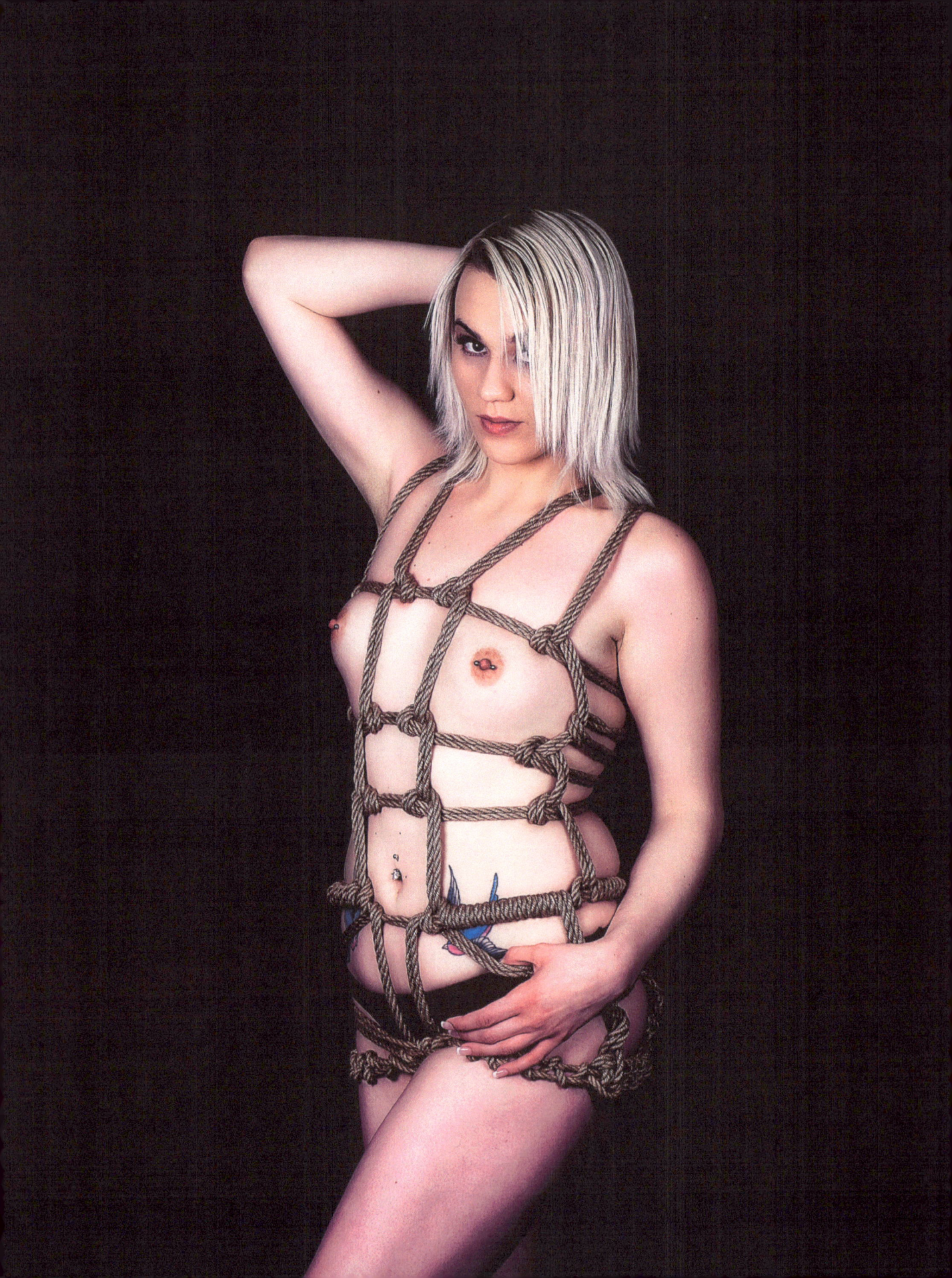

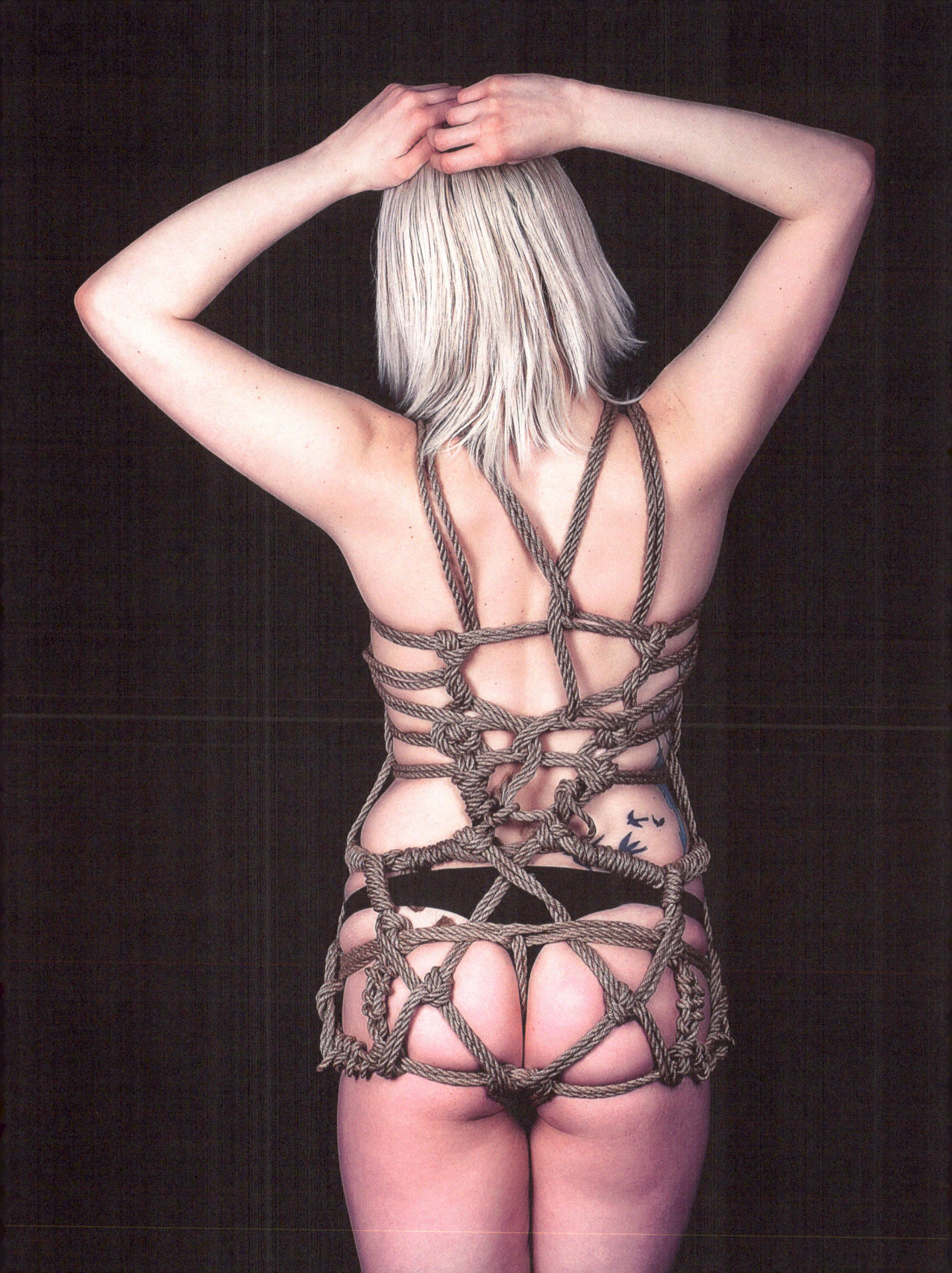

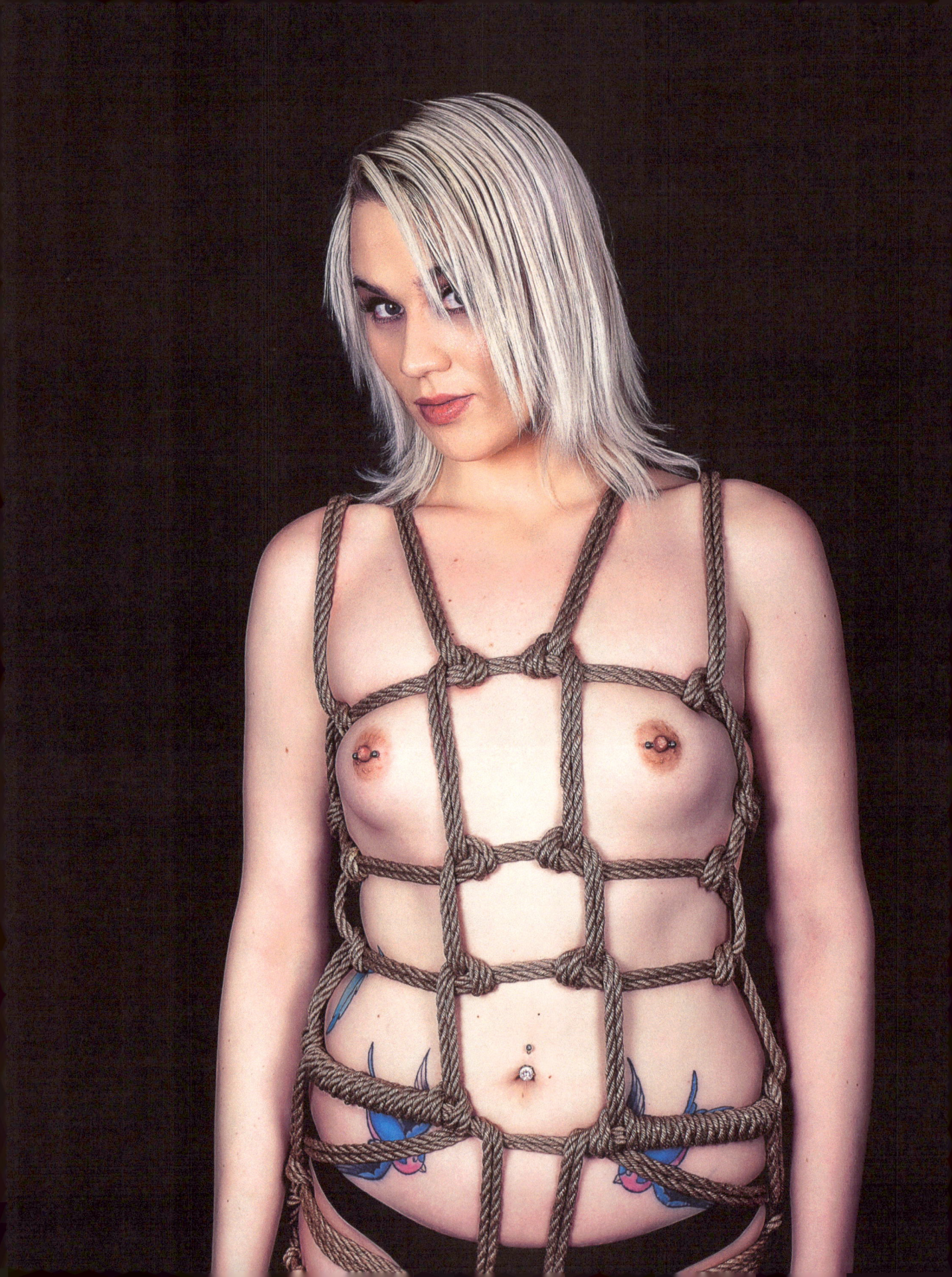

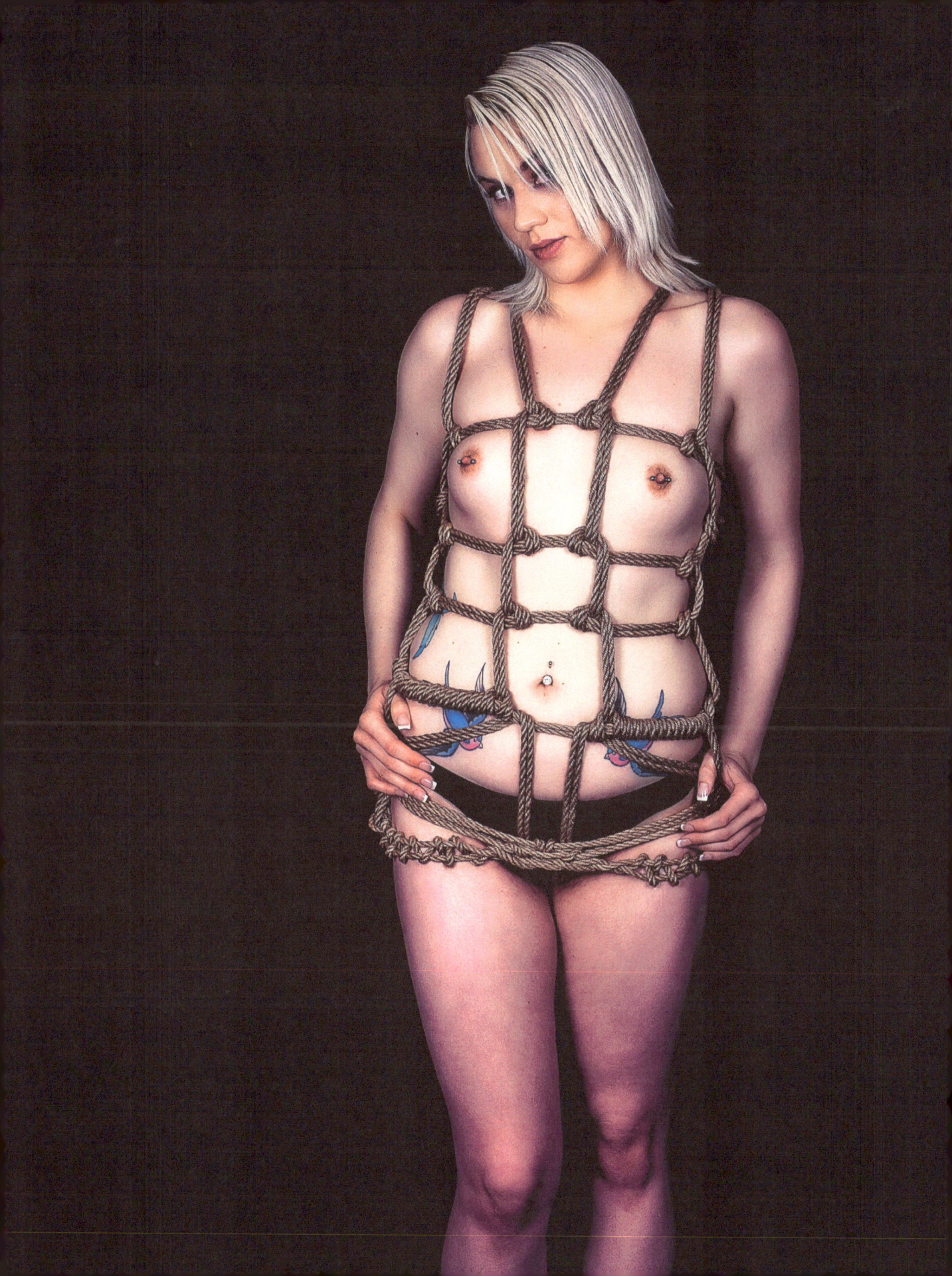

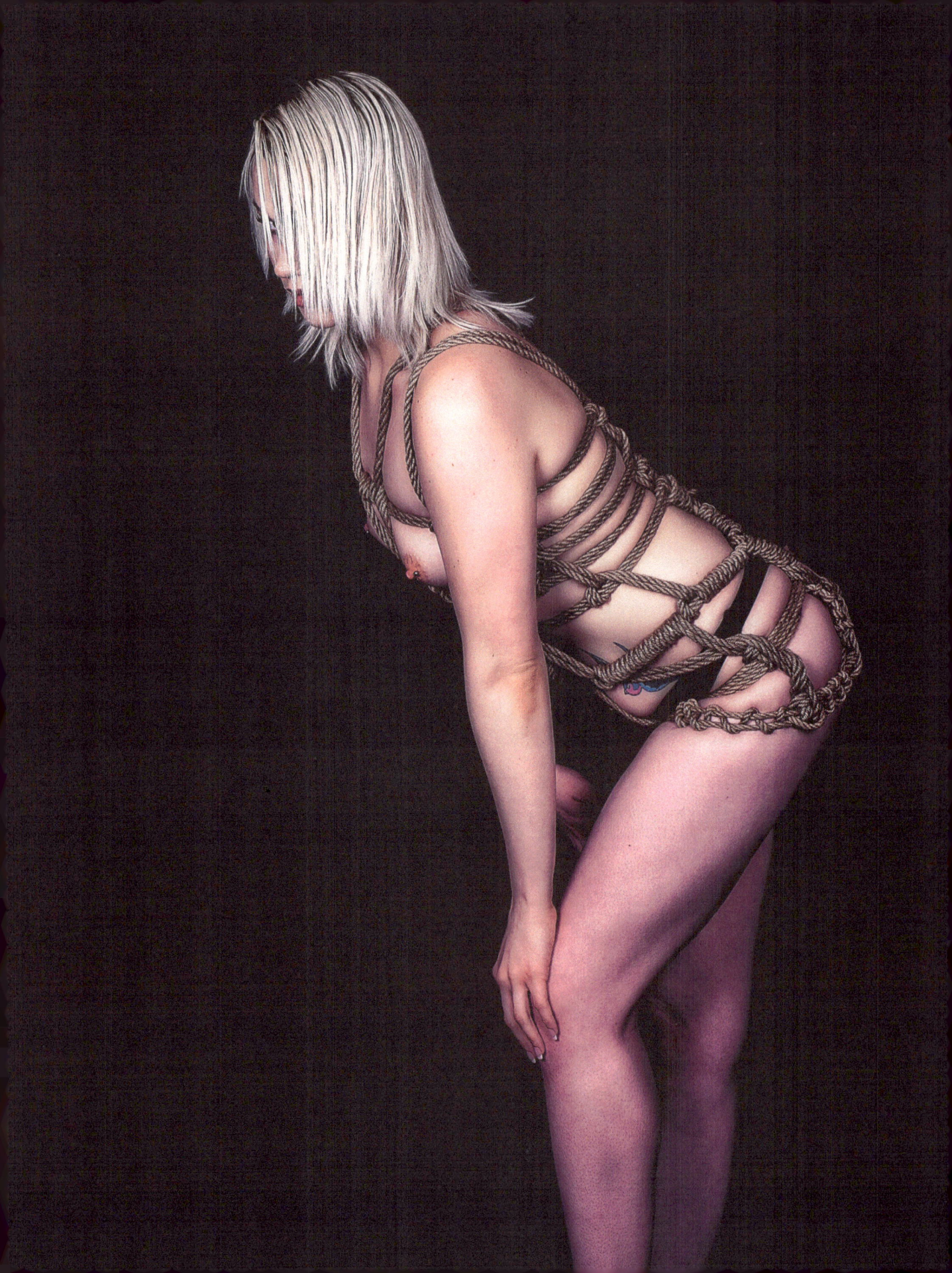

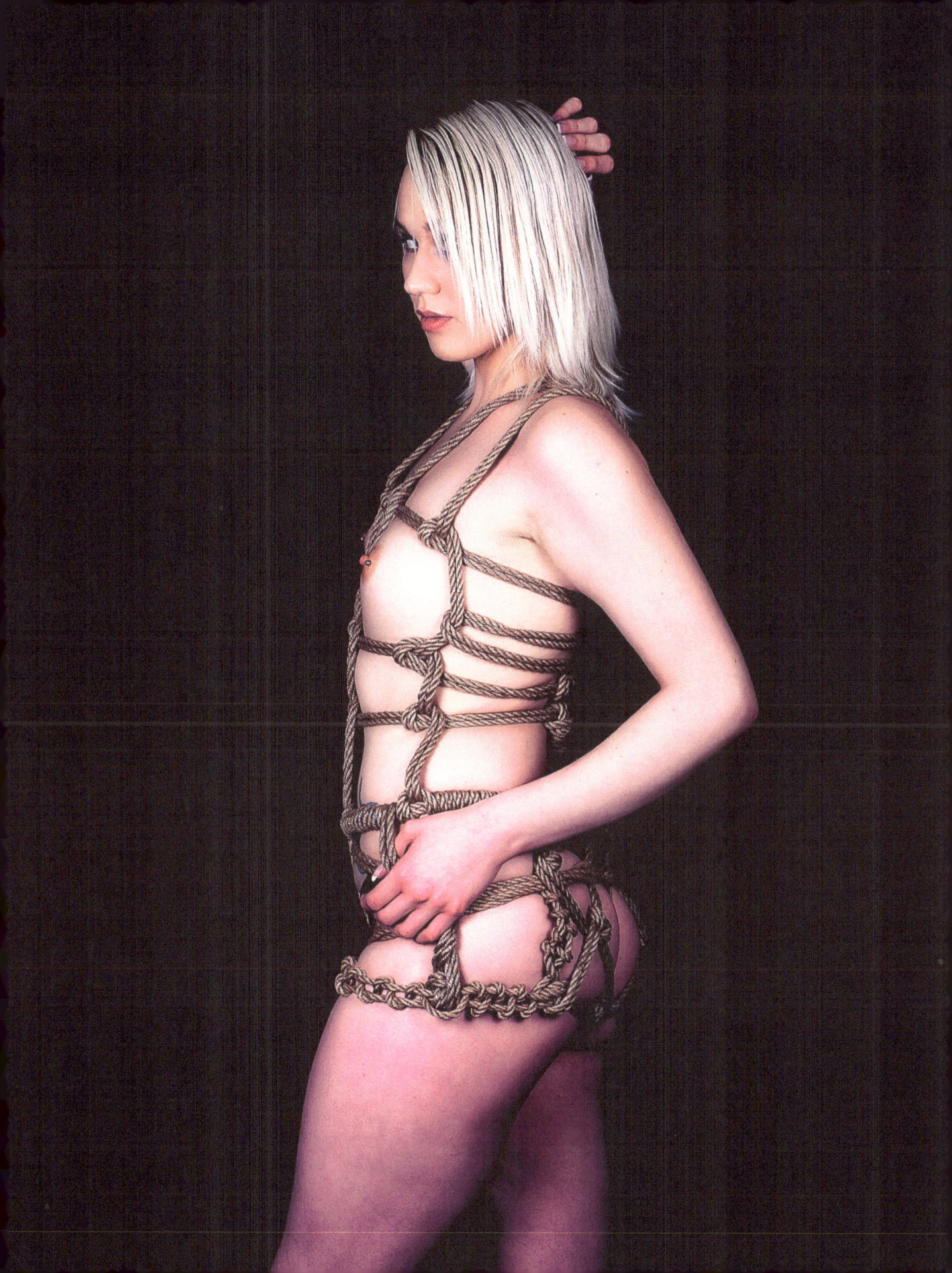

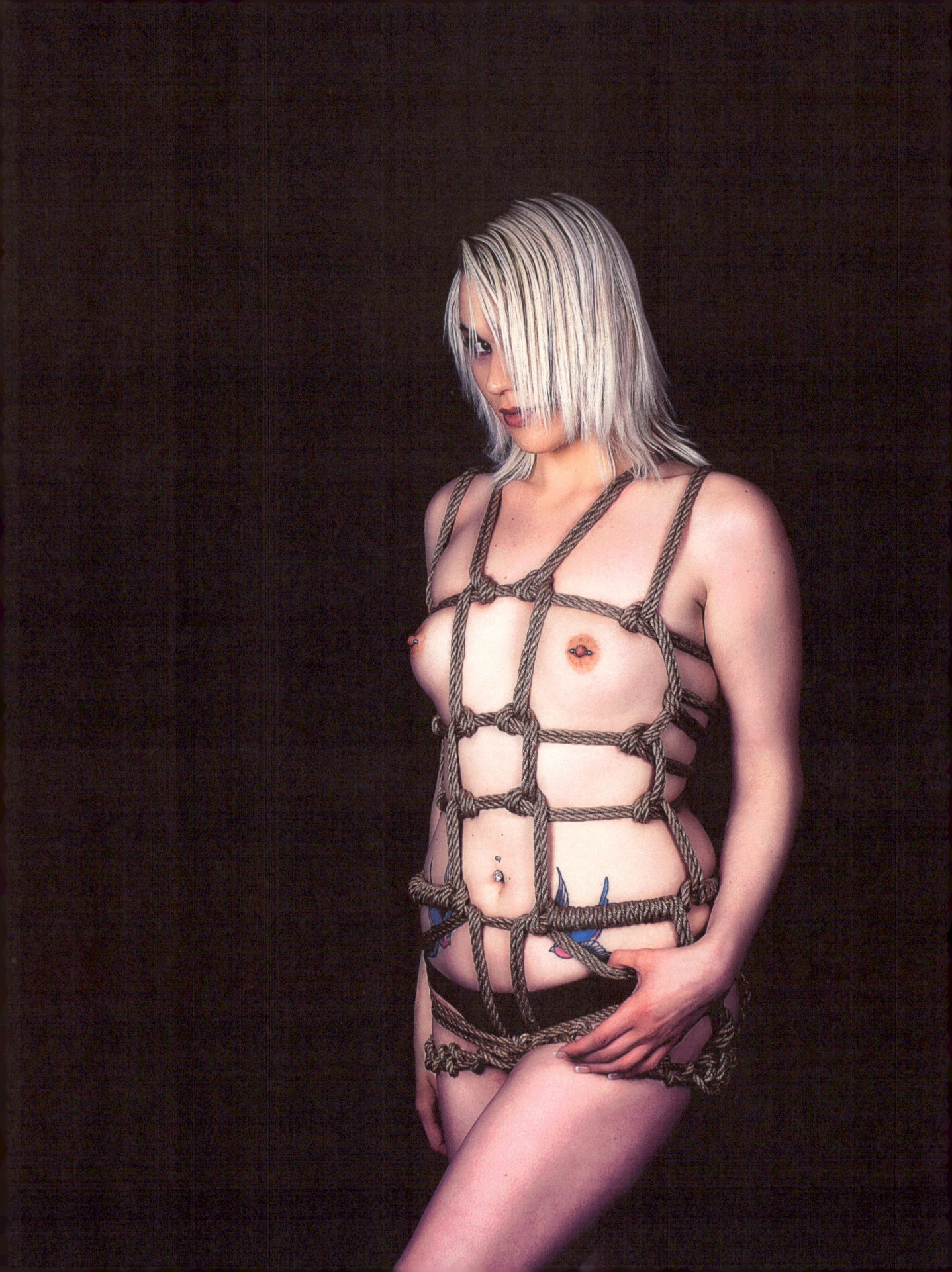

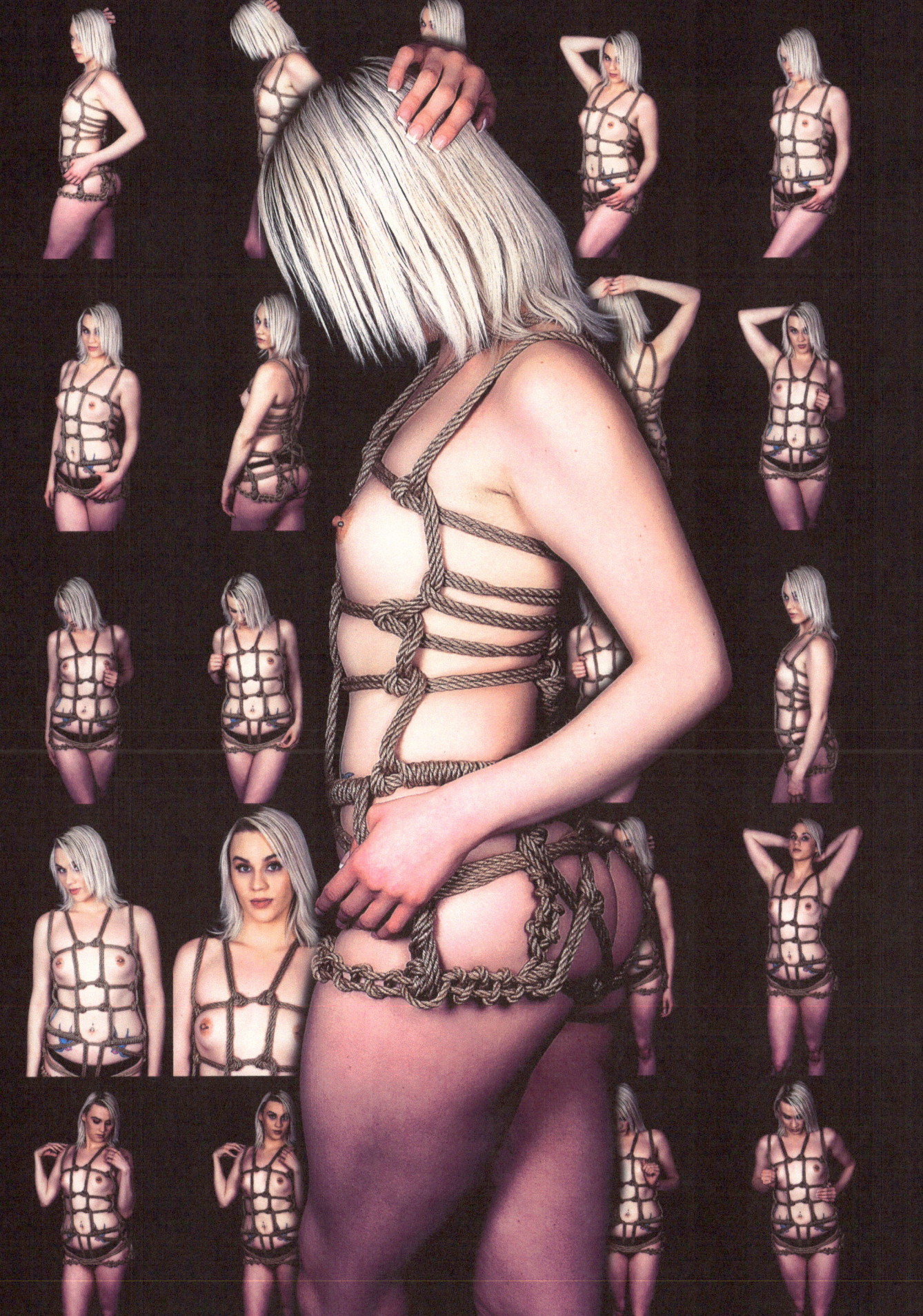

Esperanza

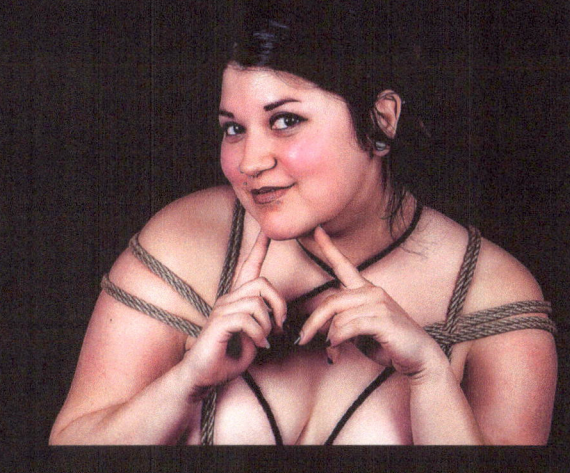

Sometimes you get lucky and bunny too adorable for her own good just shows up out of nowhere.

Q: What was your experience with bondage before this?
A: Dabbled a time or two, limited experience.

Q: What did you think of this experience?
A: It was a fun time!

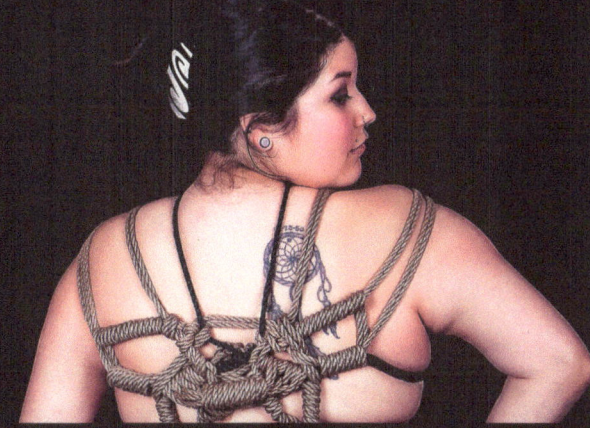

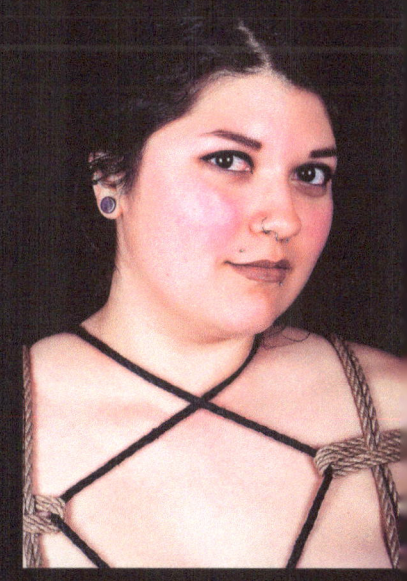

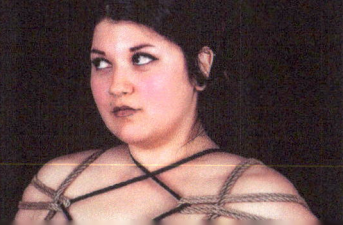

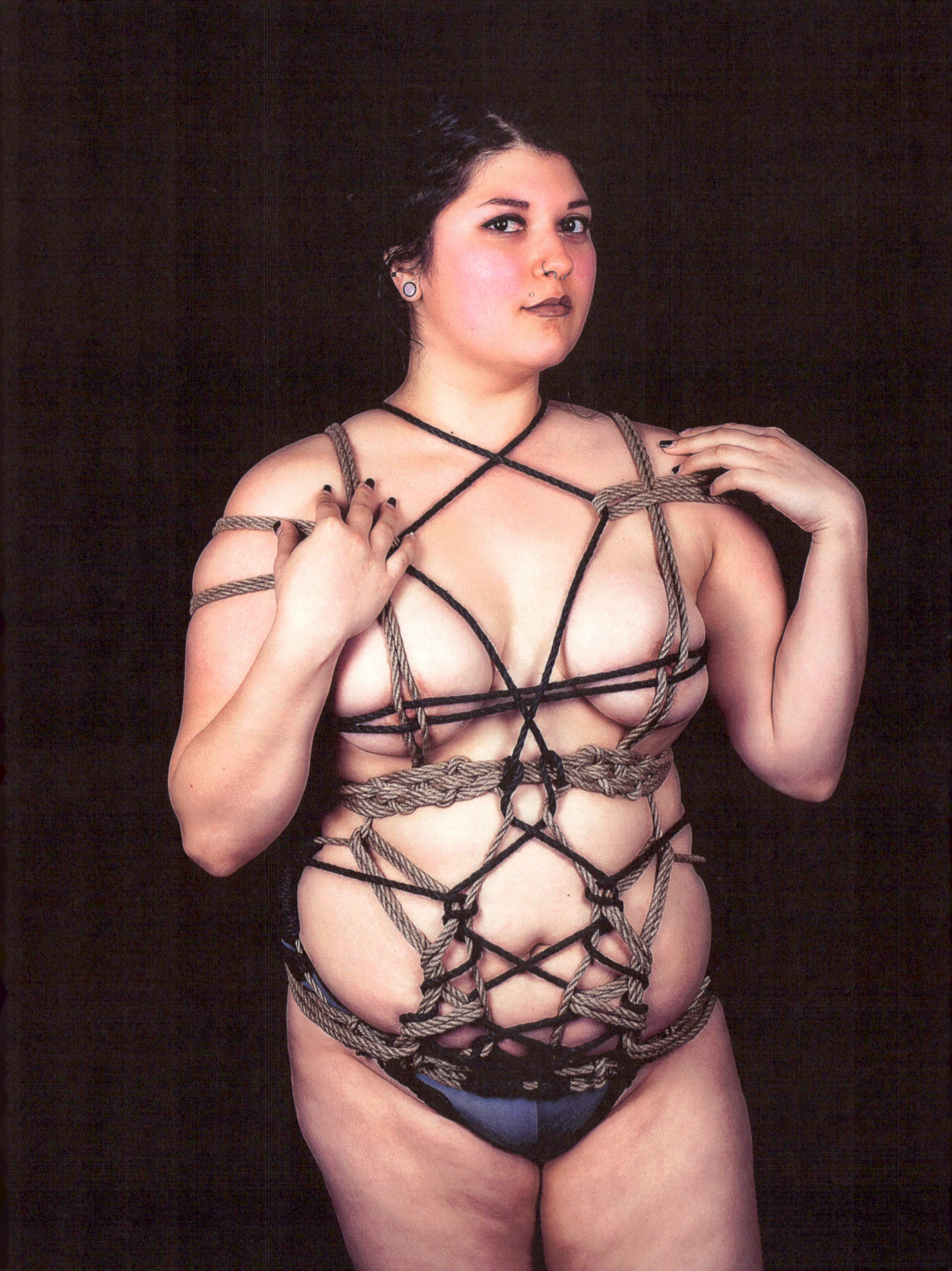

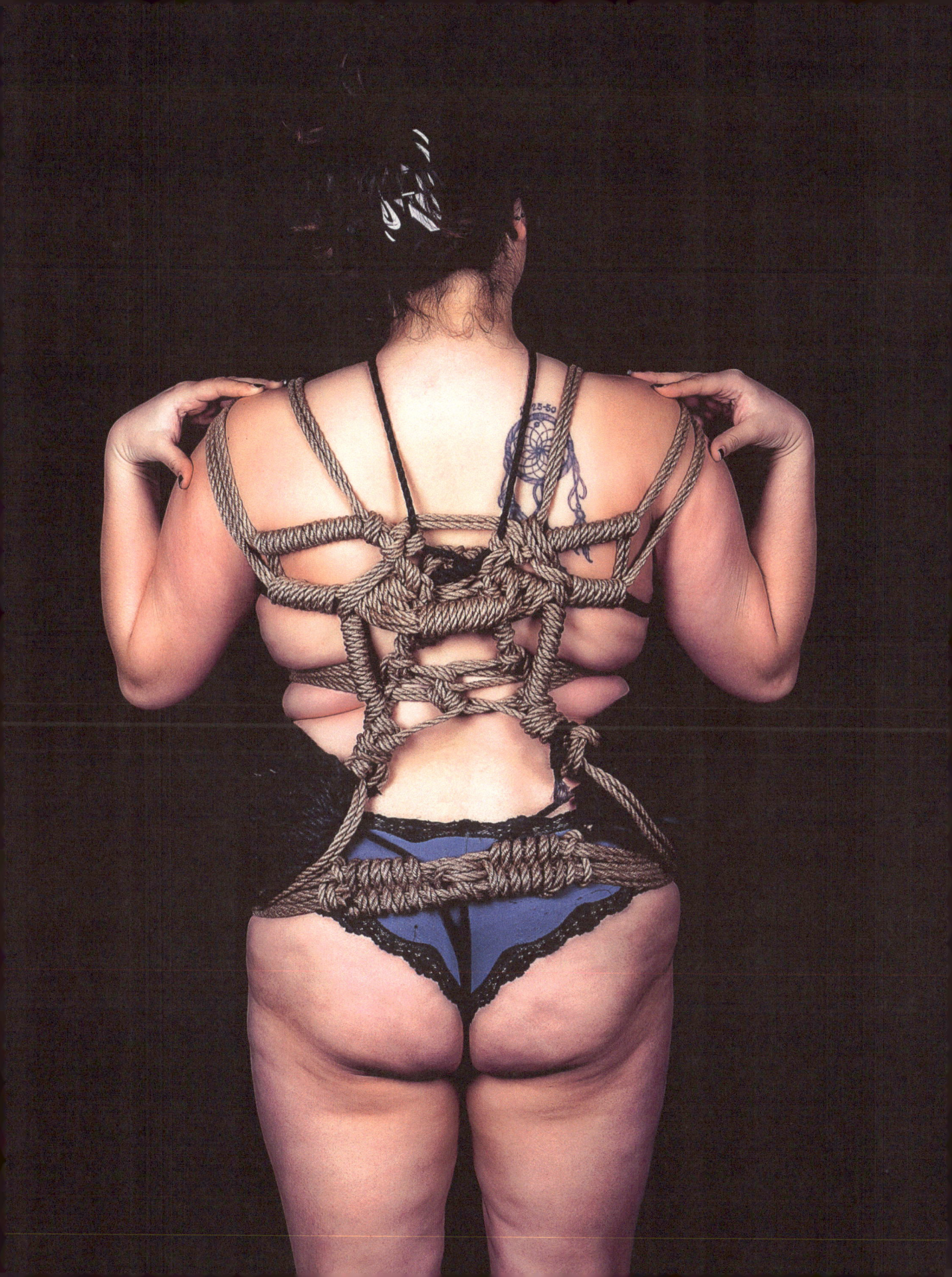

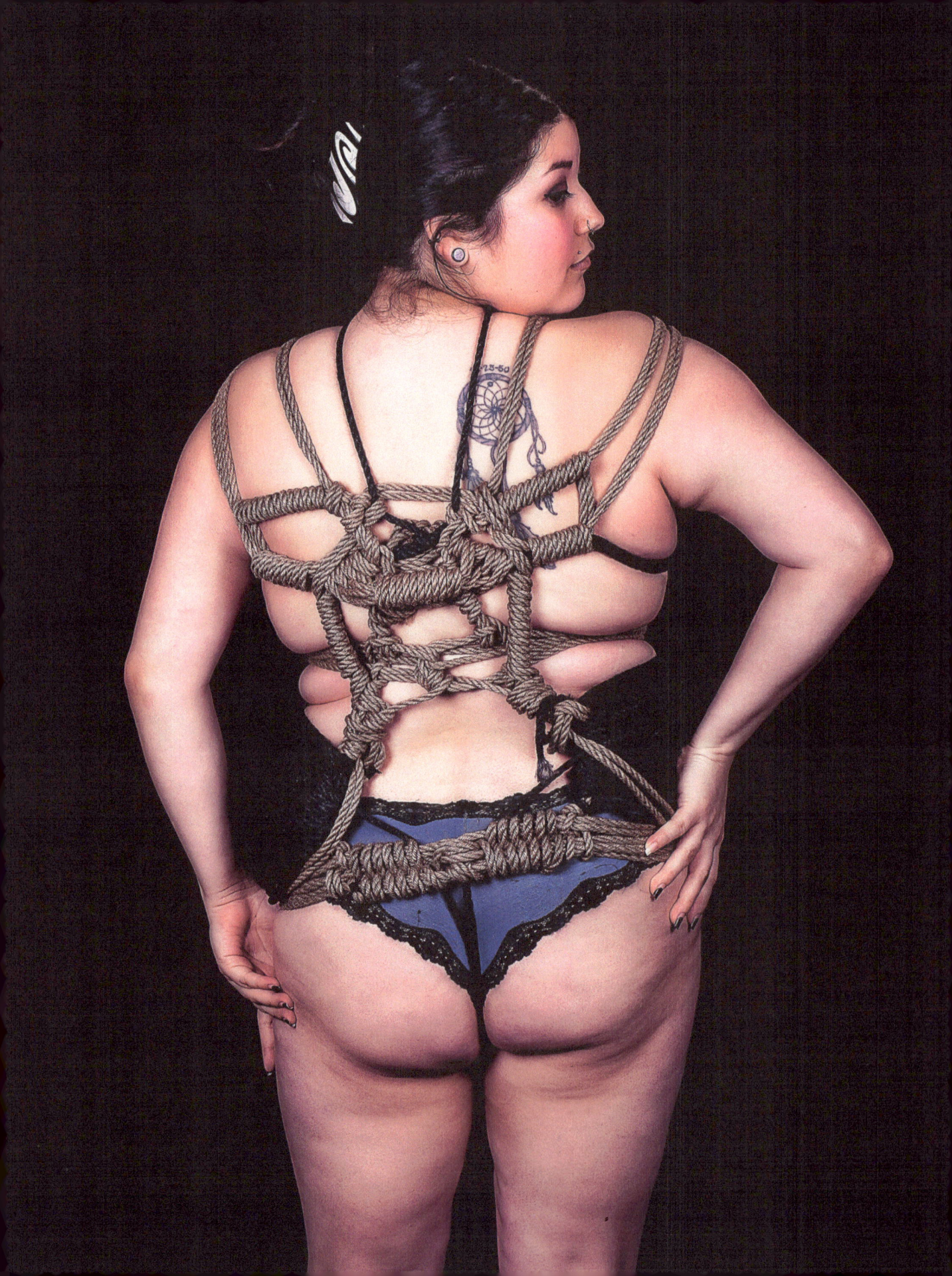

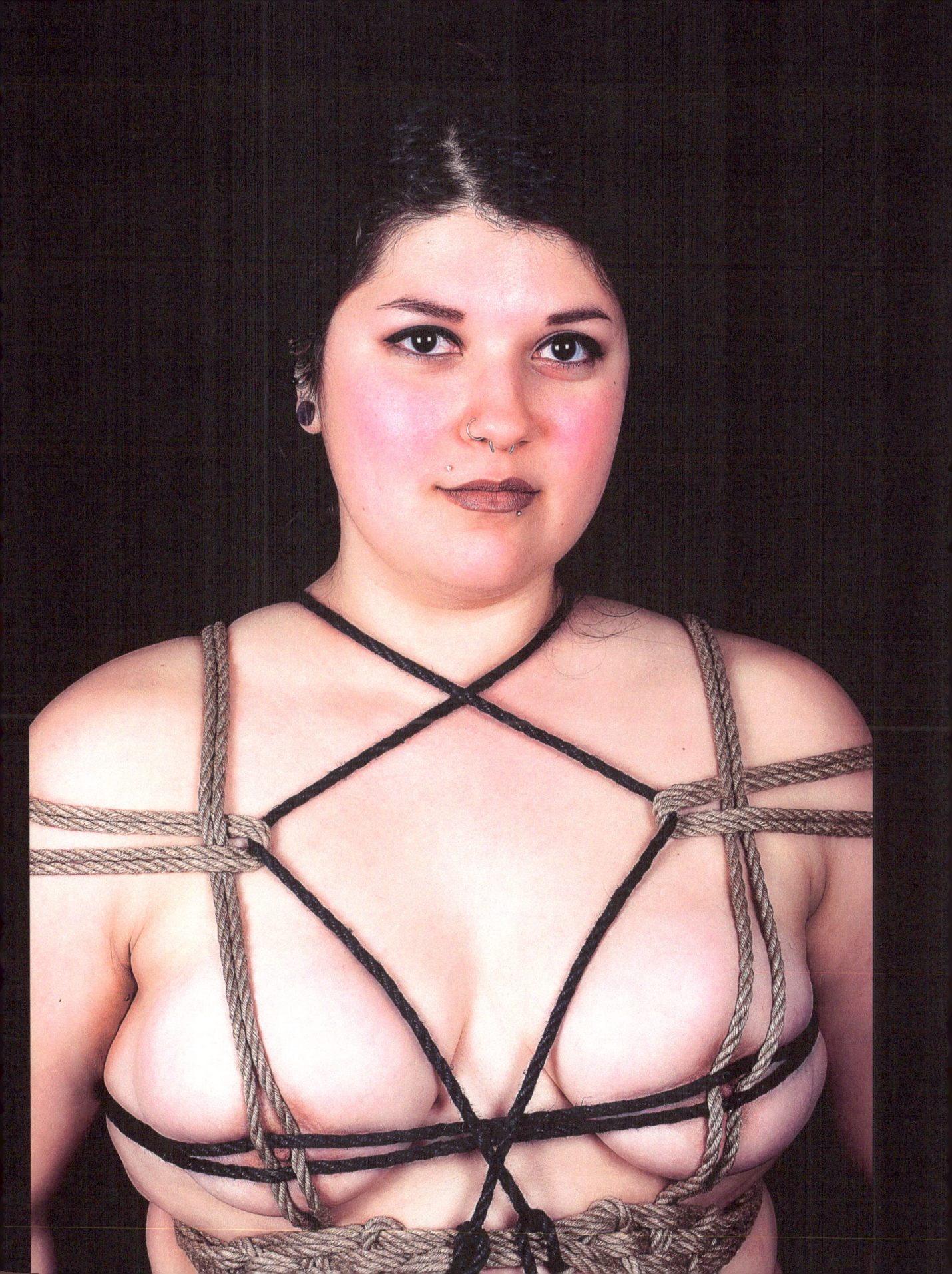

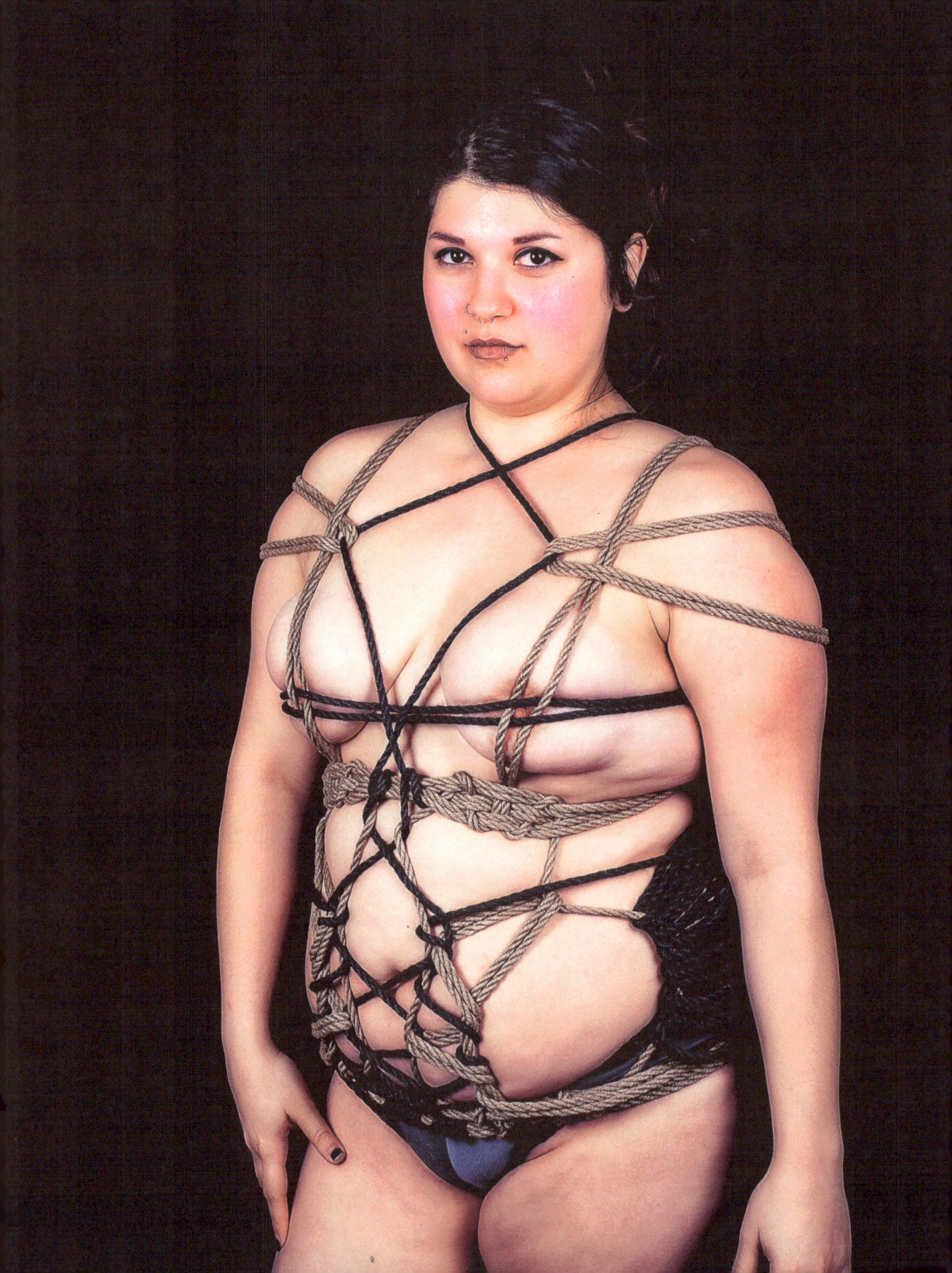

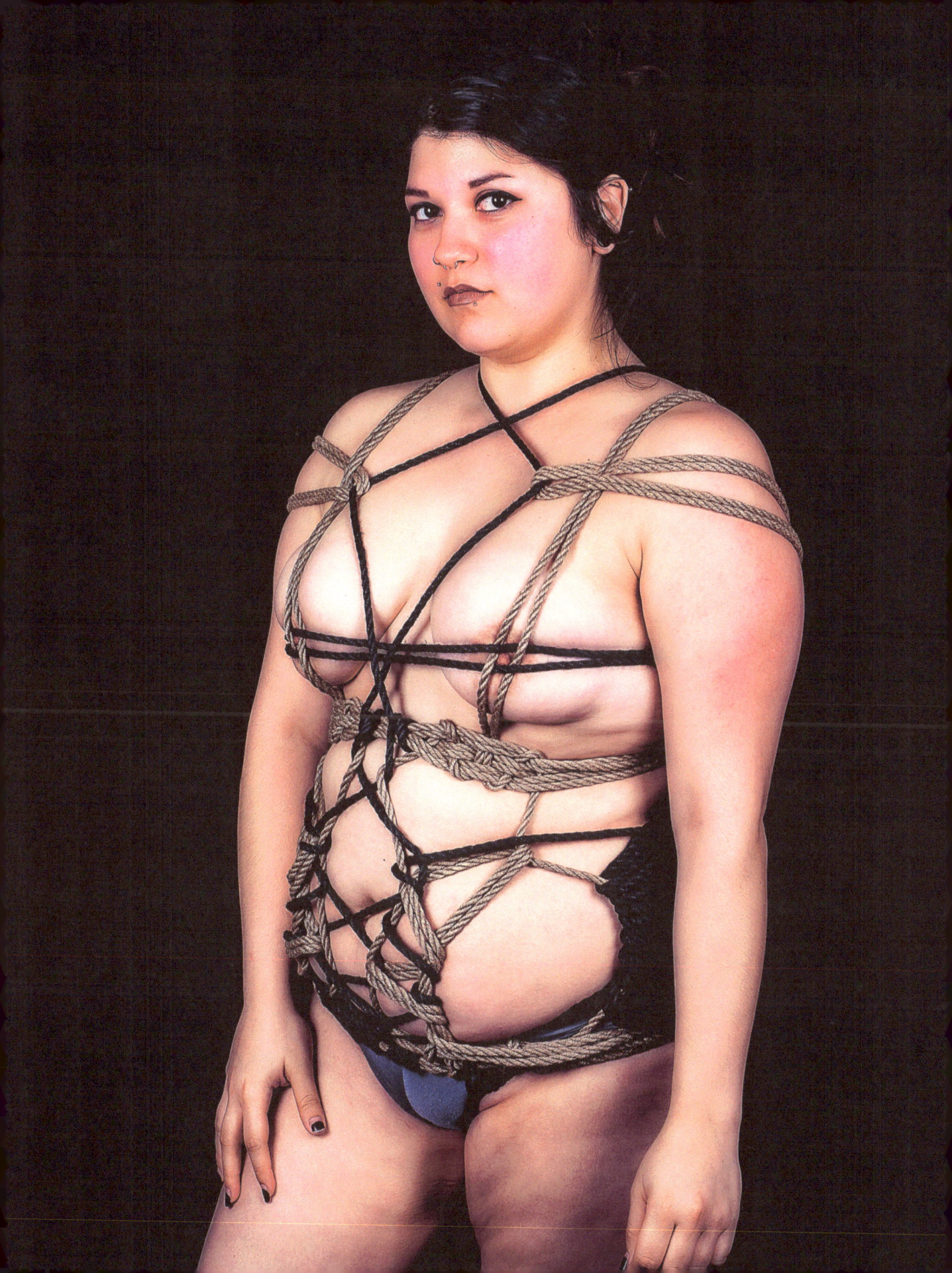

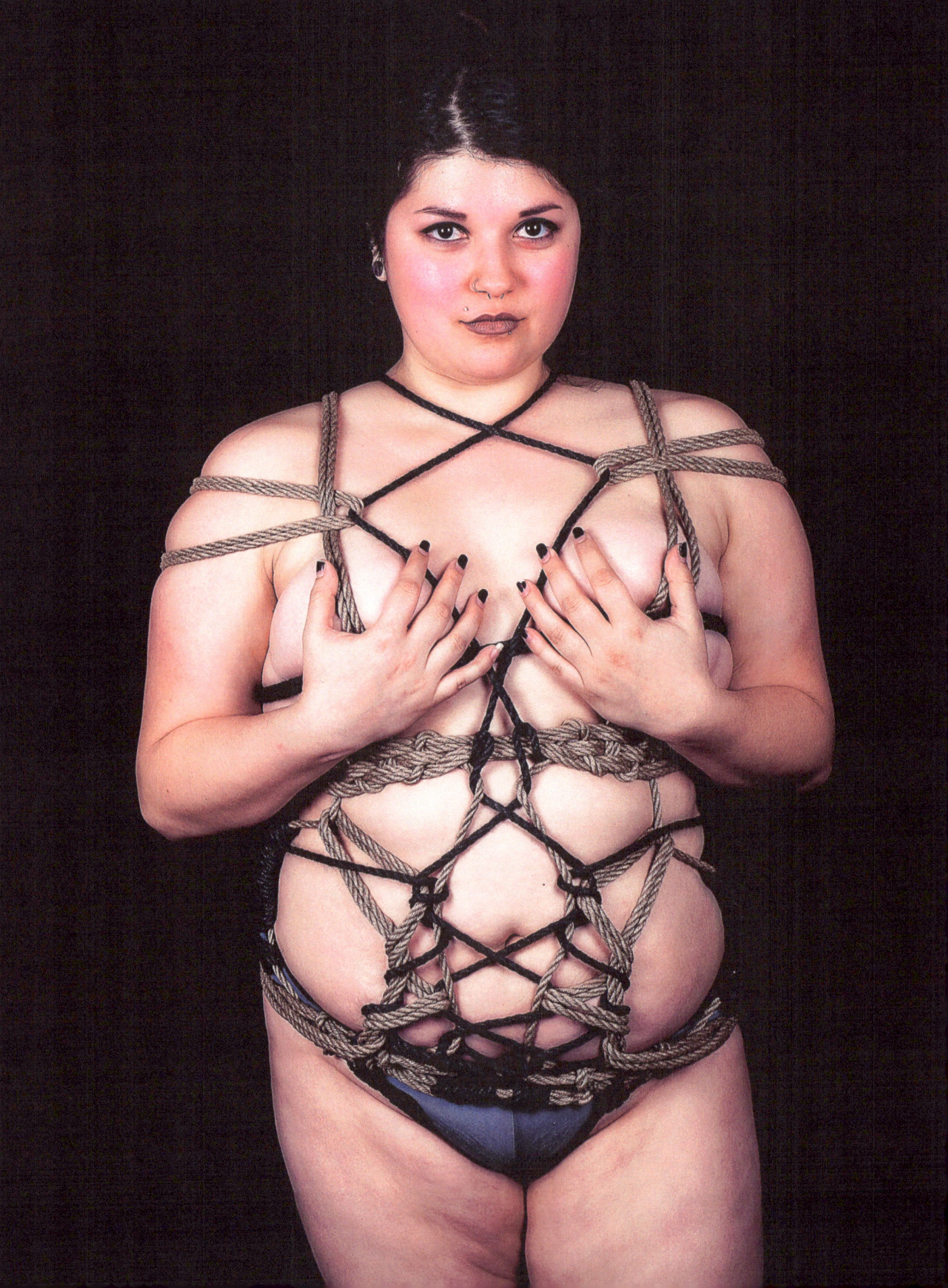

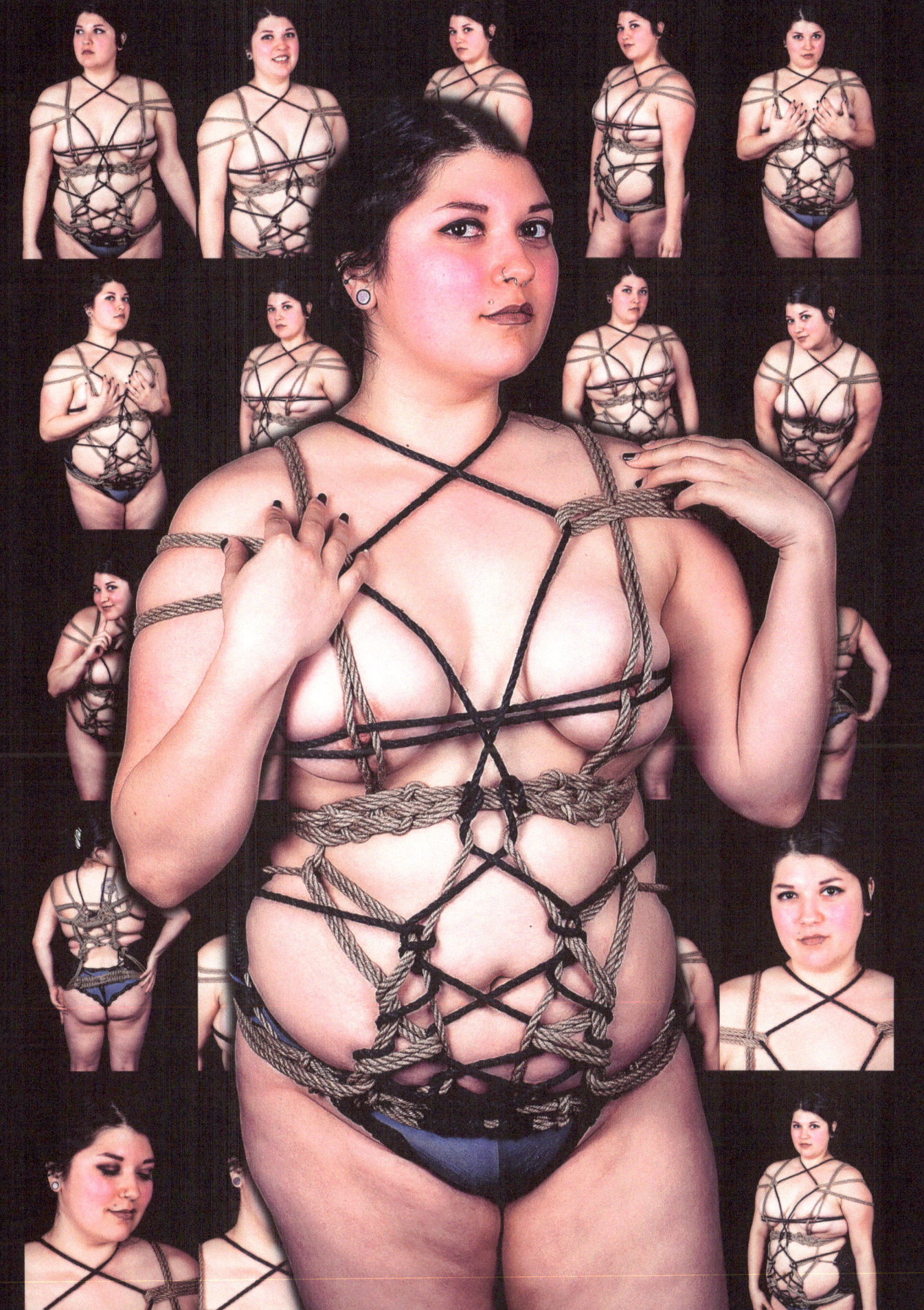

Dani

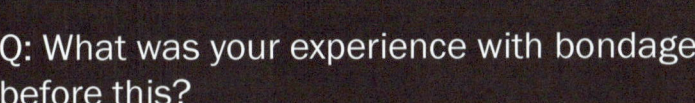

After a class one year I was doing an impromp-tu bondage party. In the middle of this a lady I had already decided was too shy for this kind of thing removed her cloths and stepped for-ward to be tied. Lesson: Never assume some-one is too shy.

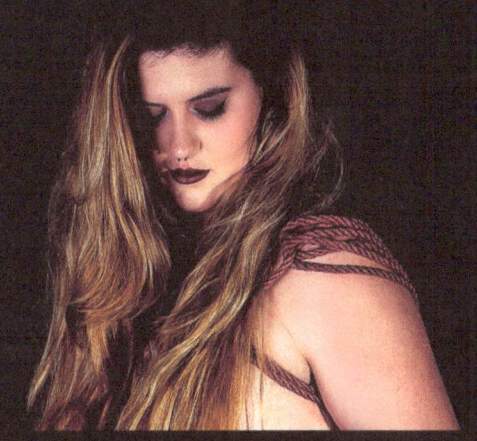

Q: What was your experience with bondage before this?
A: I'd previously done a few shoots.

Q: What did you think of this experience?
A: It was great. It was very comfortable and fun.

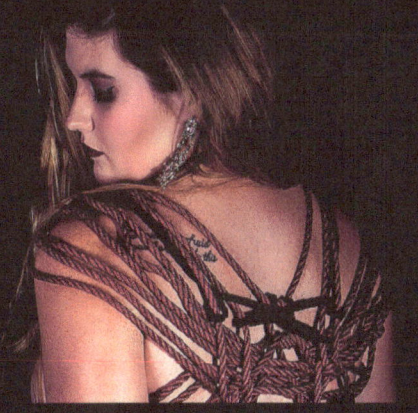

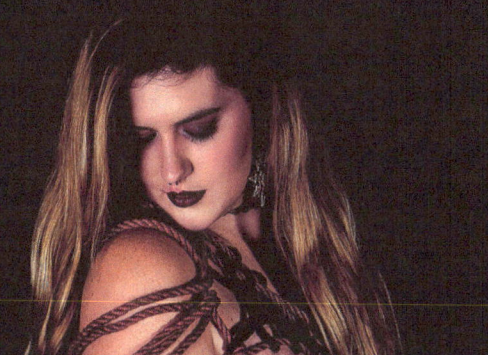

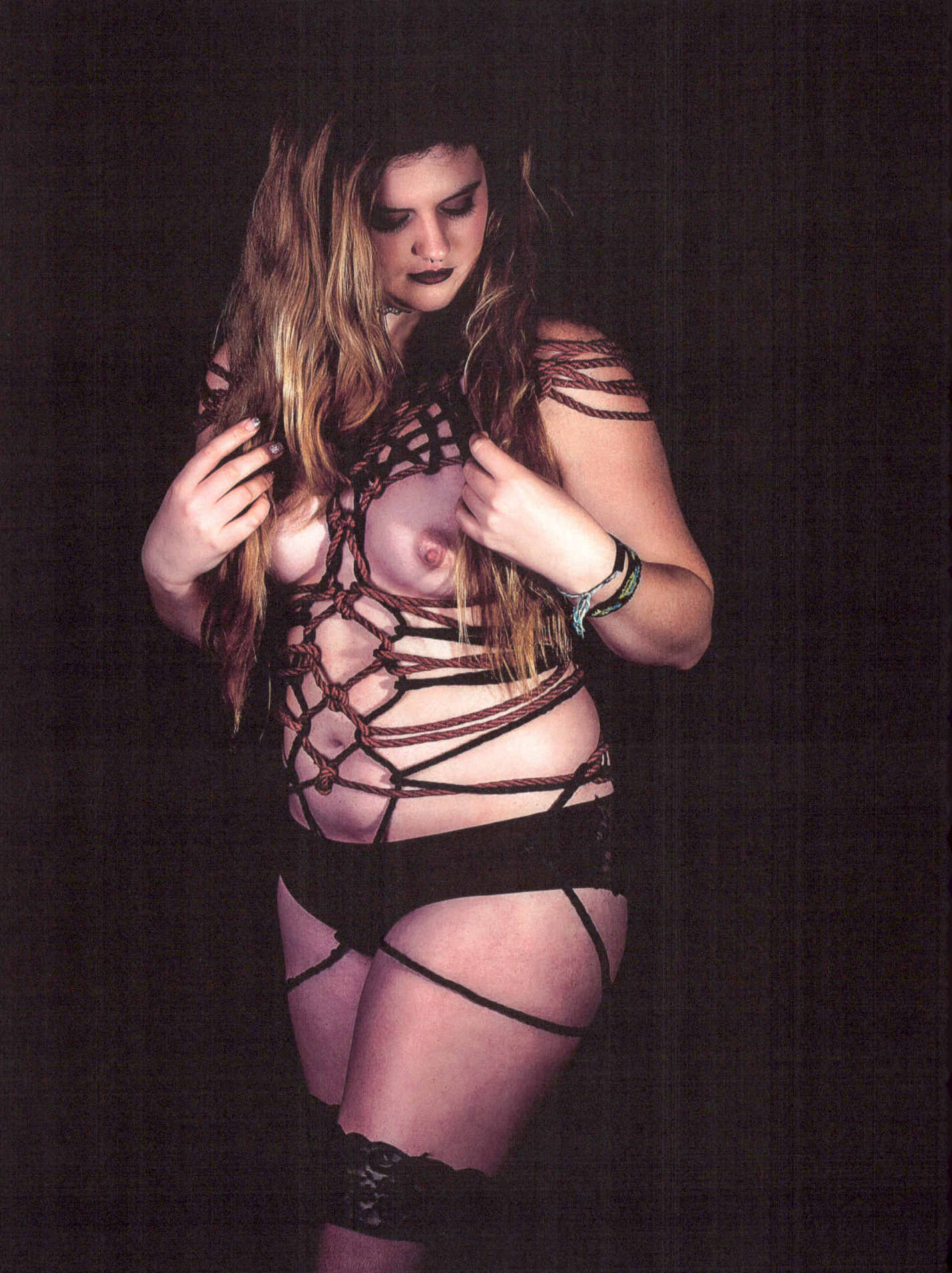

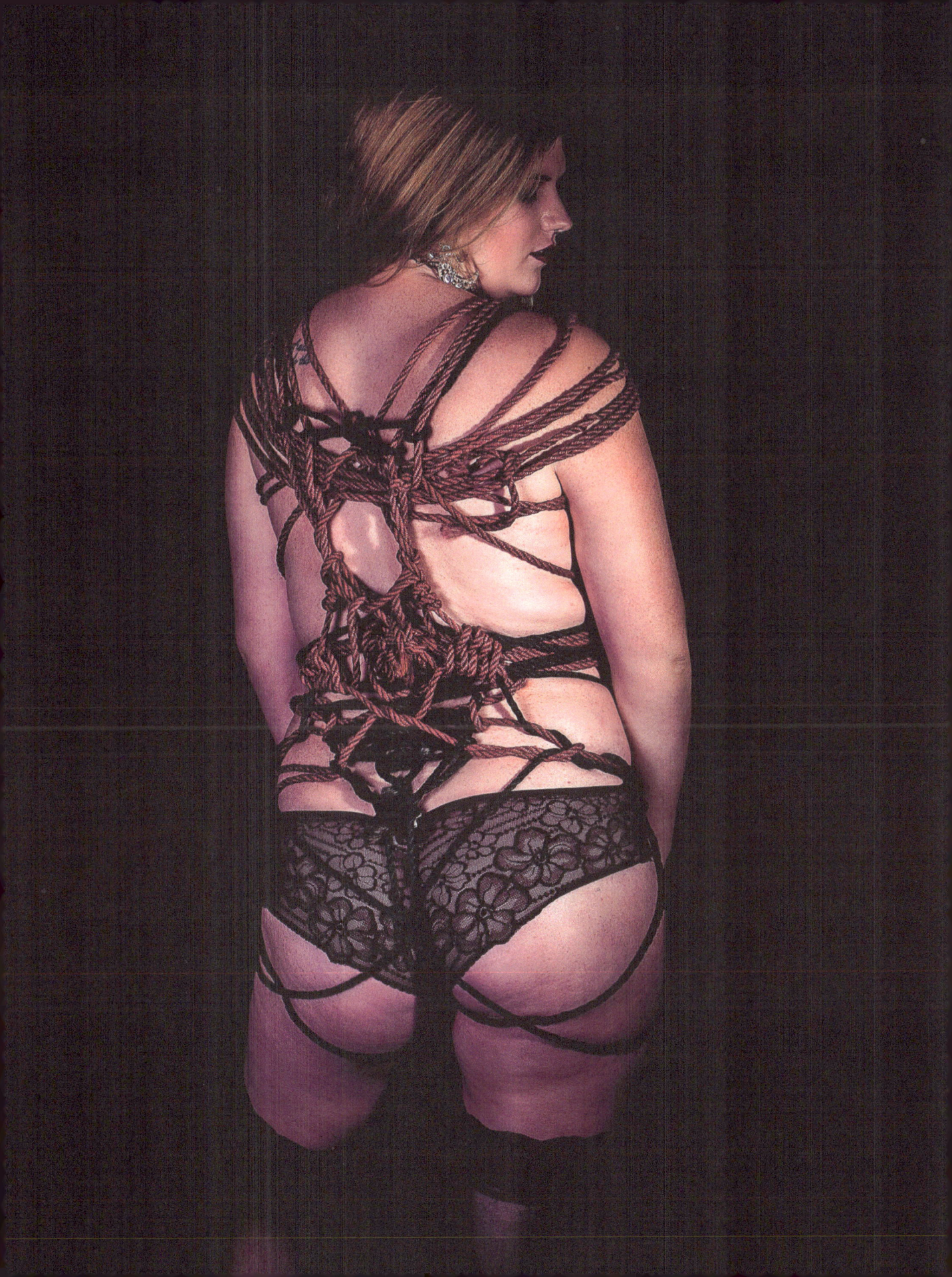

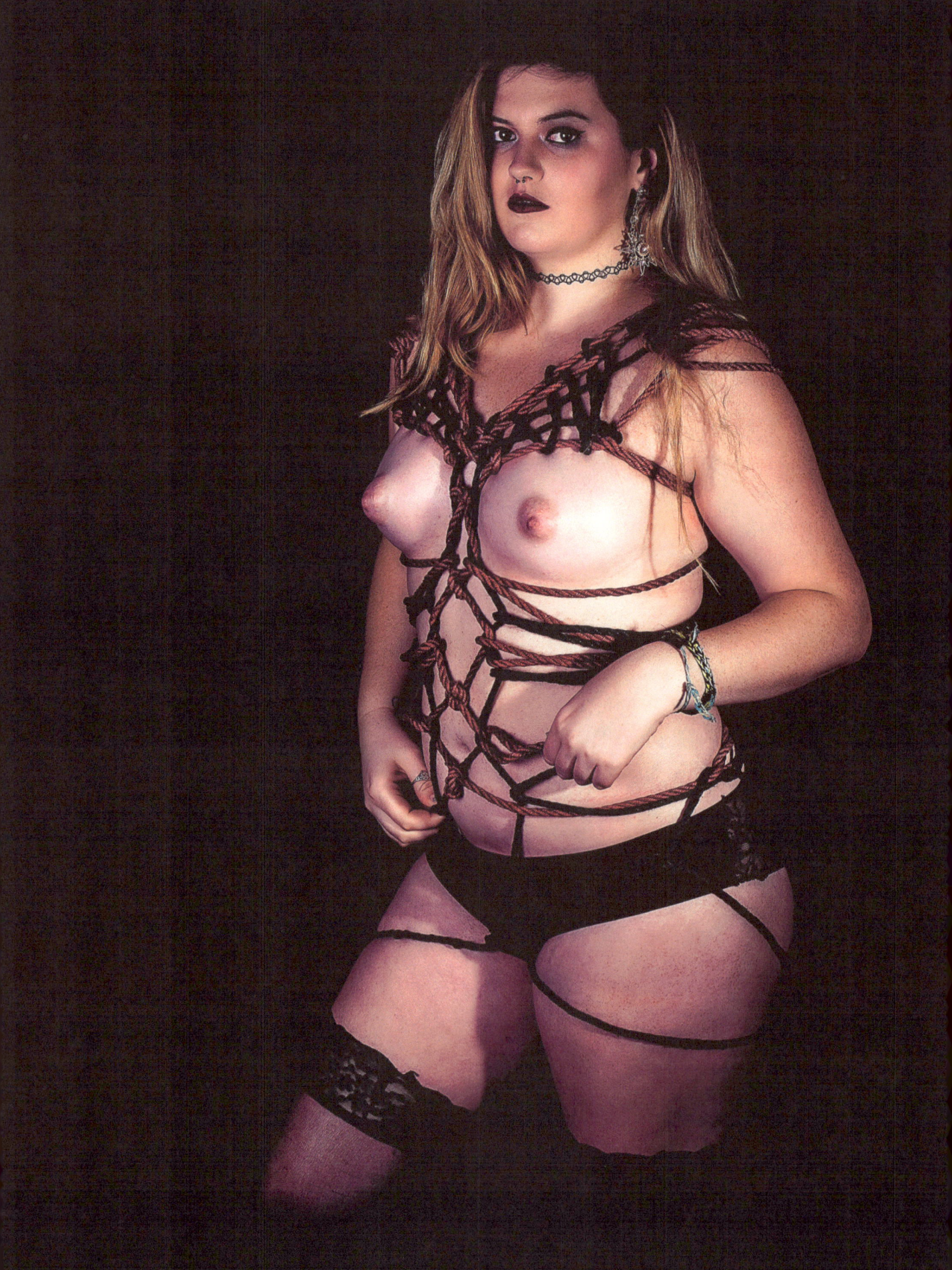

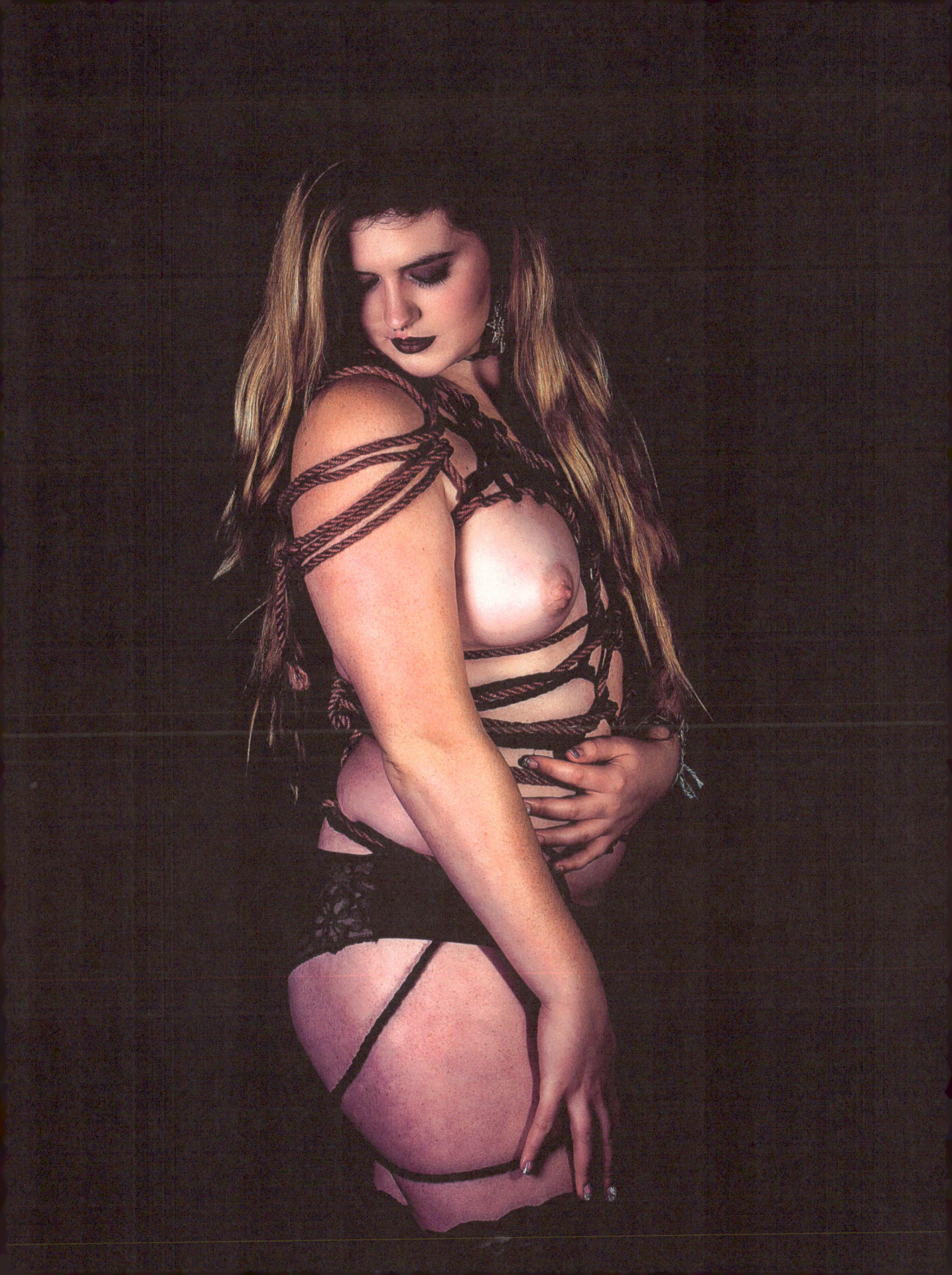

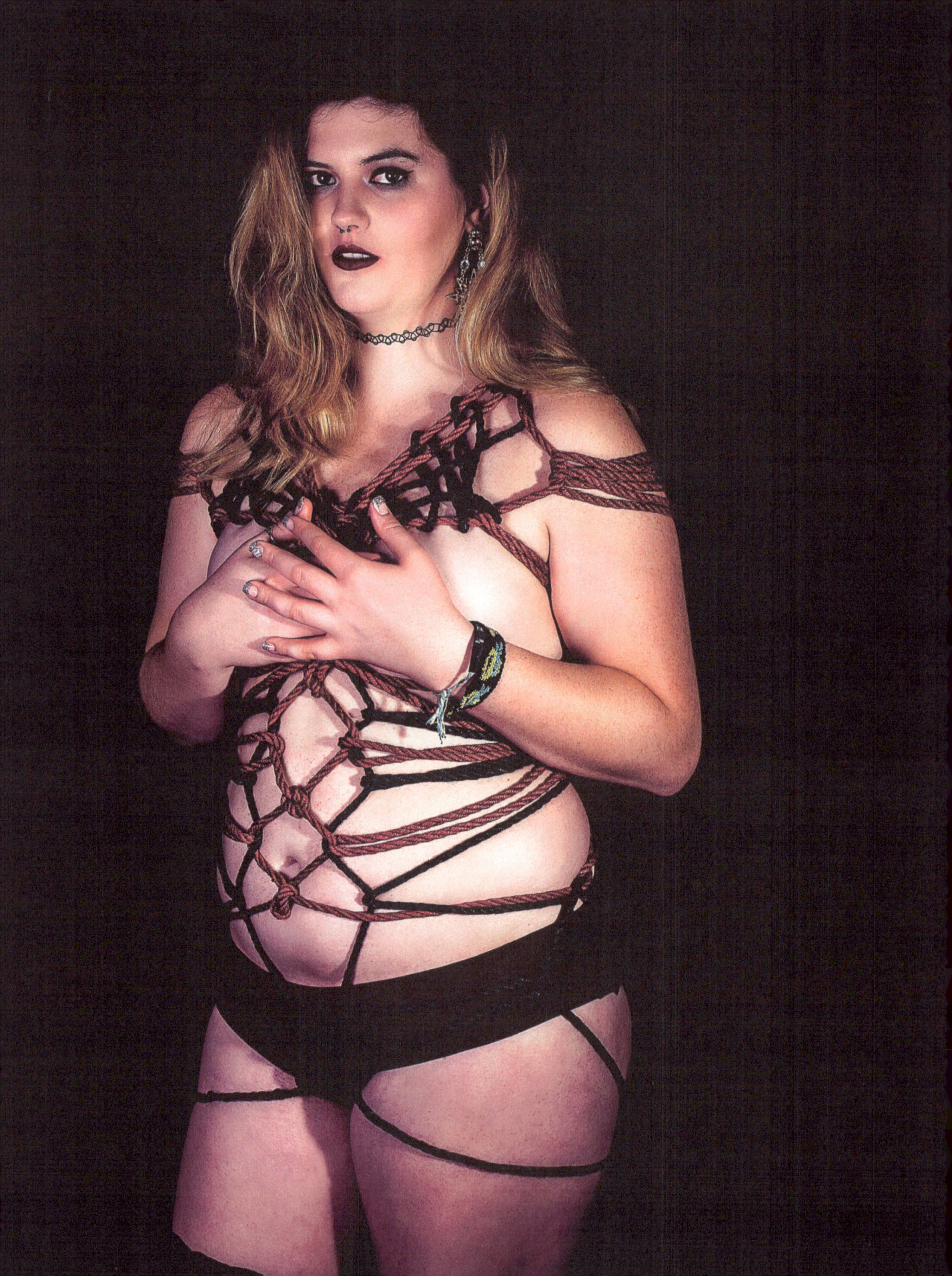

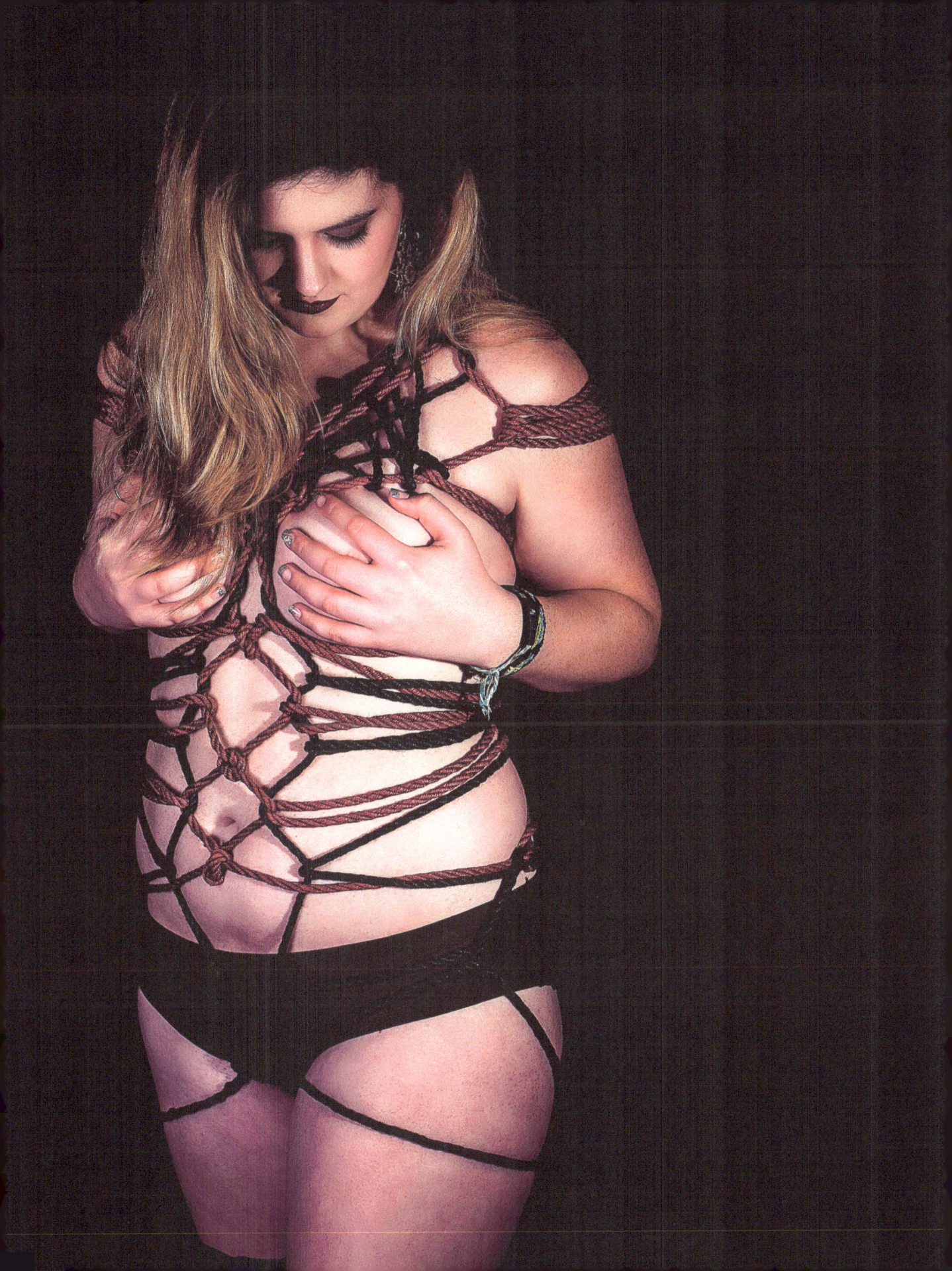

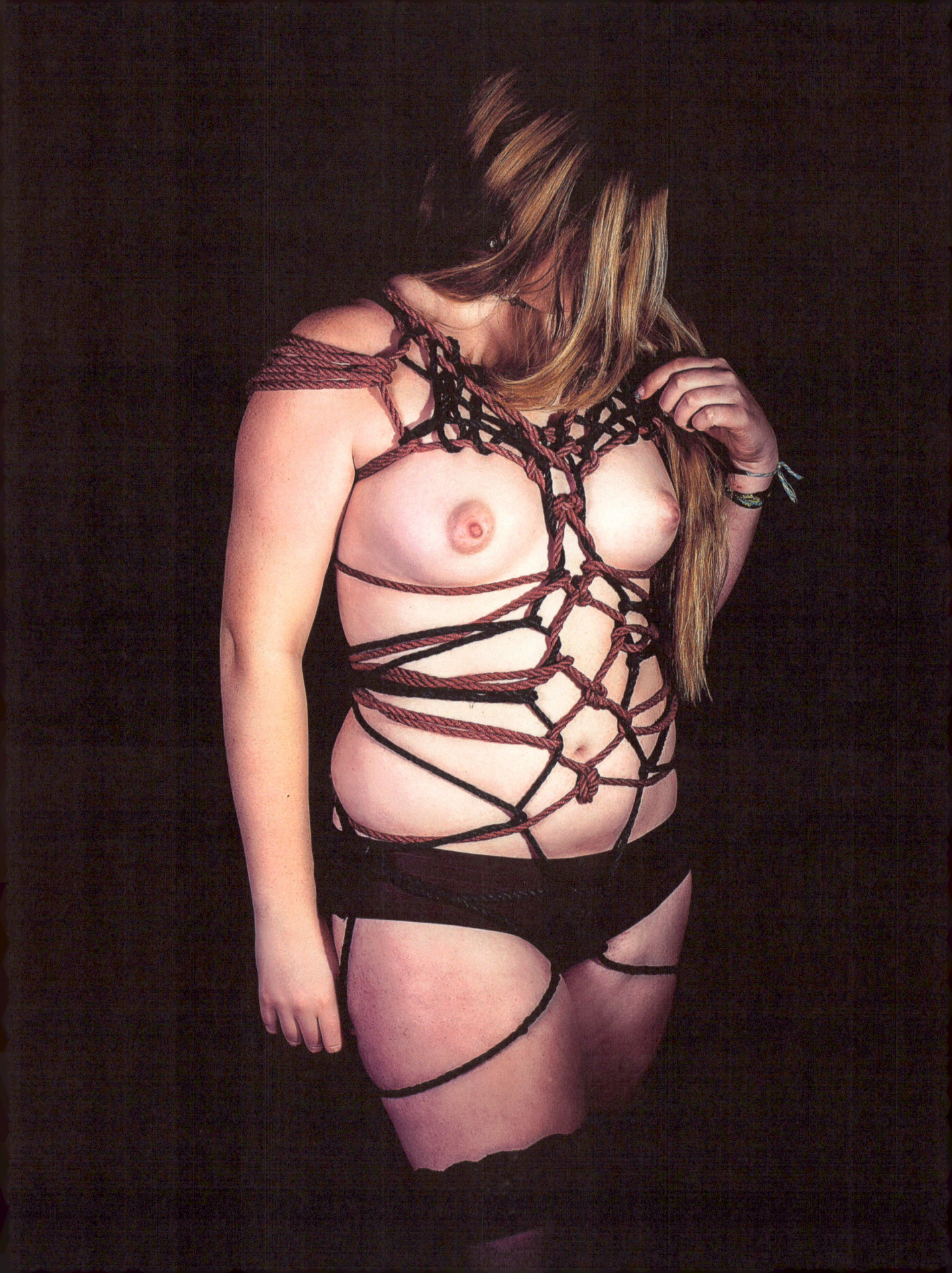

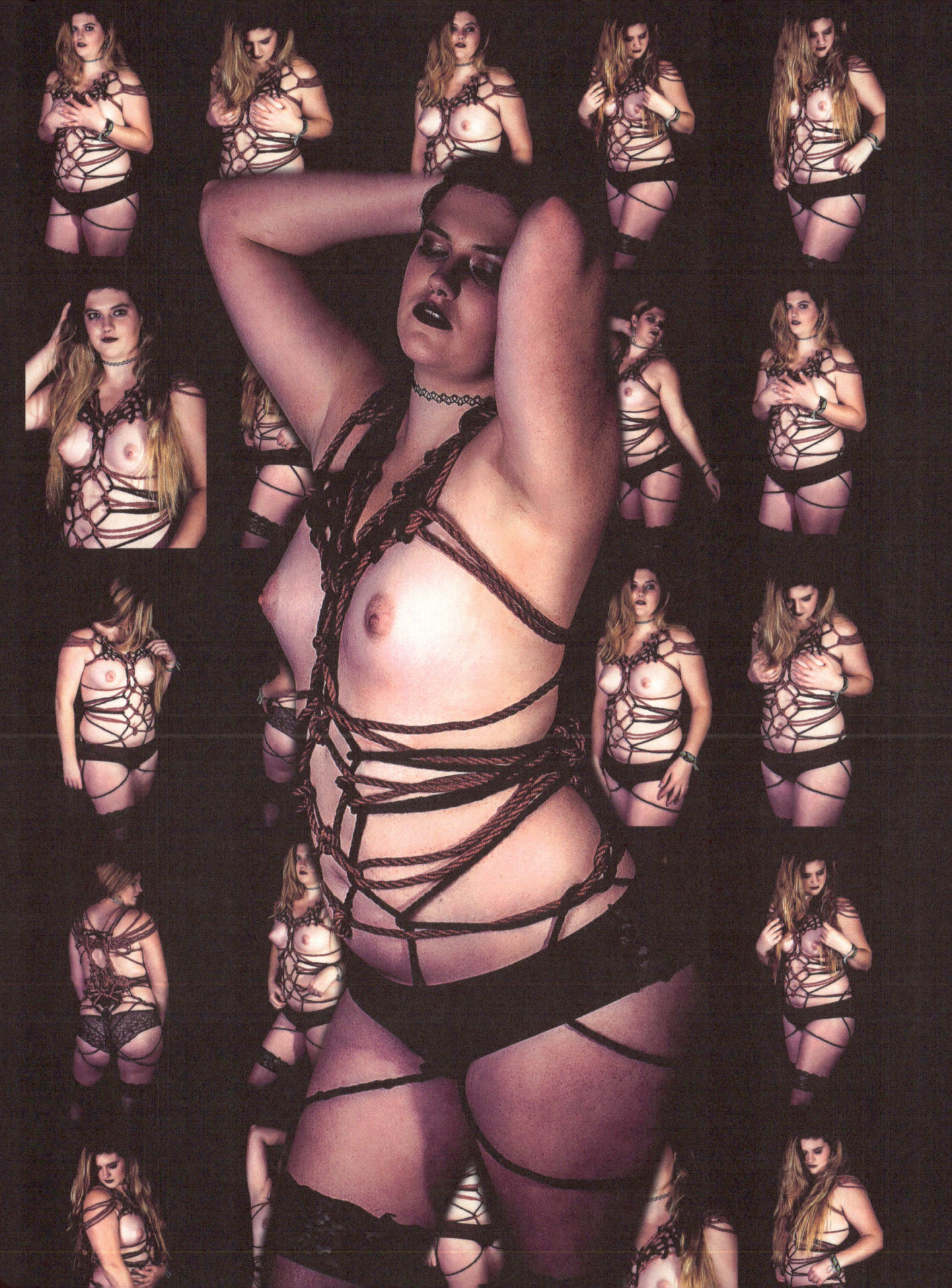

Ginger

Some people seem to just be built for rope.

Q: What was your experience with bondage before this?
A: None

Q: Was did you think about this experience?
A: It was completely professional, courteous experience that I don't always encounter on other (non-bondage) photo shoots.

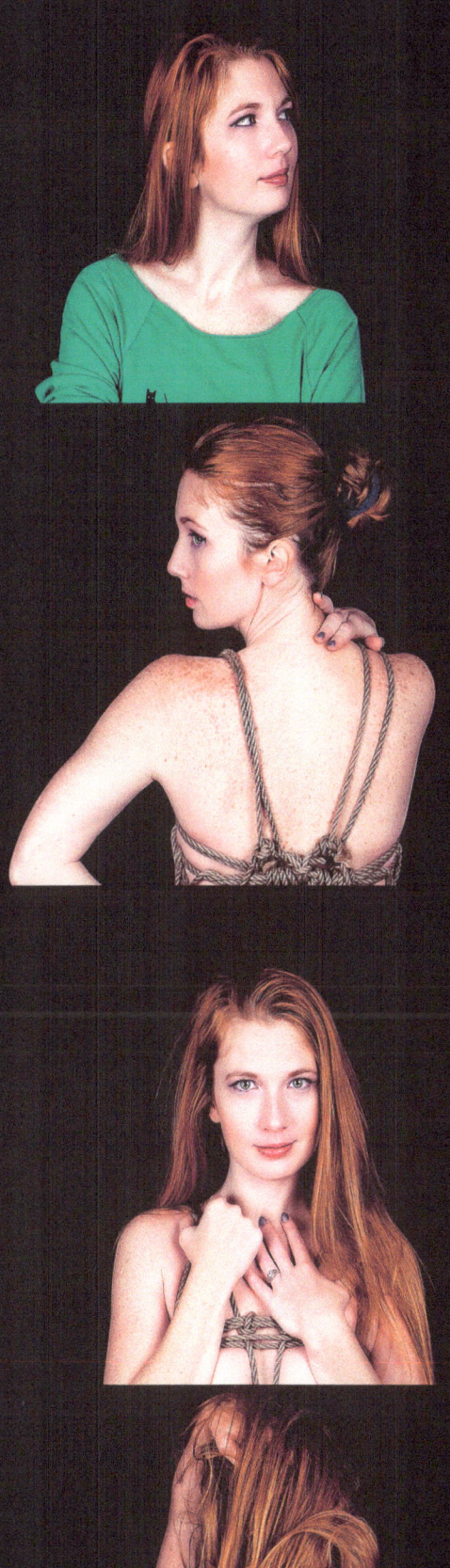

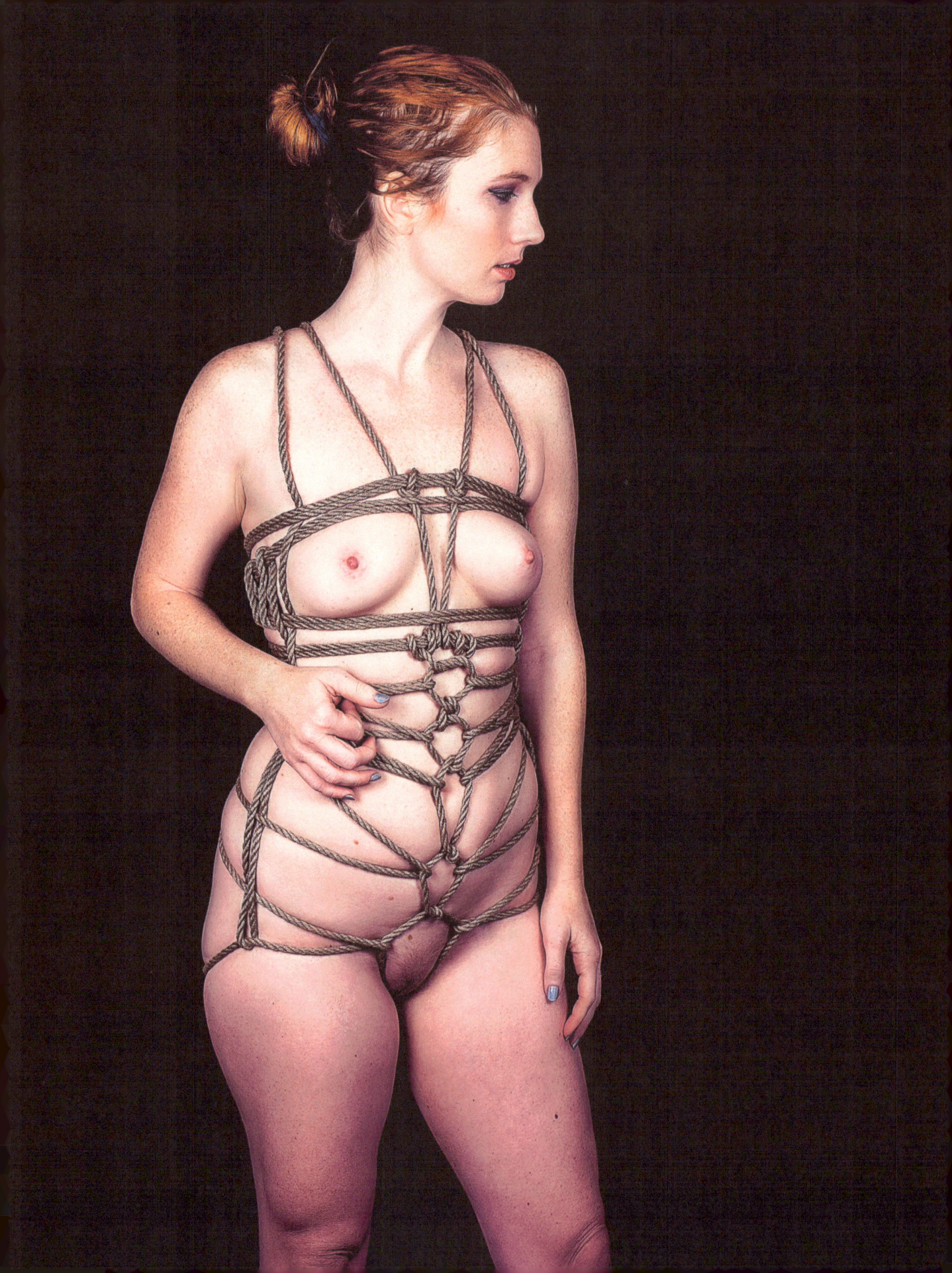

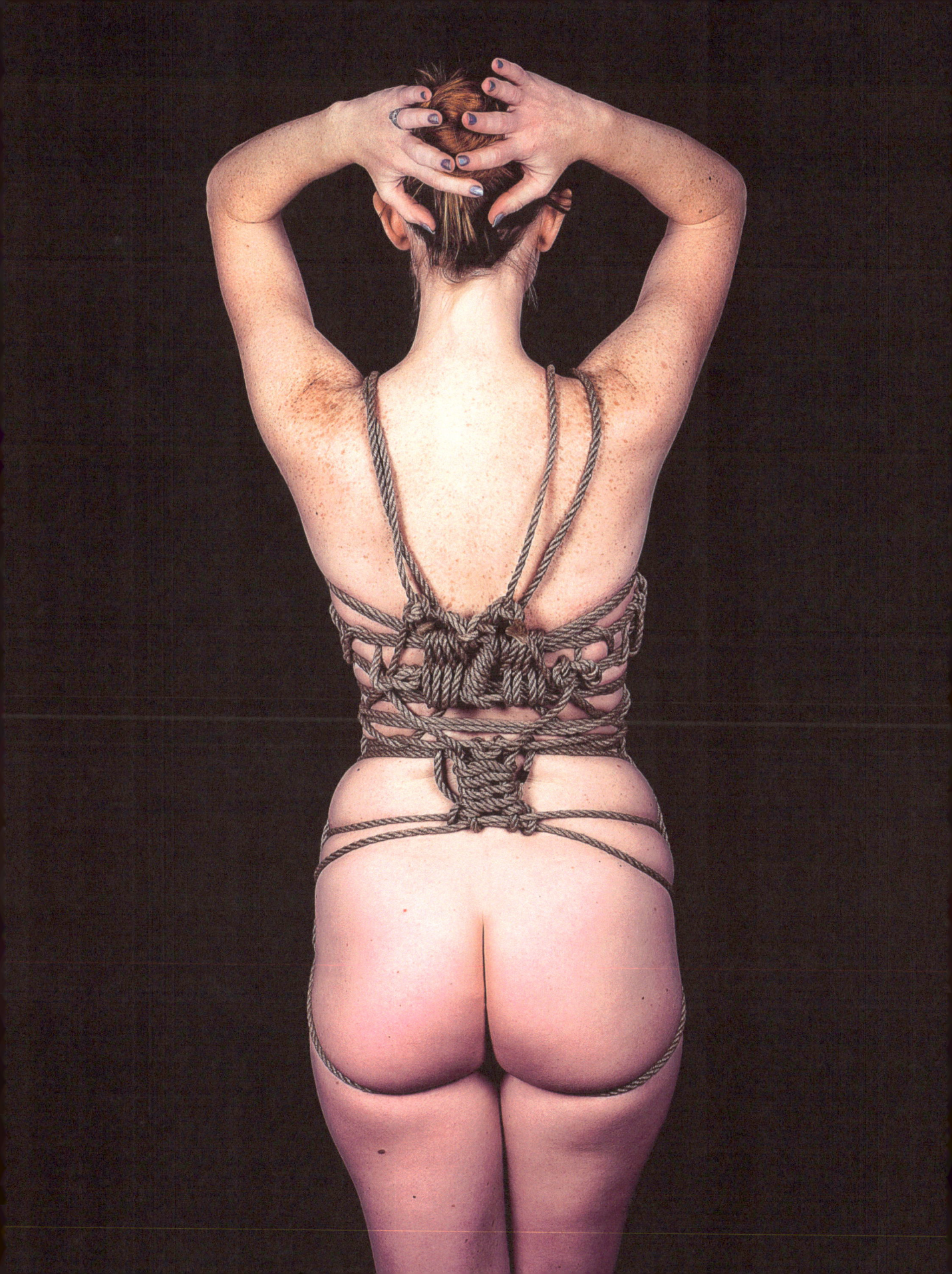

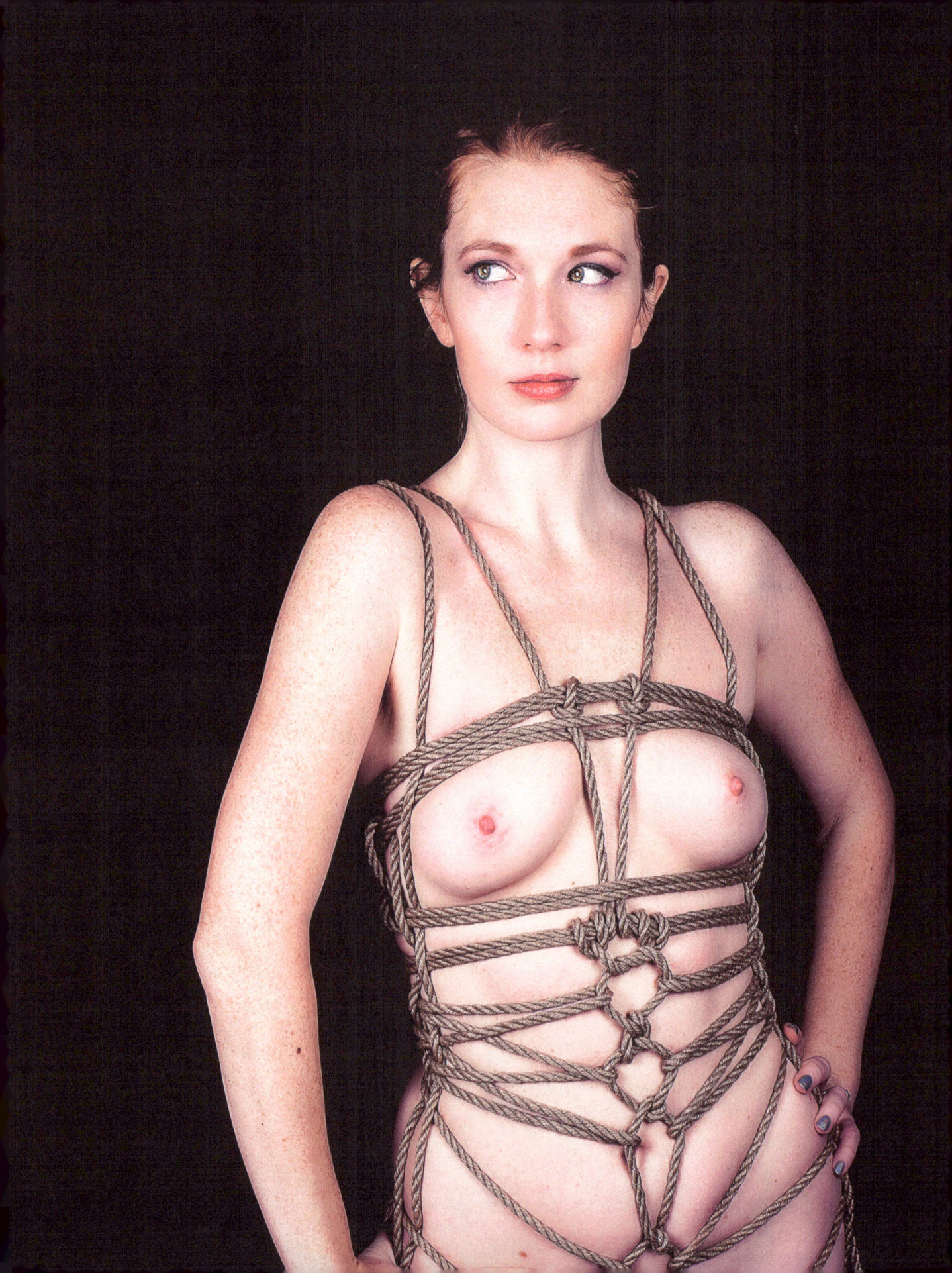

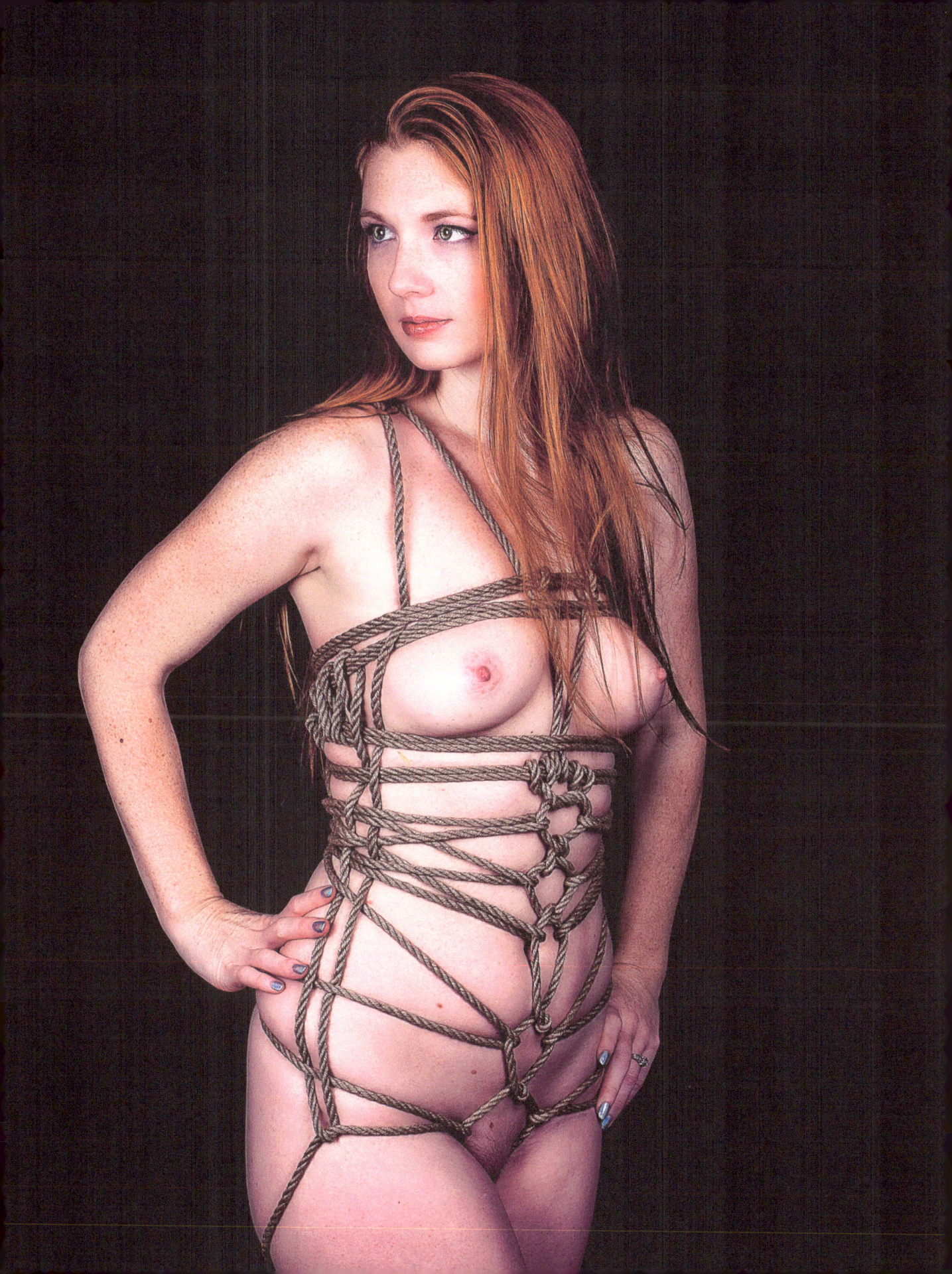

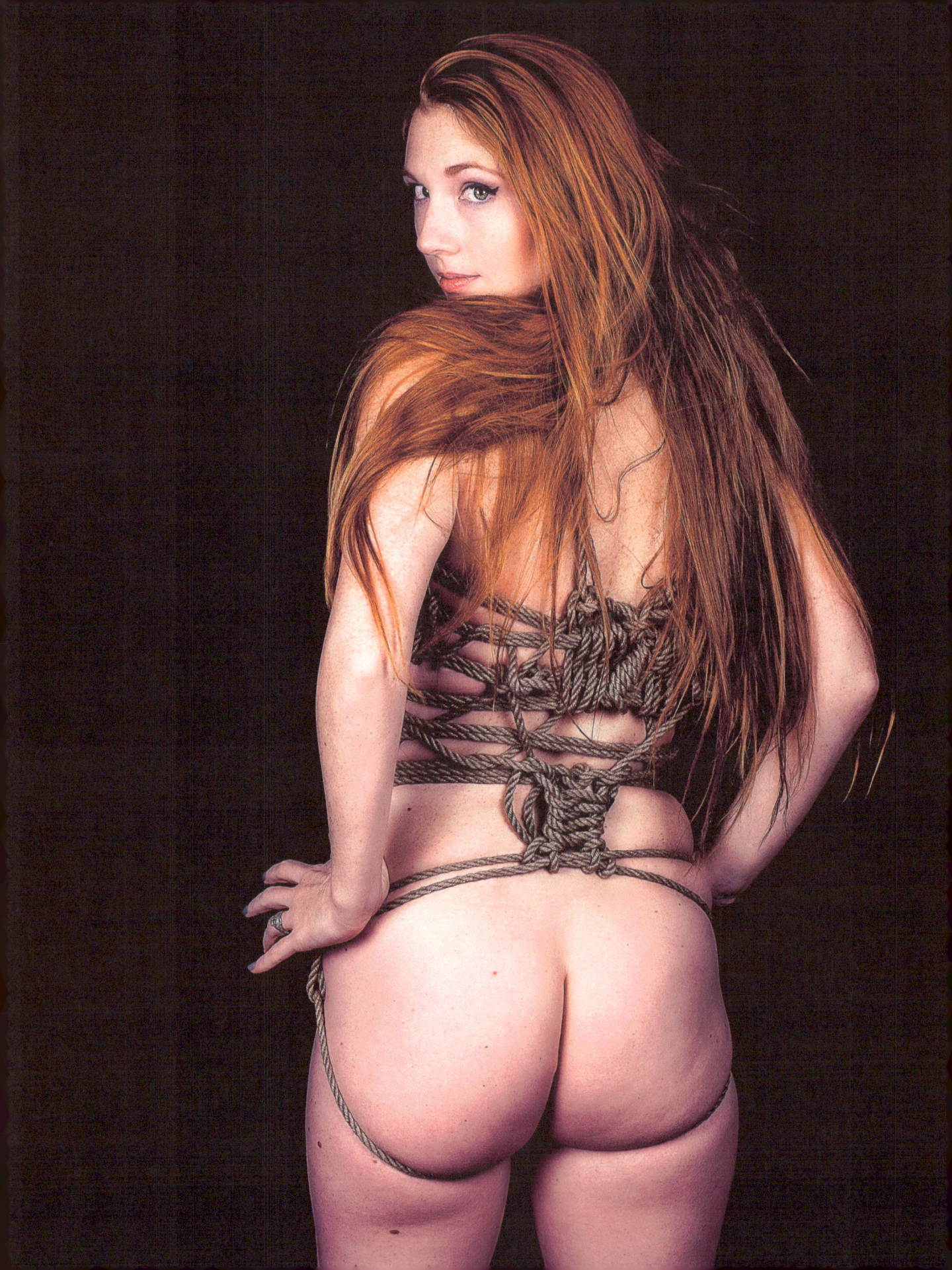

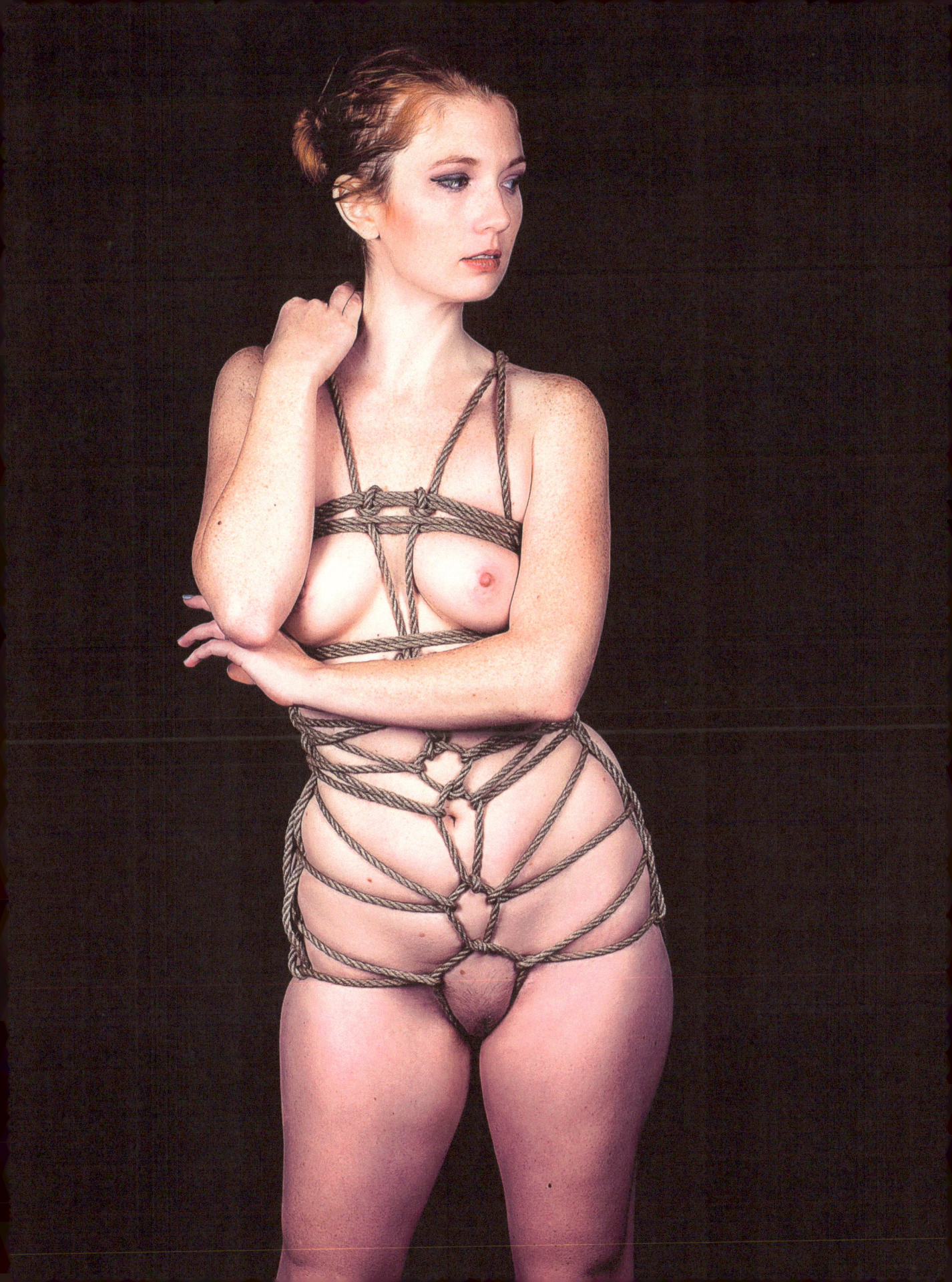

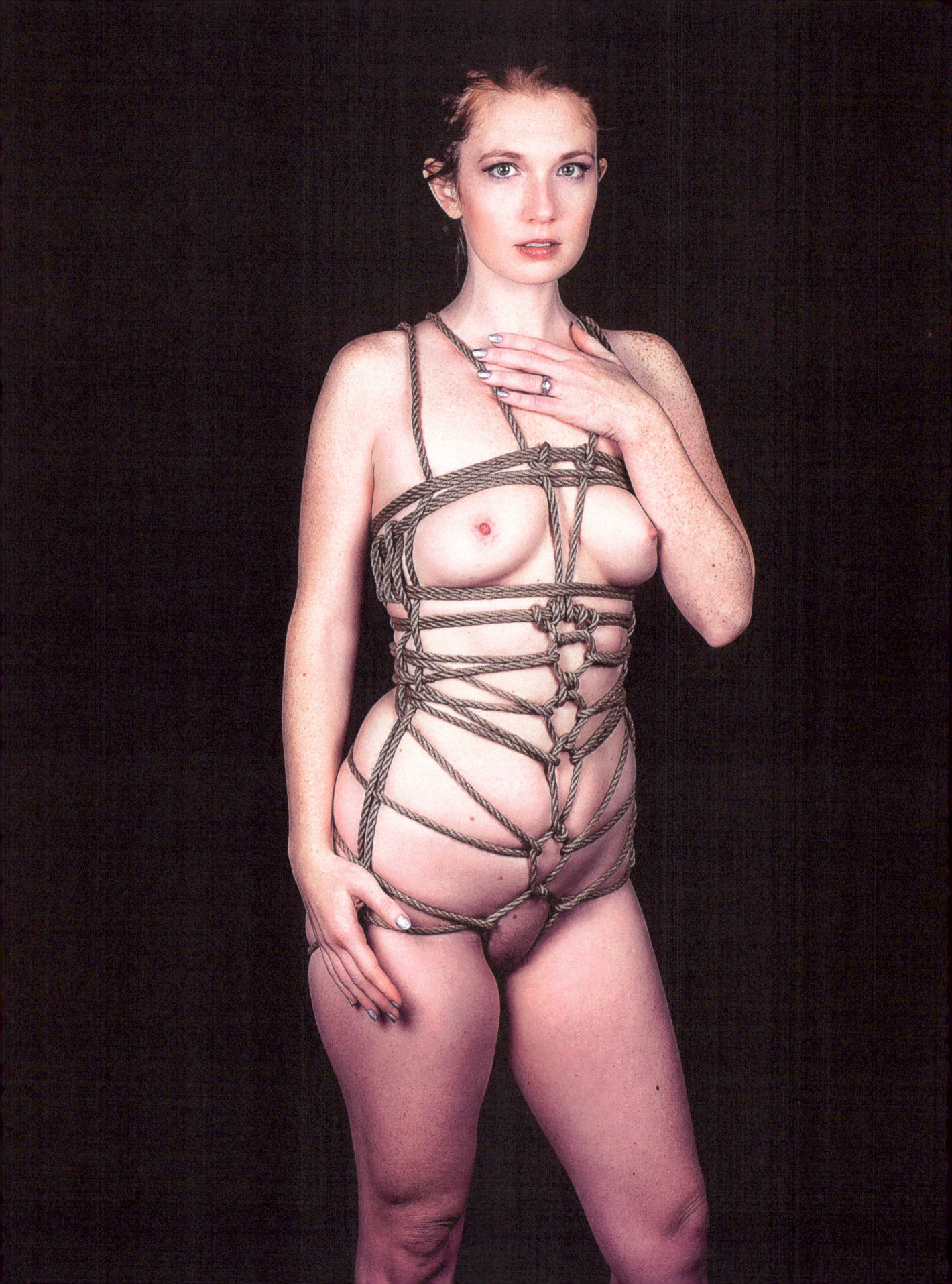

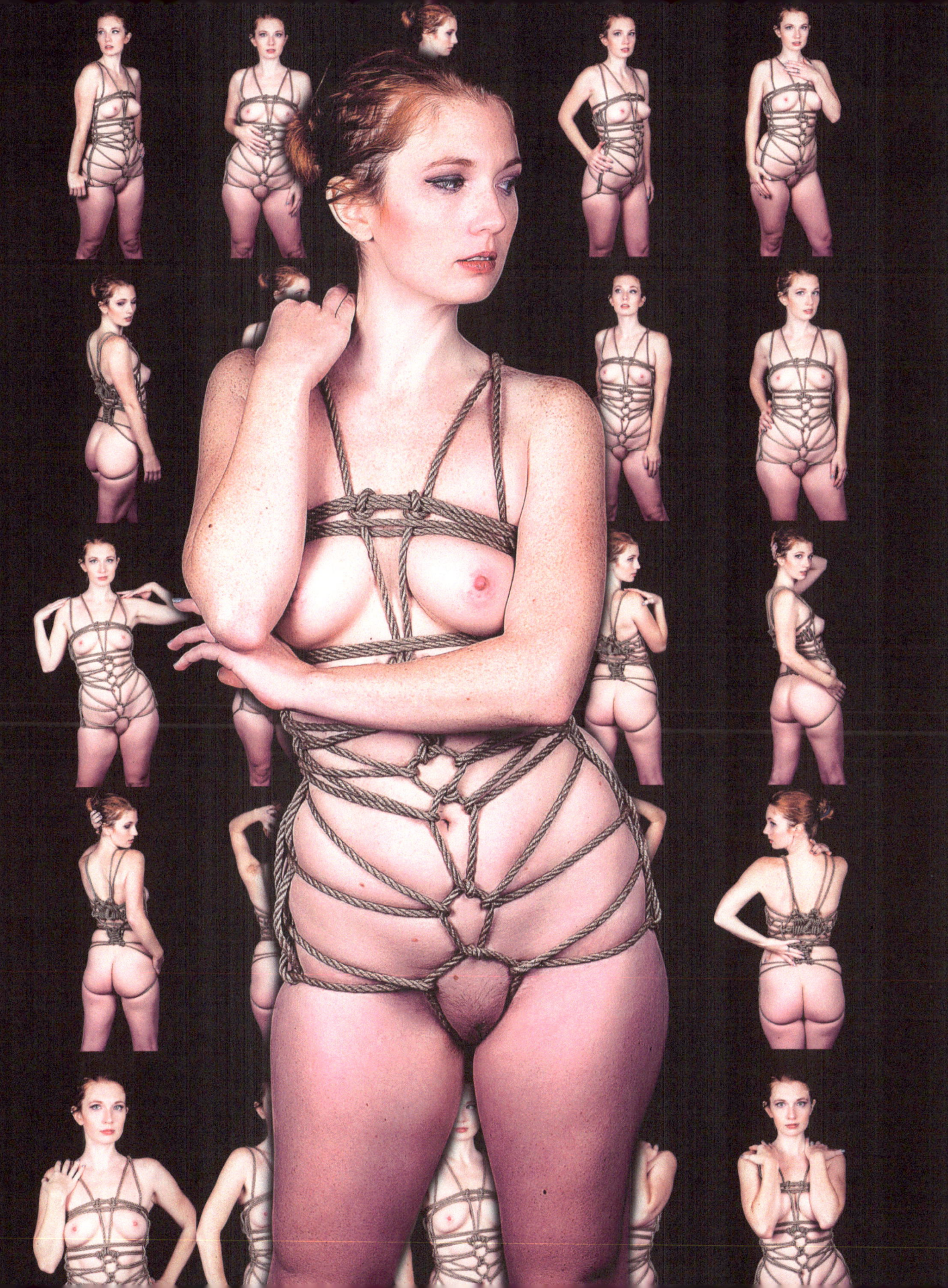

Lindsey H

There is nothing more powerful than a pretty girl who knows how to pout.

Q: What was your experience with bondage before this?
A: None

Q: How did you feel about this experience?
A: It was very pleasant and I got to learn a lot of new stuff too.

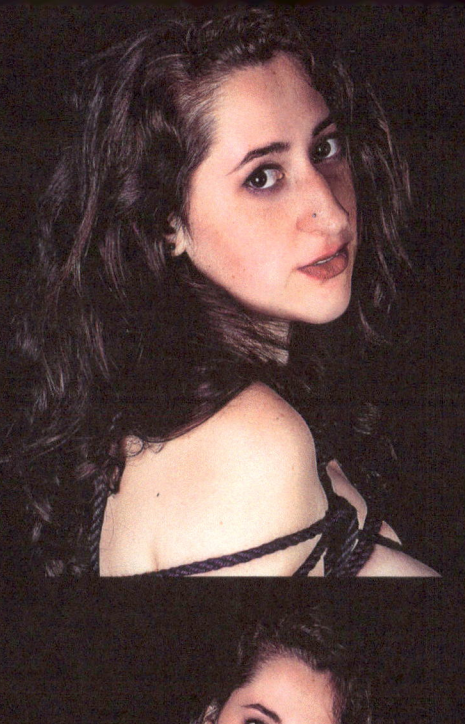

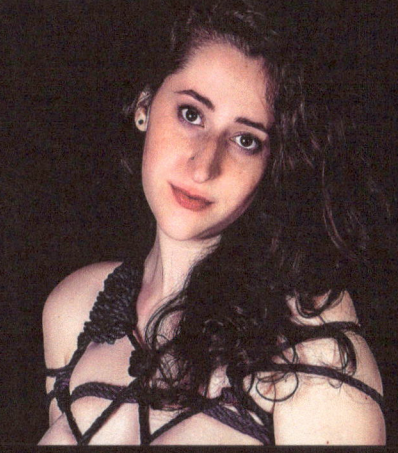

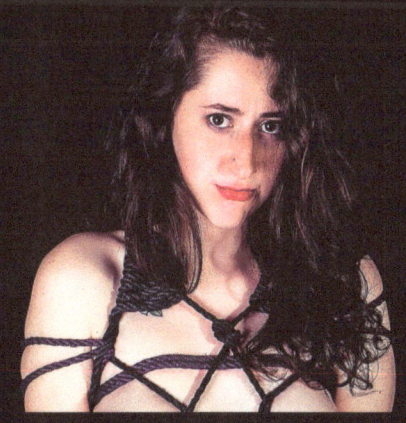

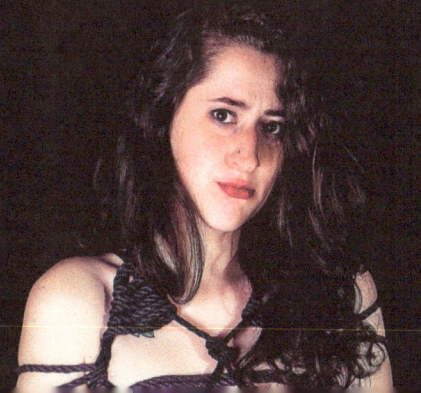

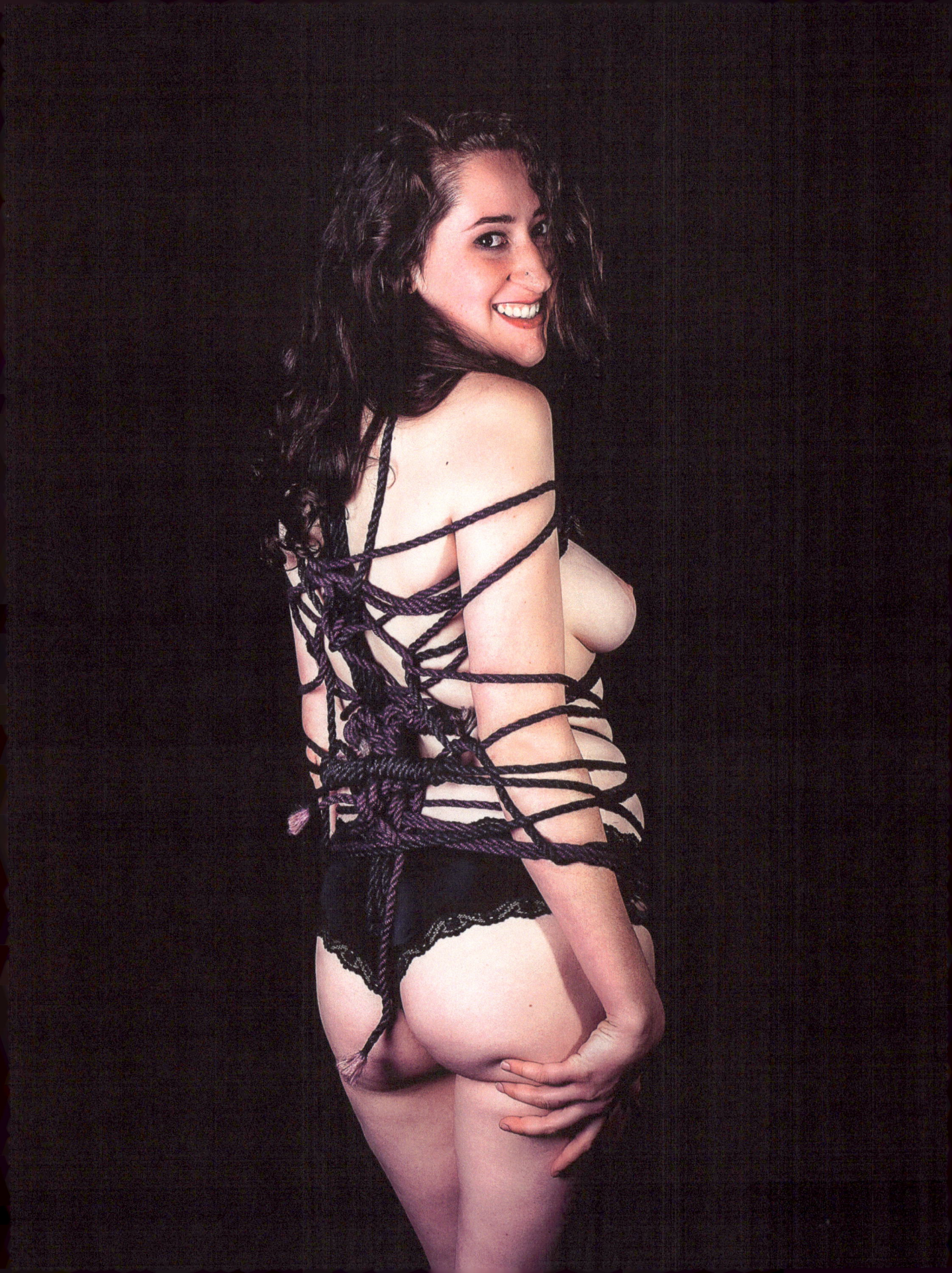

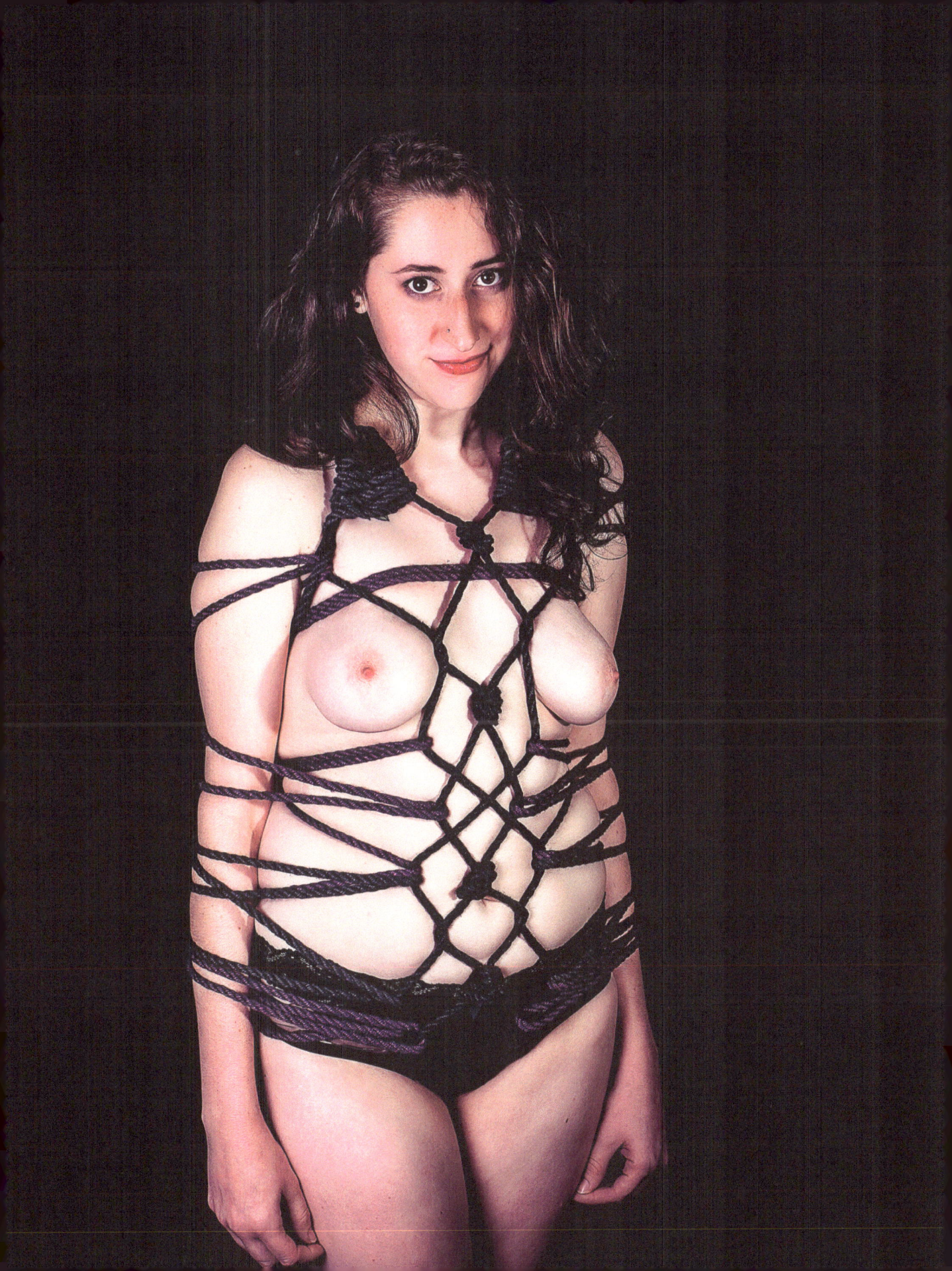

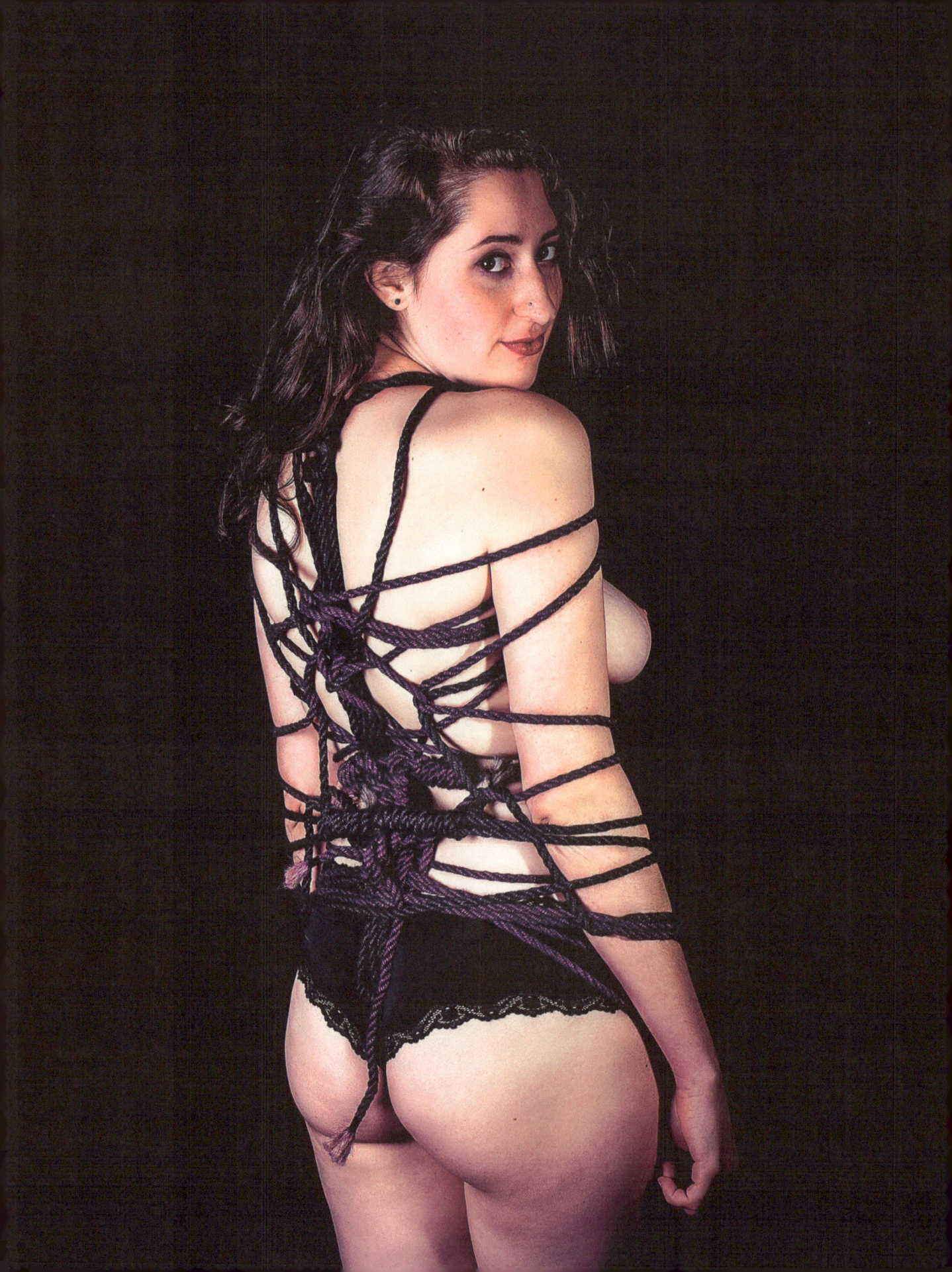

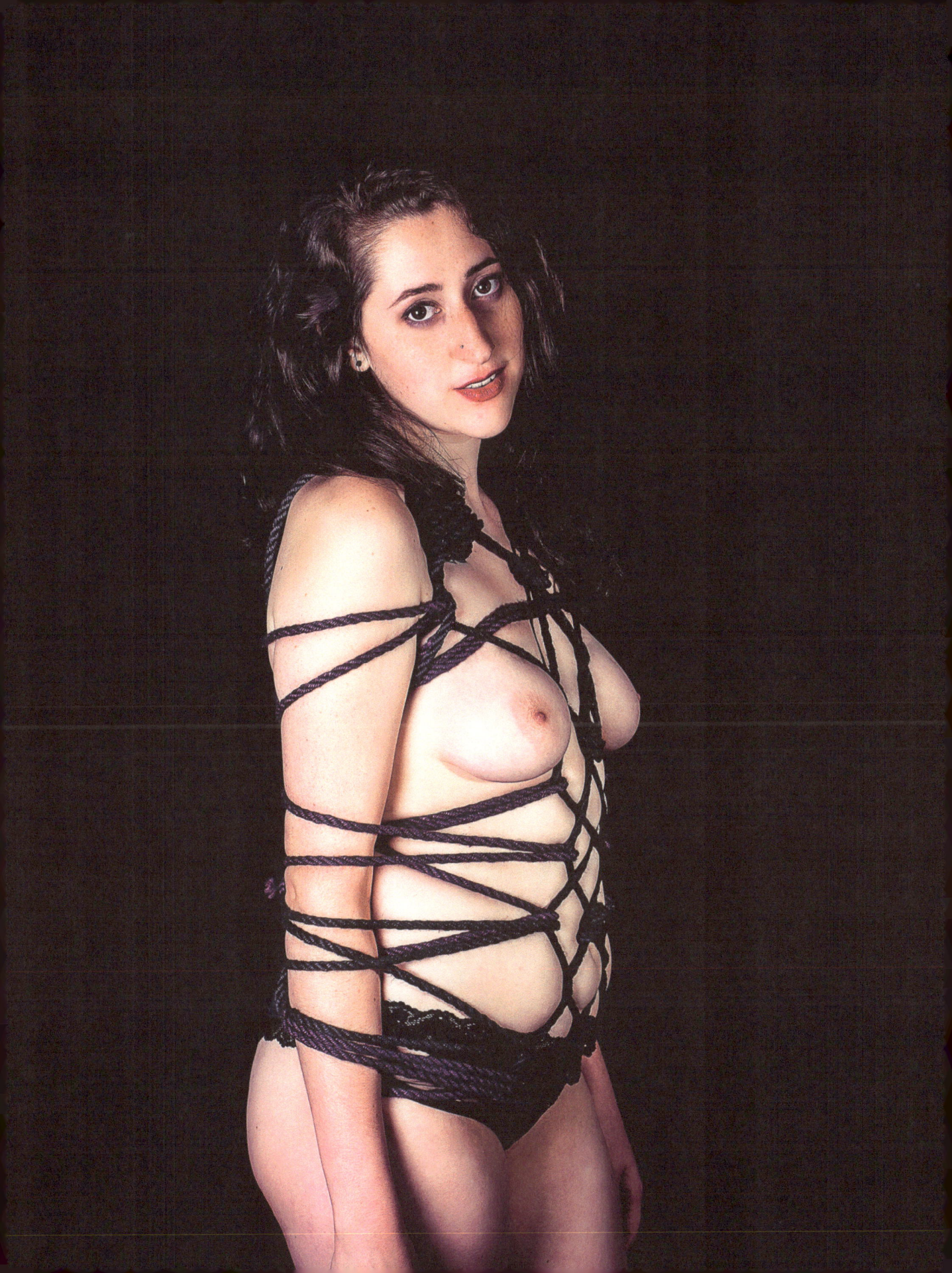

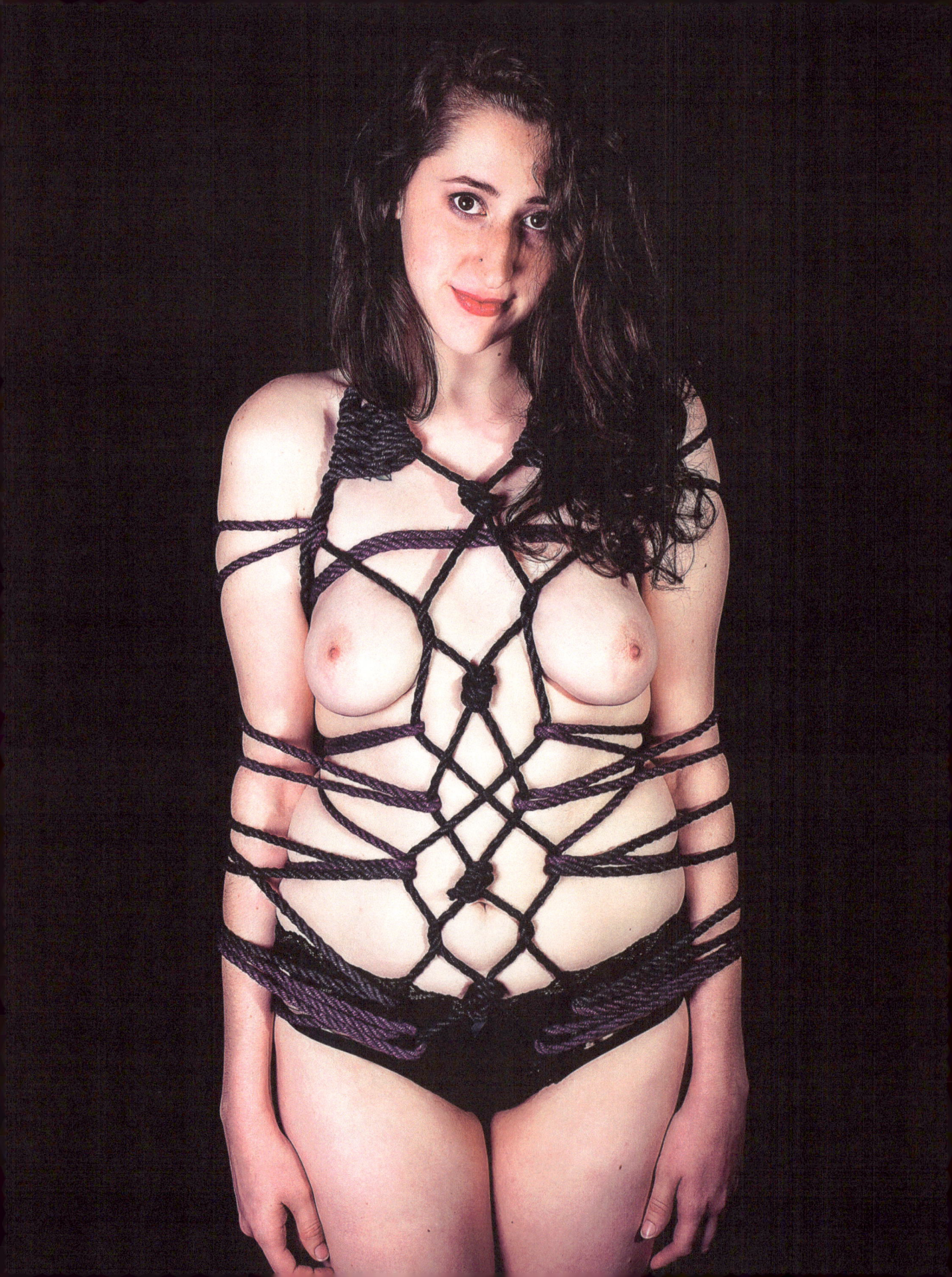

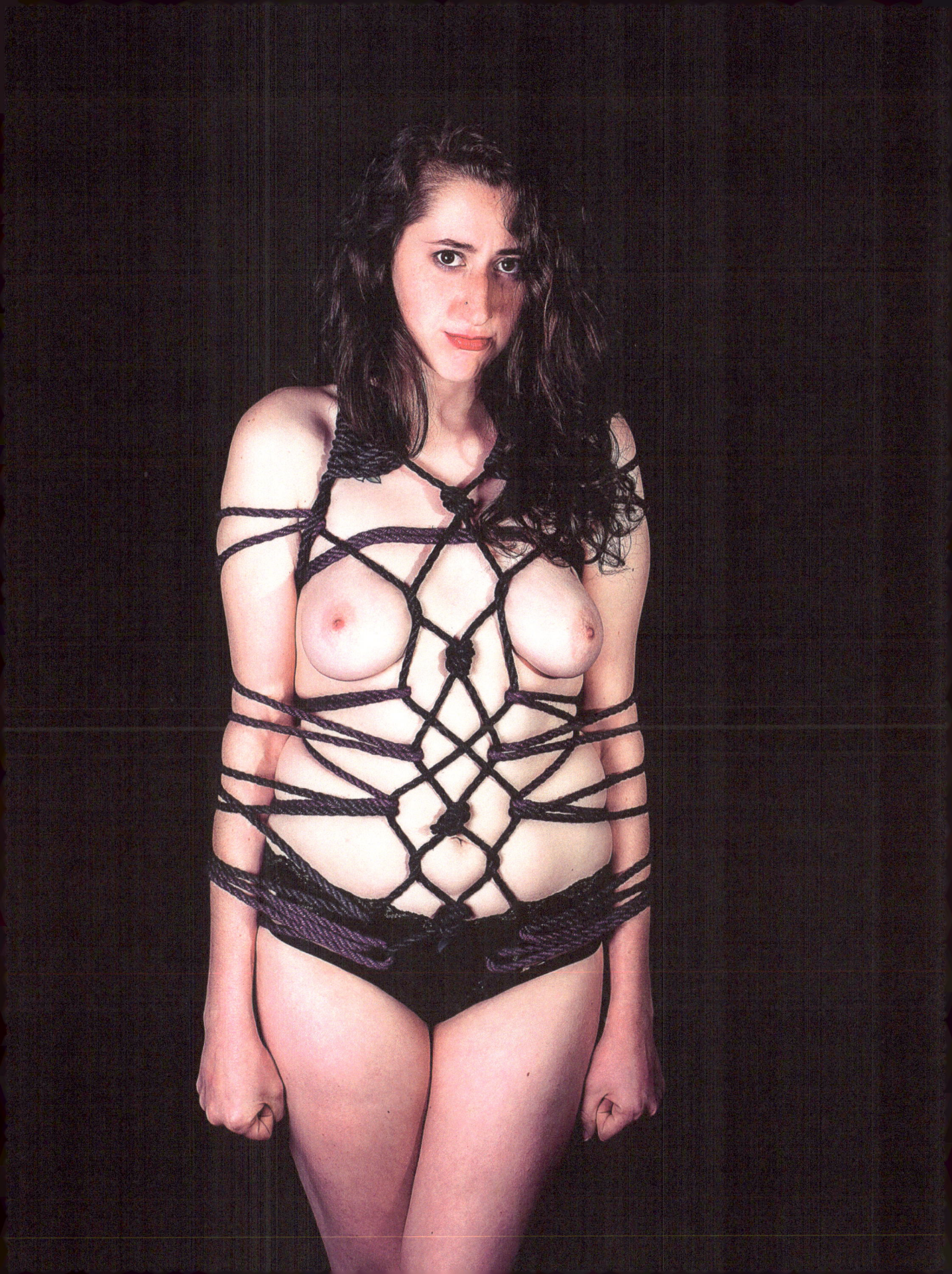

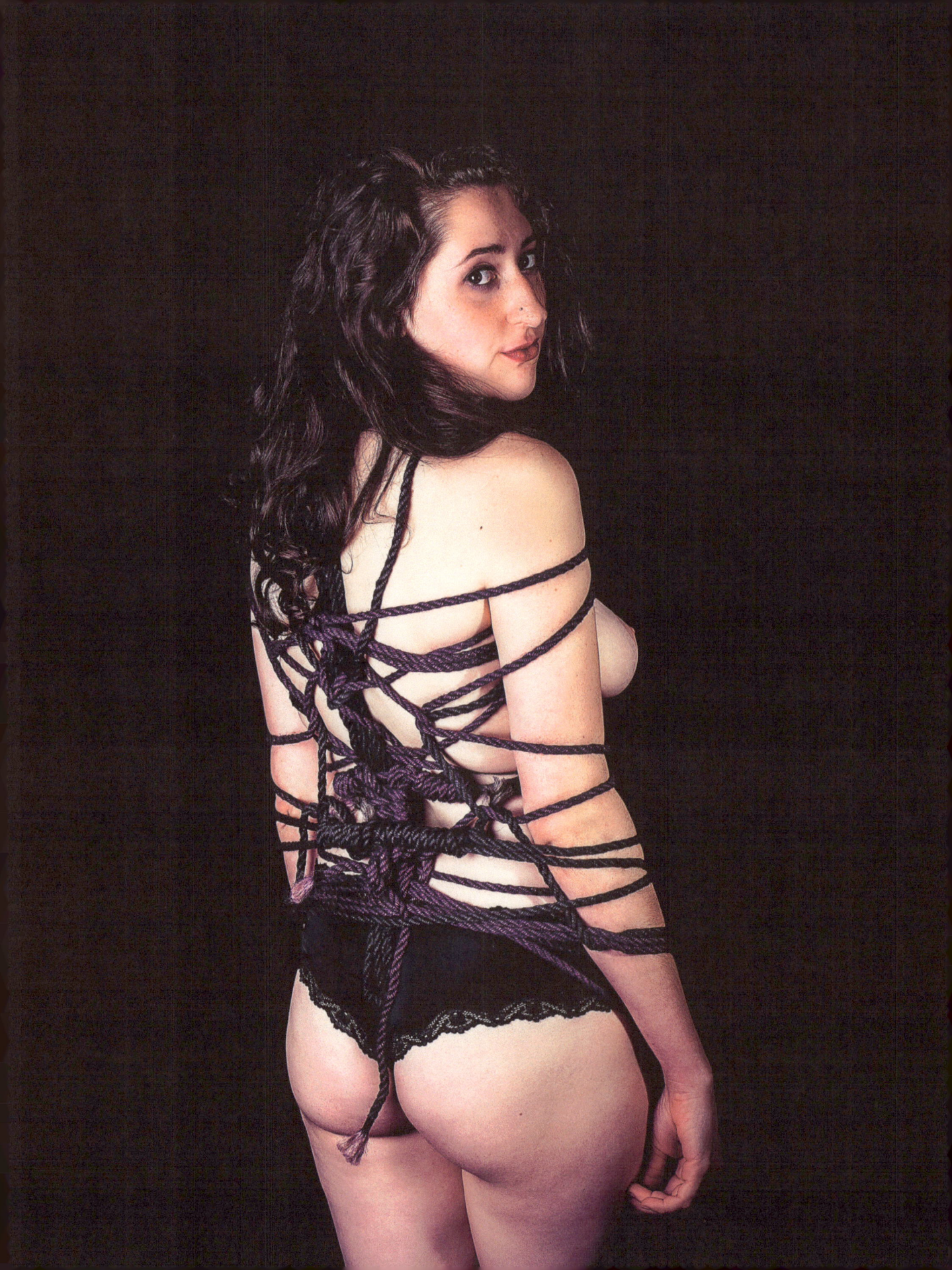

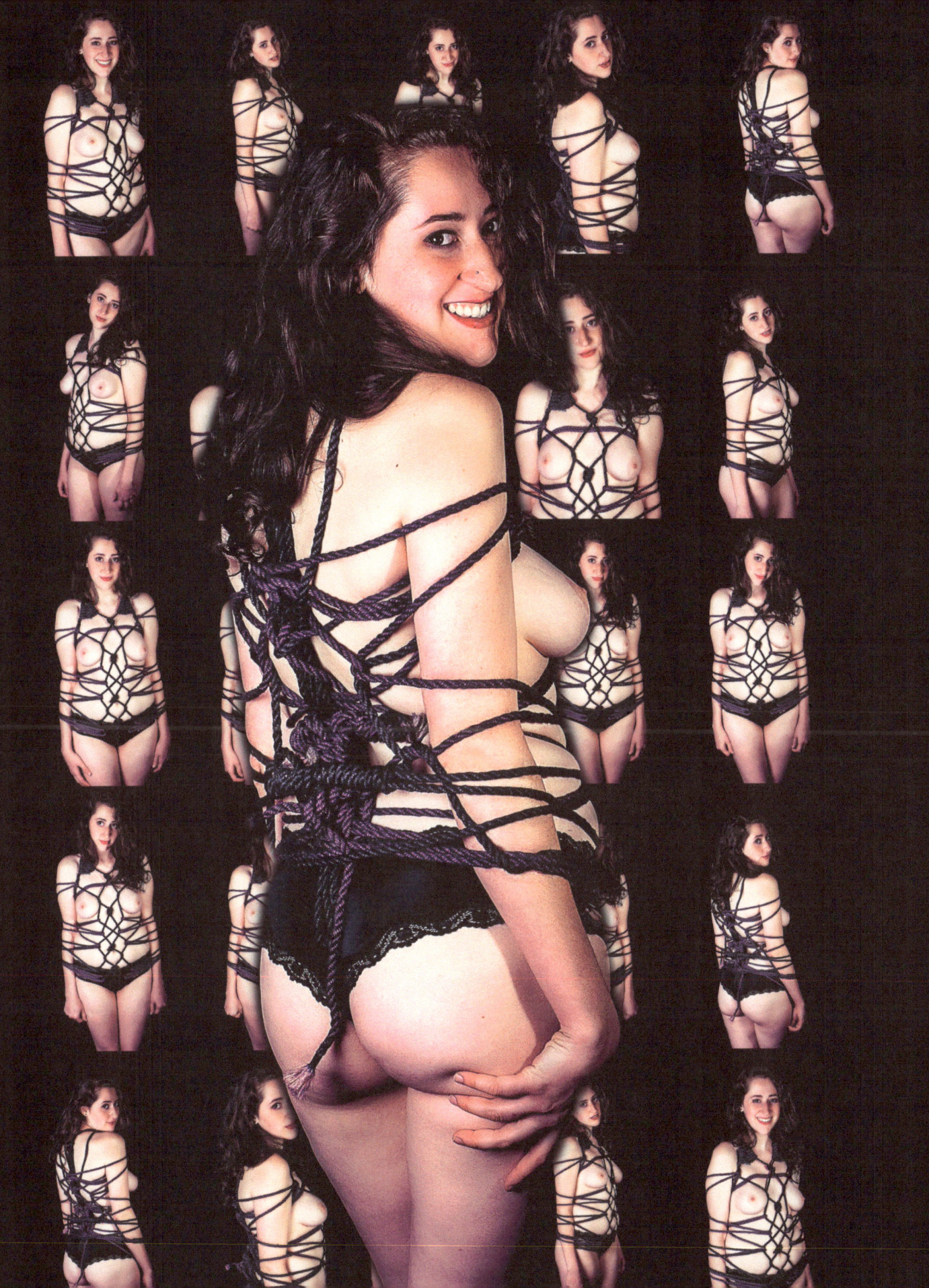

Heather

Warriors can be beautiful too. Very beautiful.

Q: What was your experience with bondage before this?
A: Non-existent

Q: What did you think about this experience?
A: Fun and comfortable!

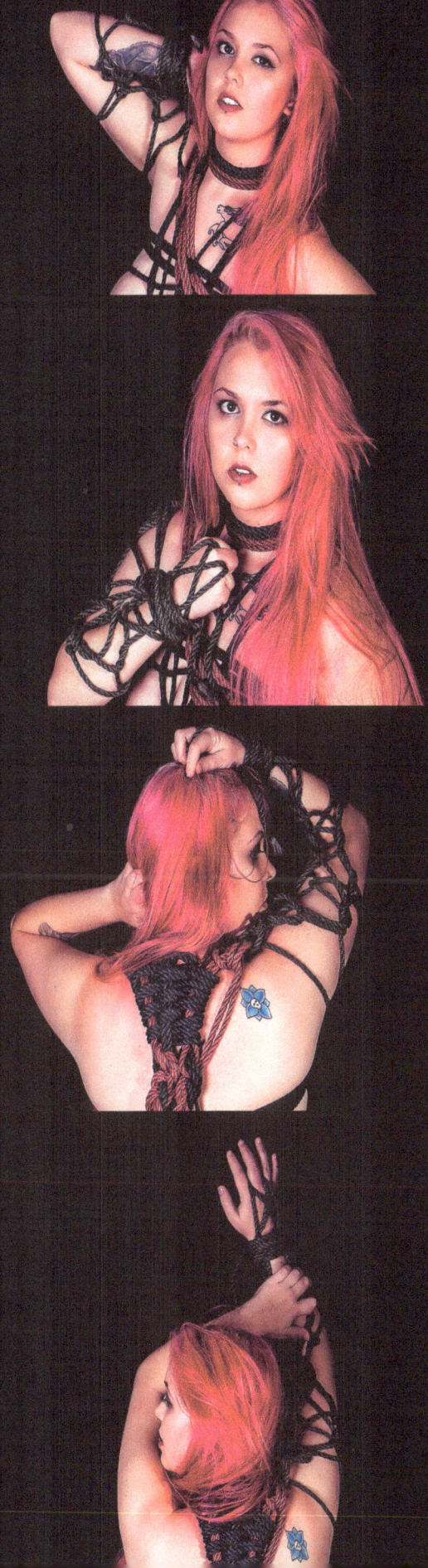

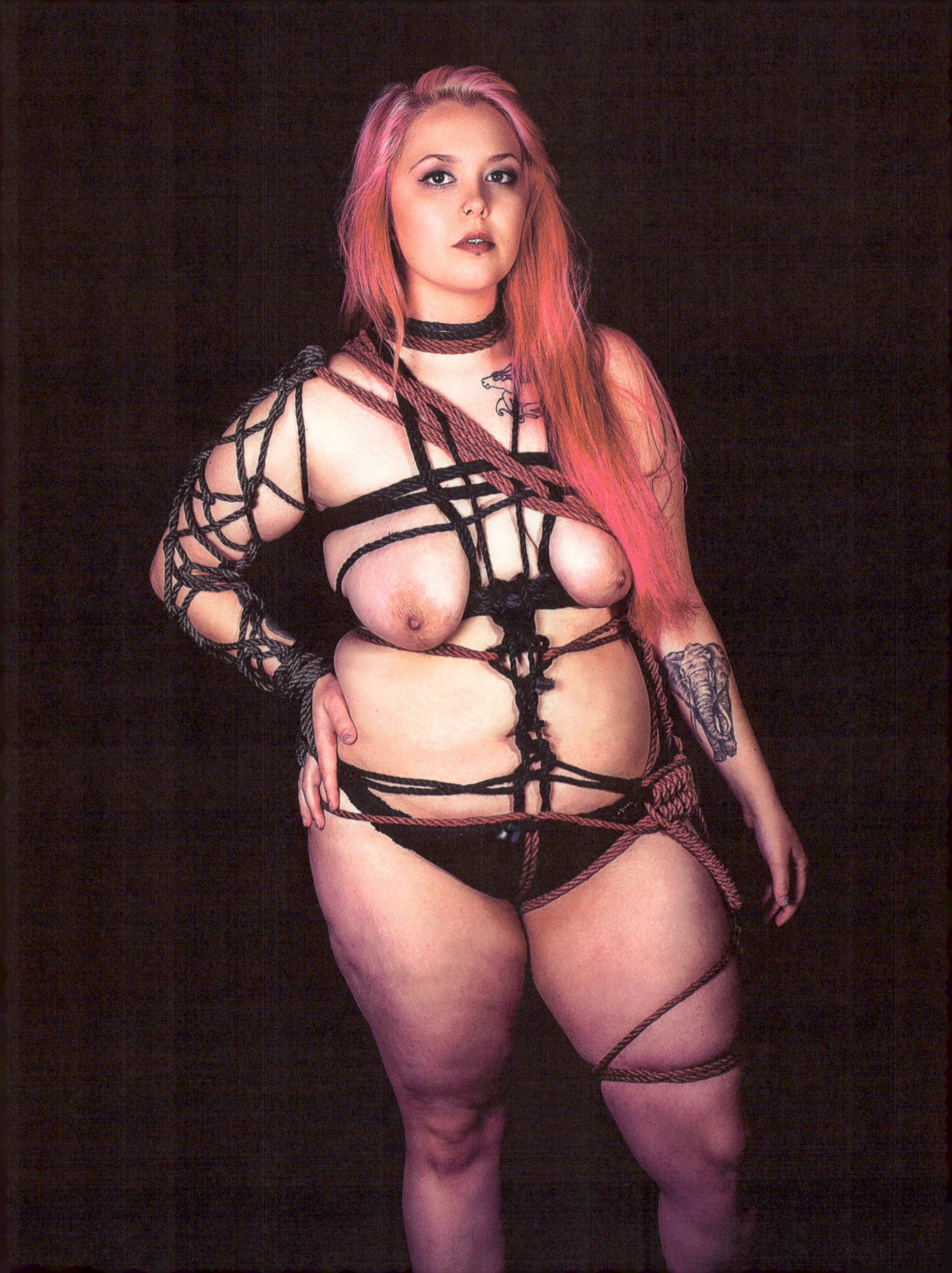

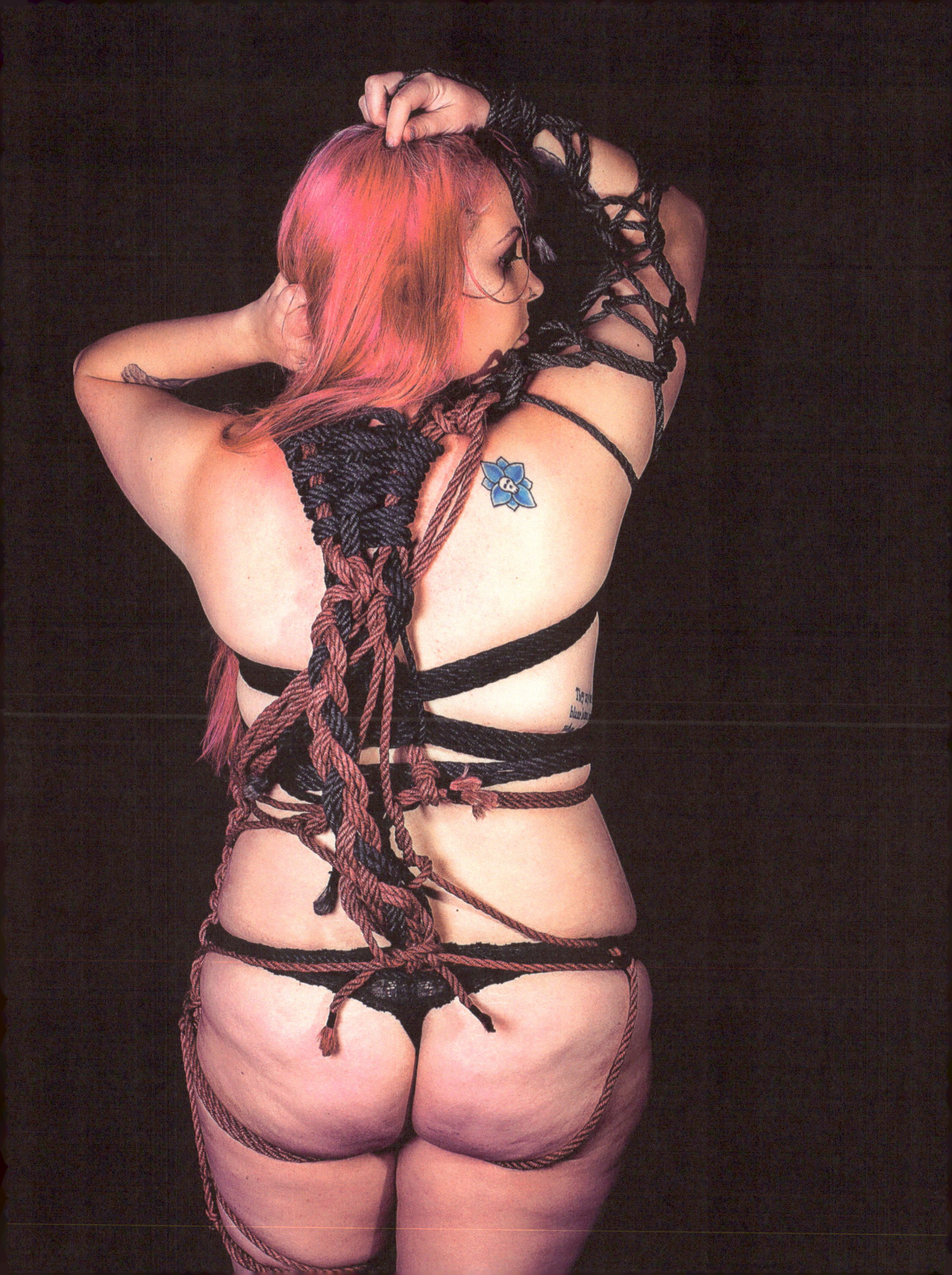

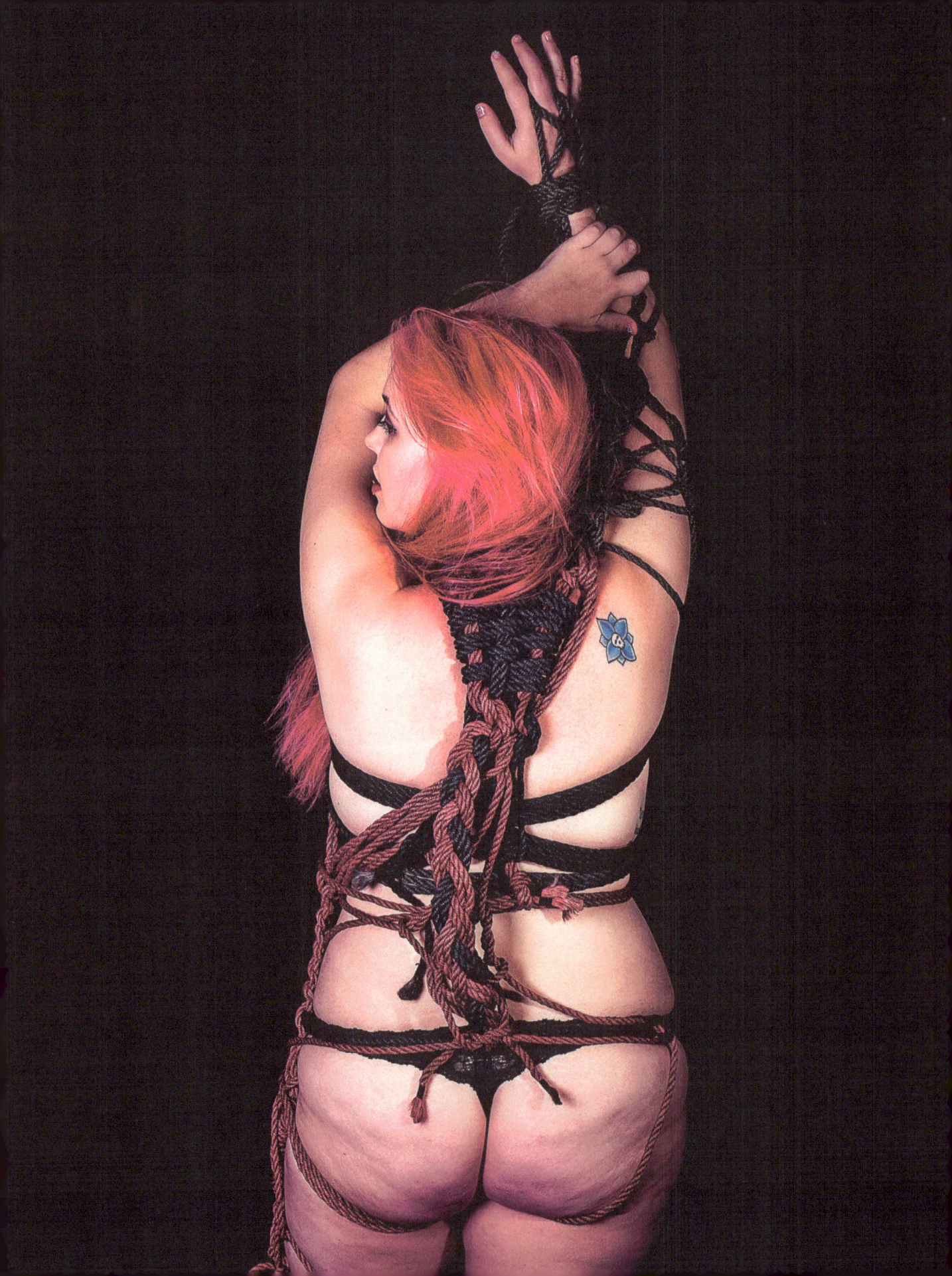

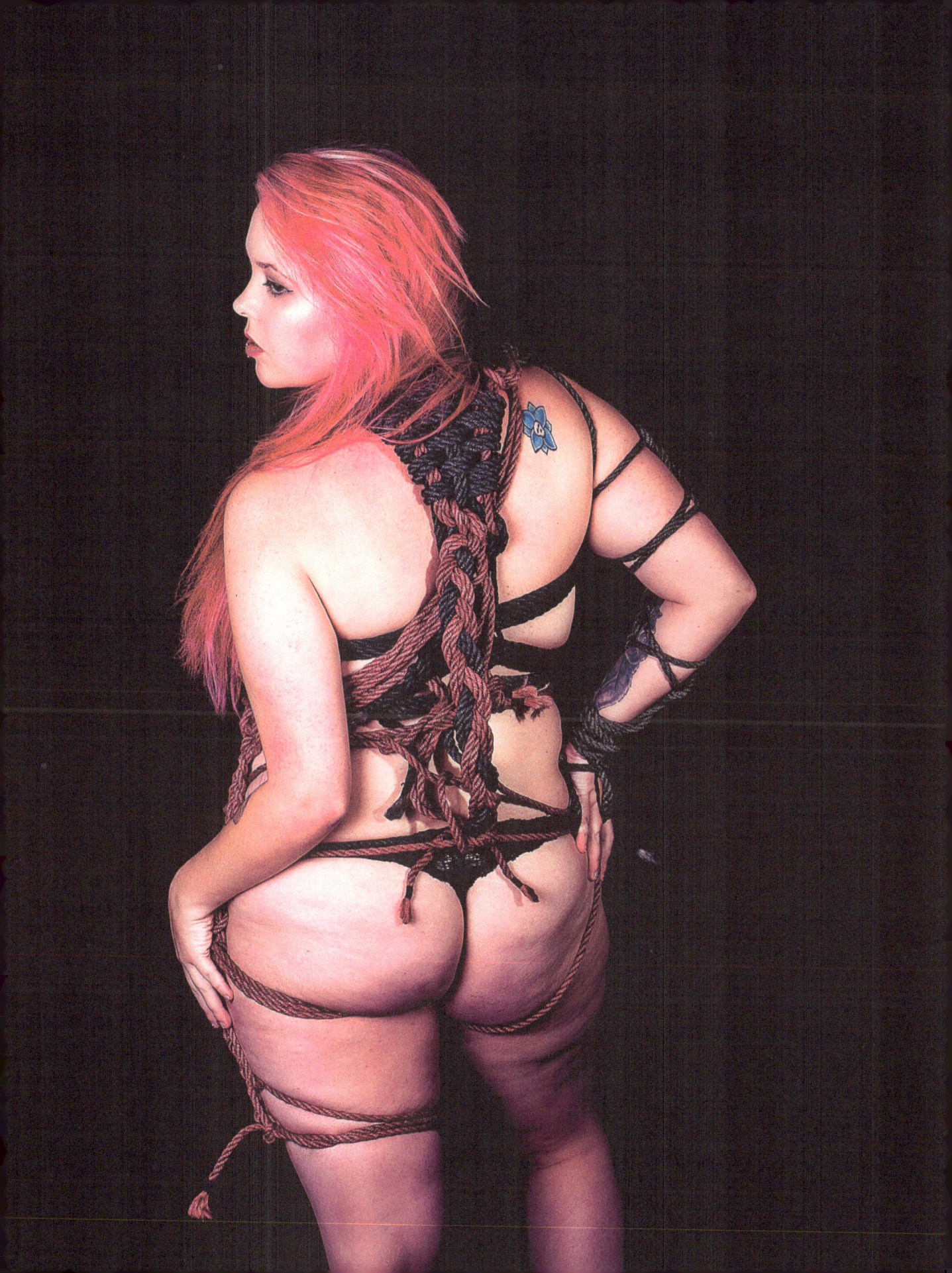

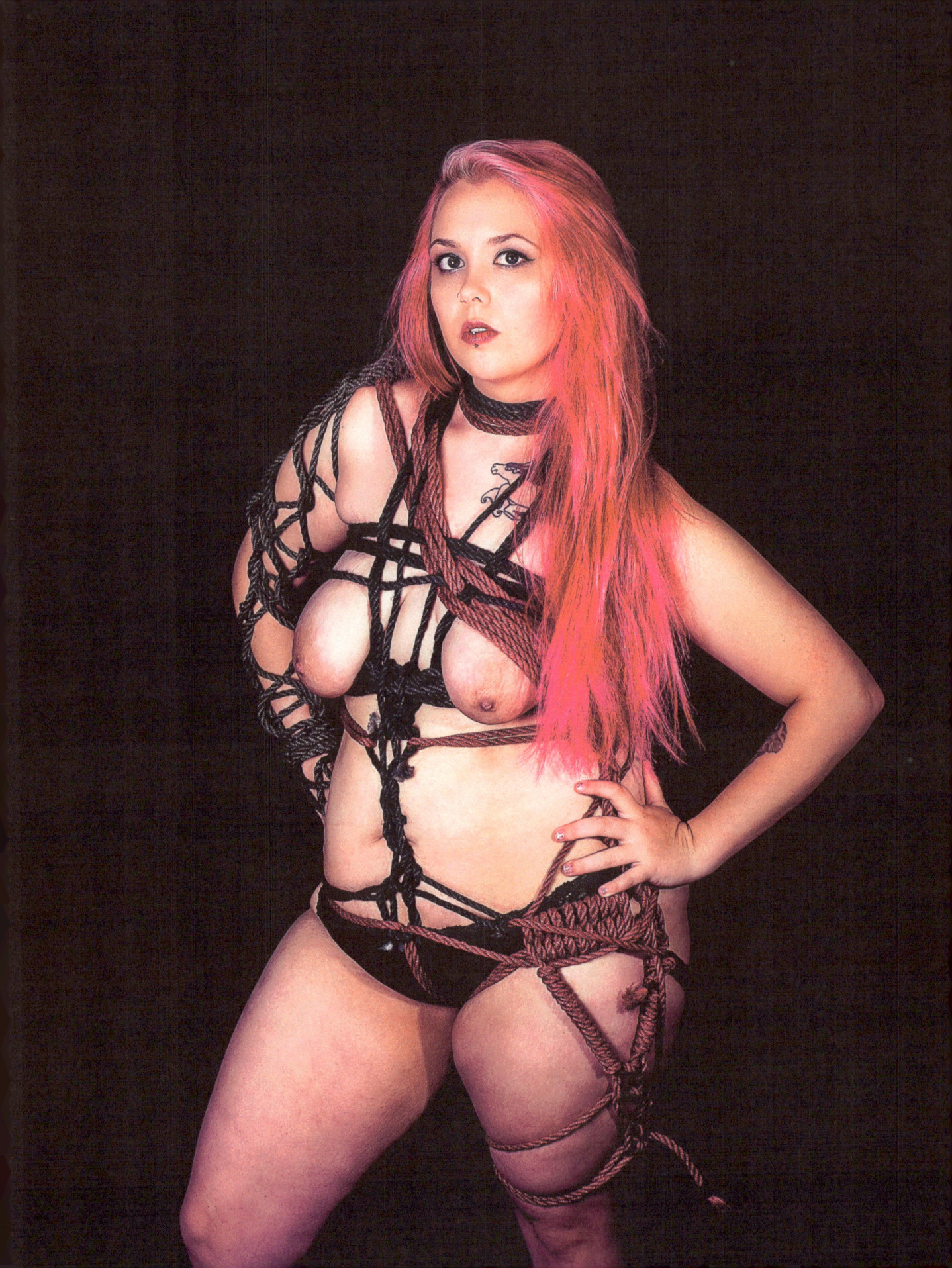

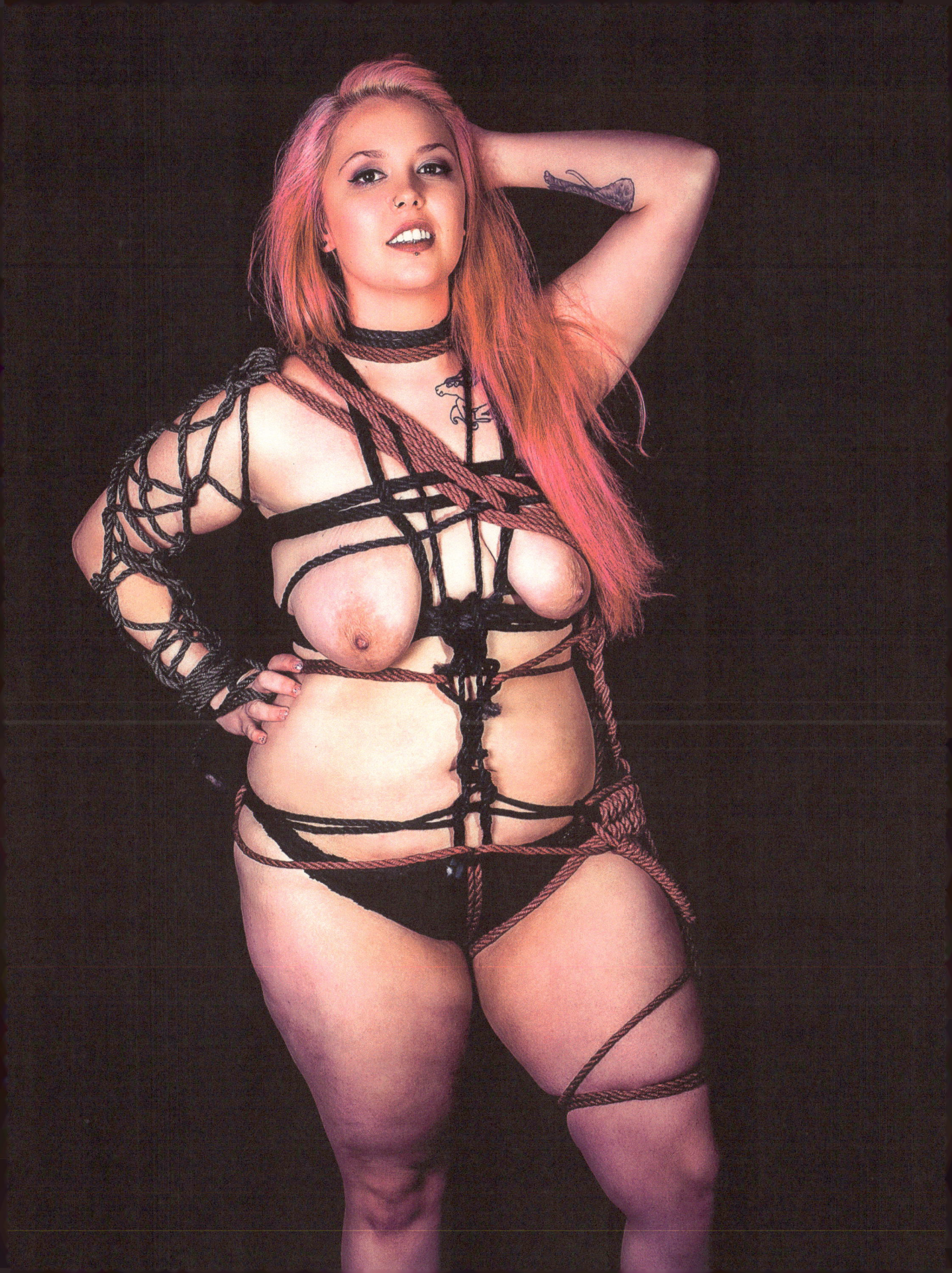

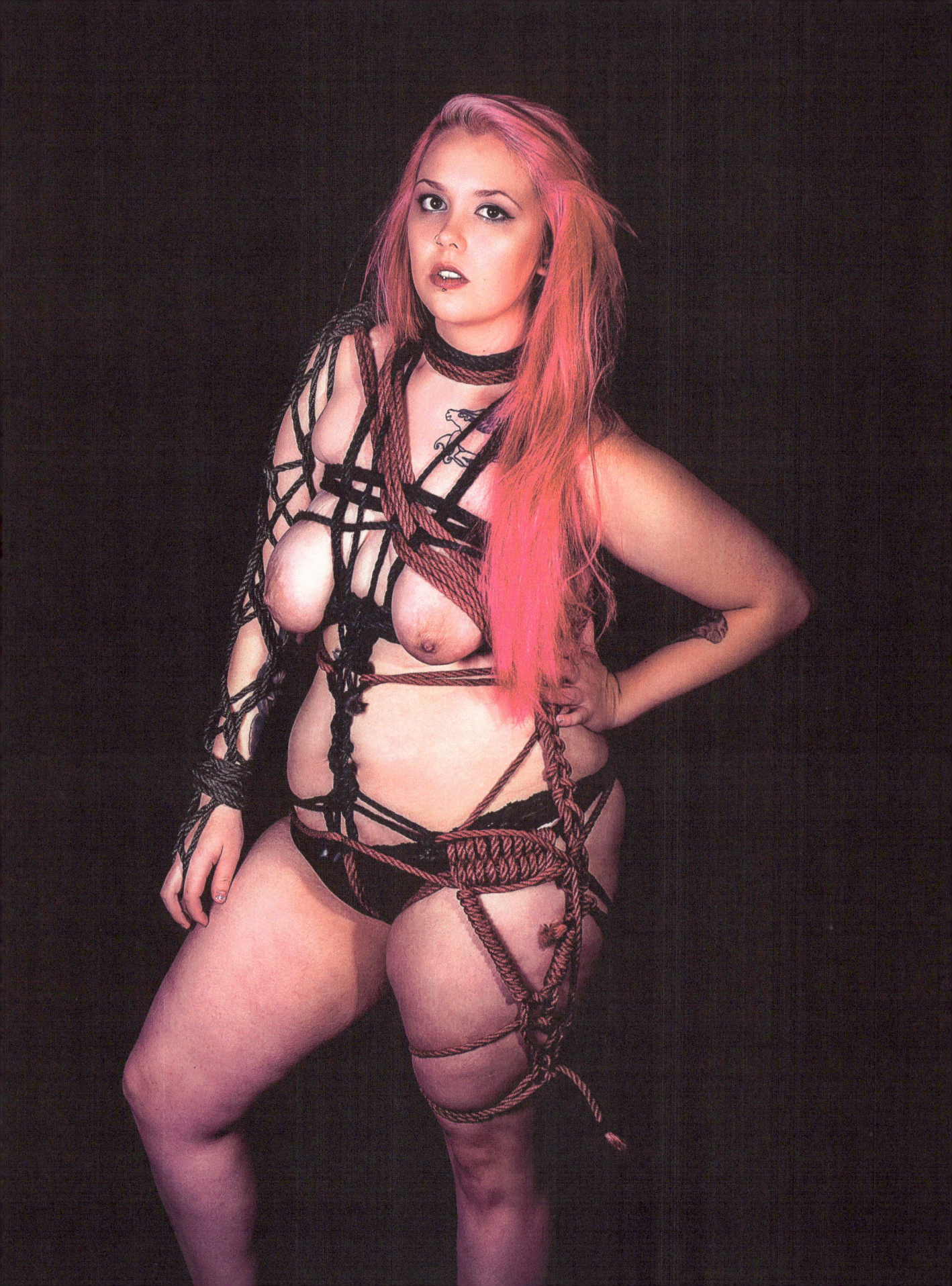

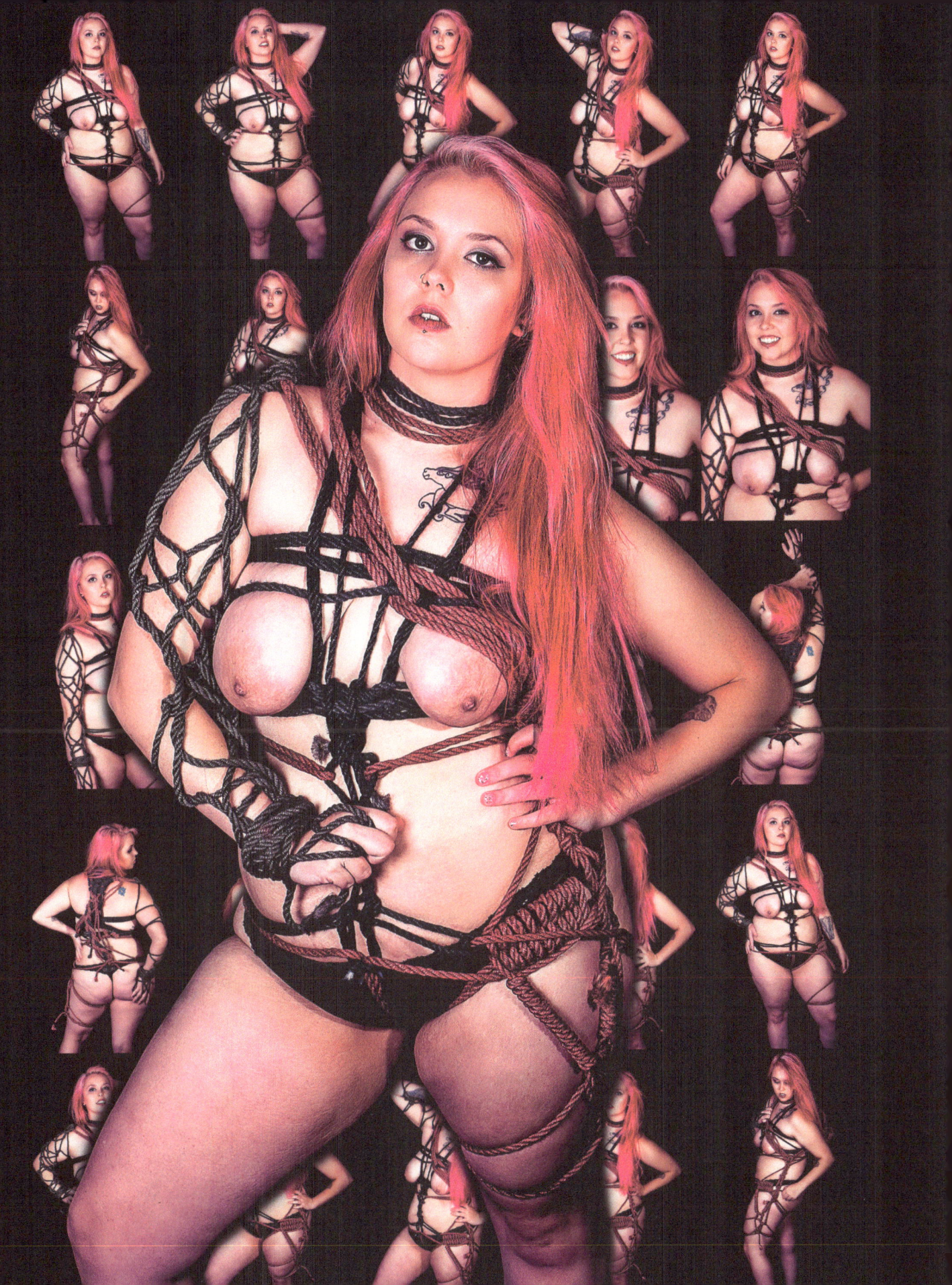

Claire

Often times the bunny is as appreciative of the rigger as the rigger is of the bunny.

Q: What was your experience with bondage before this?
A: Limited

Q: What did you think of this experience?
A: I loved it and tried it again at home!

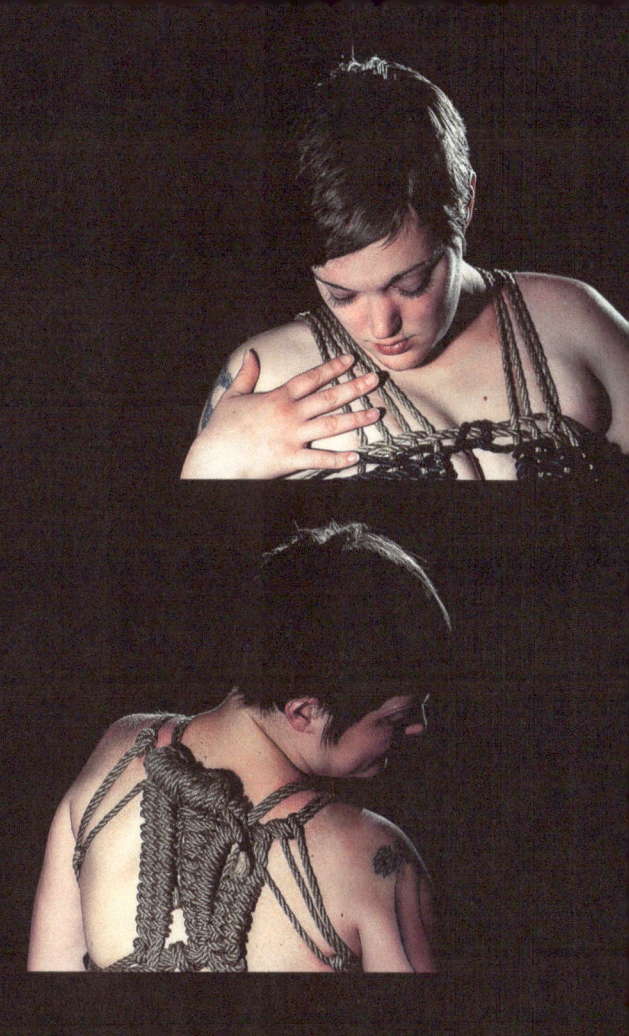

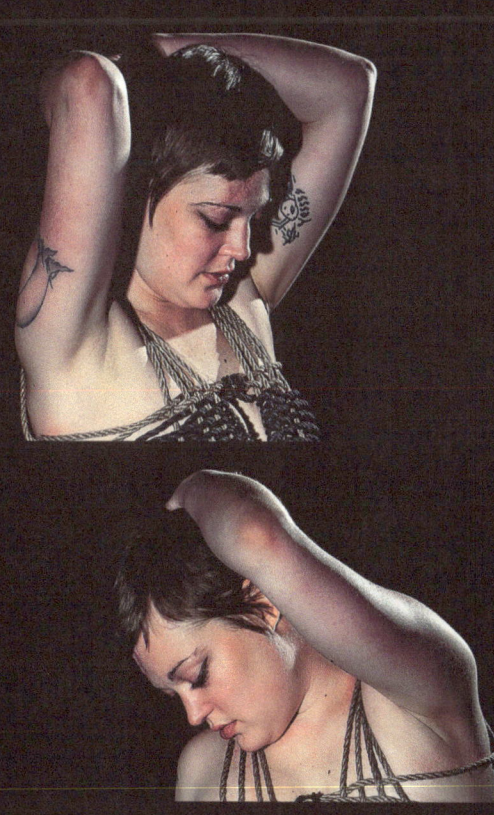

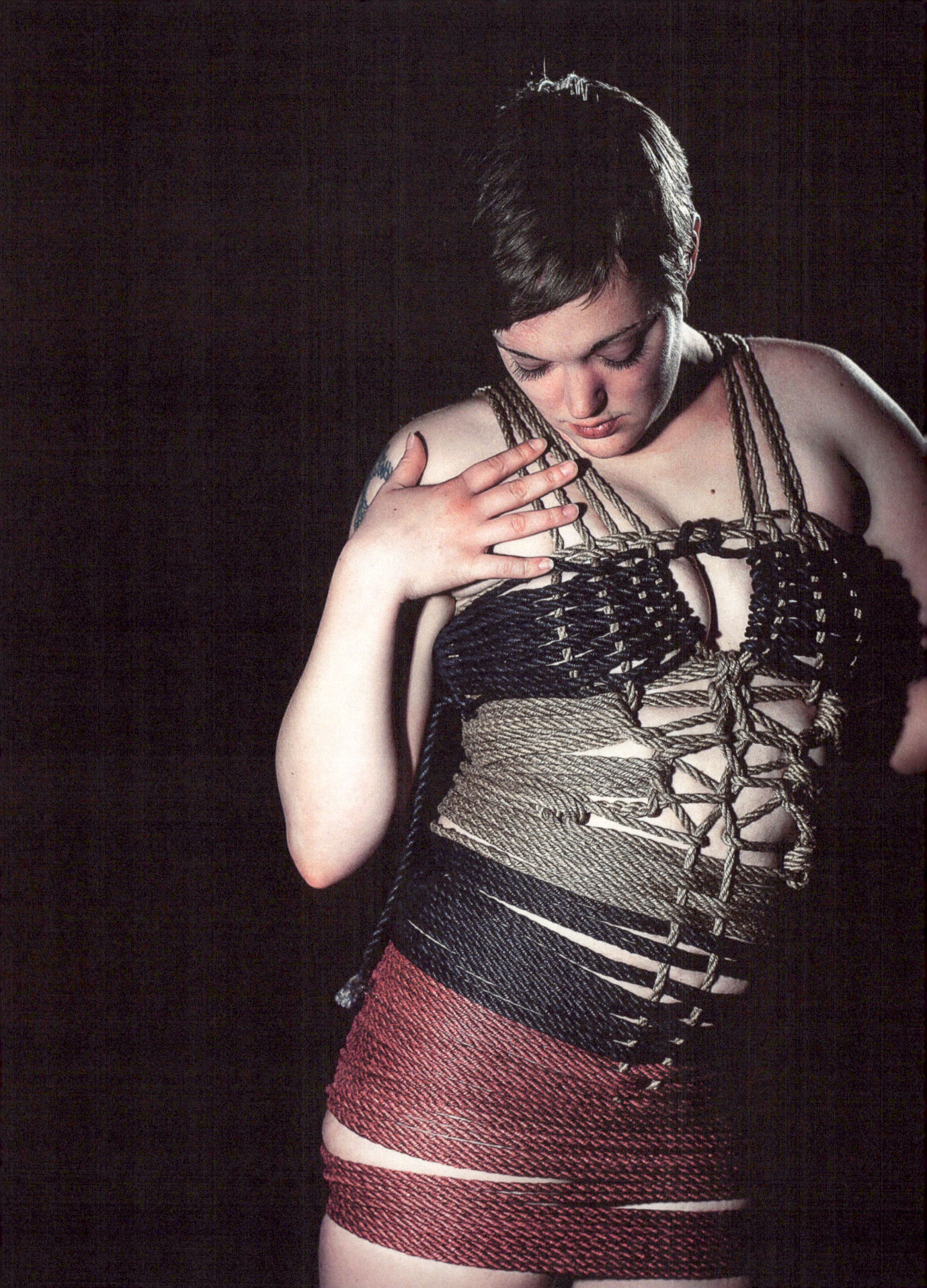

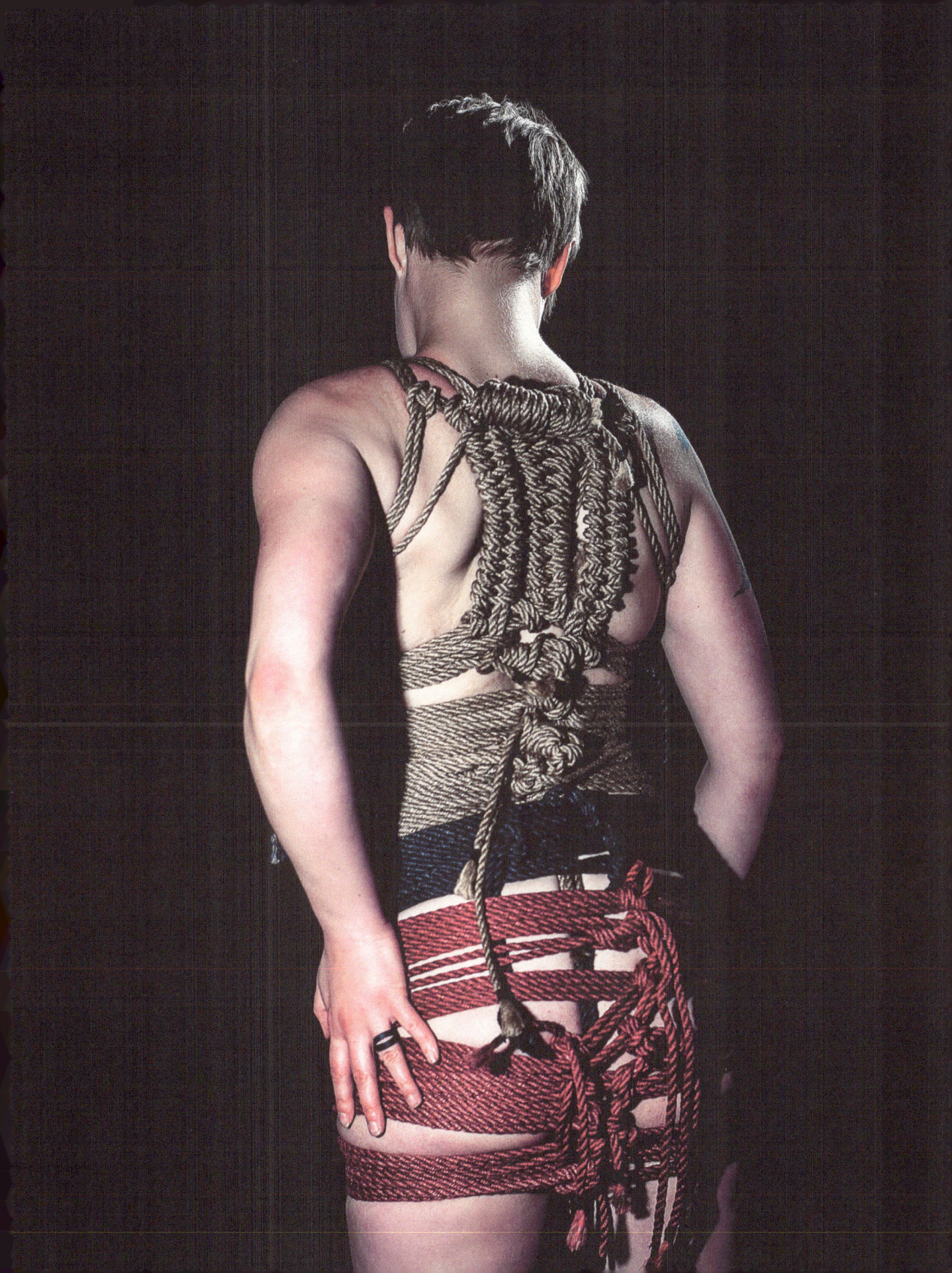

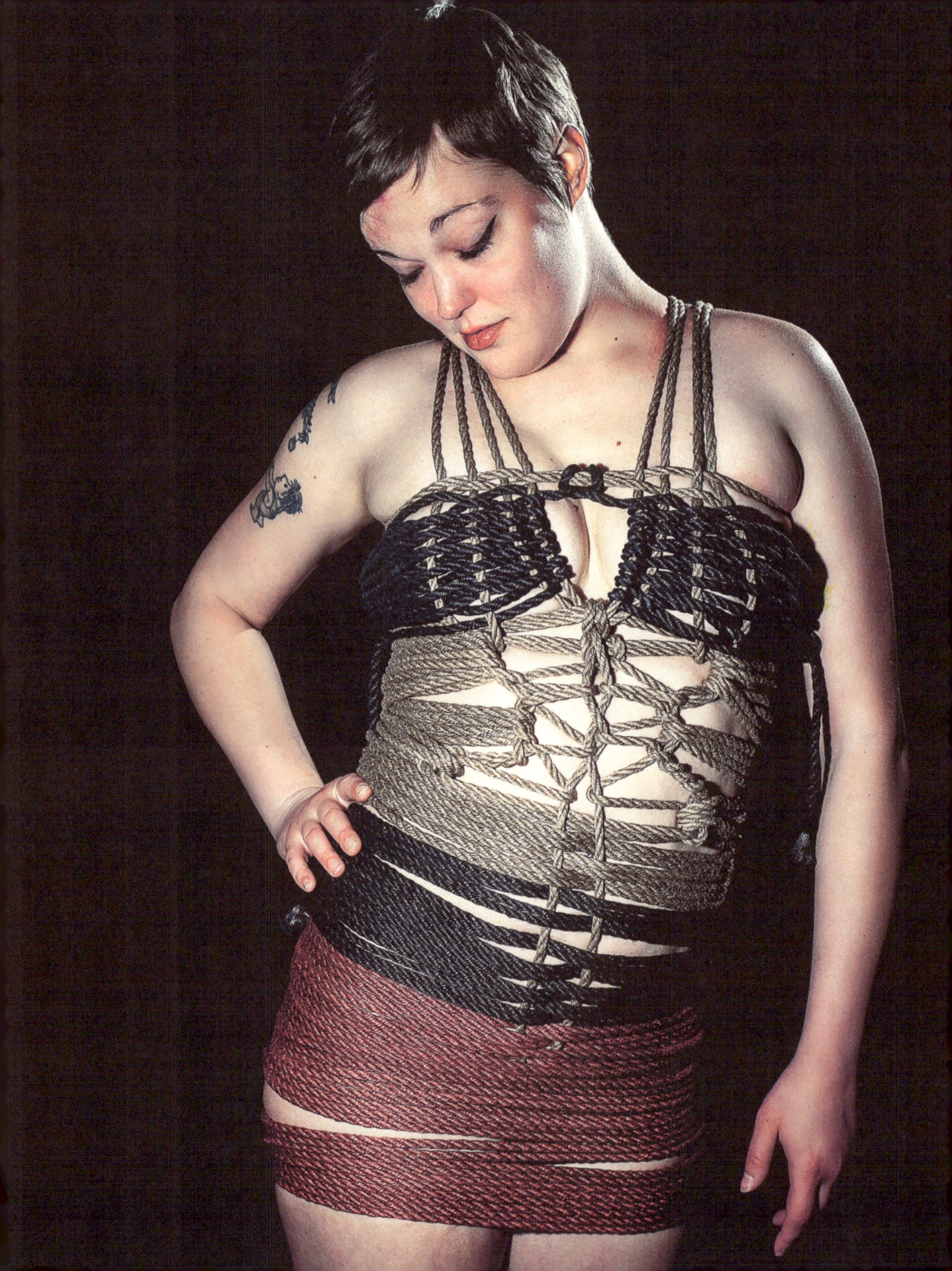

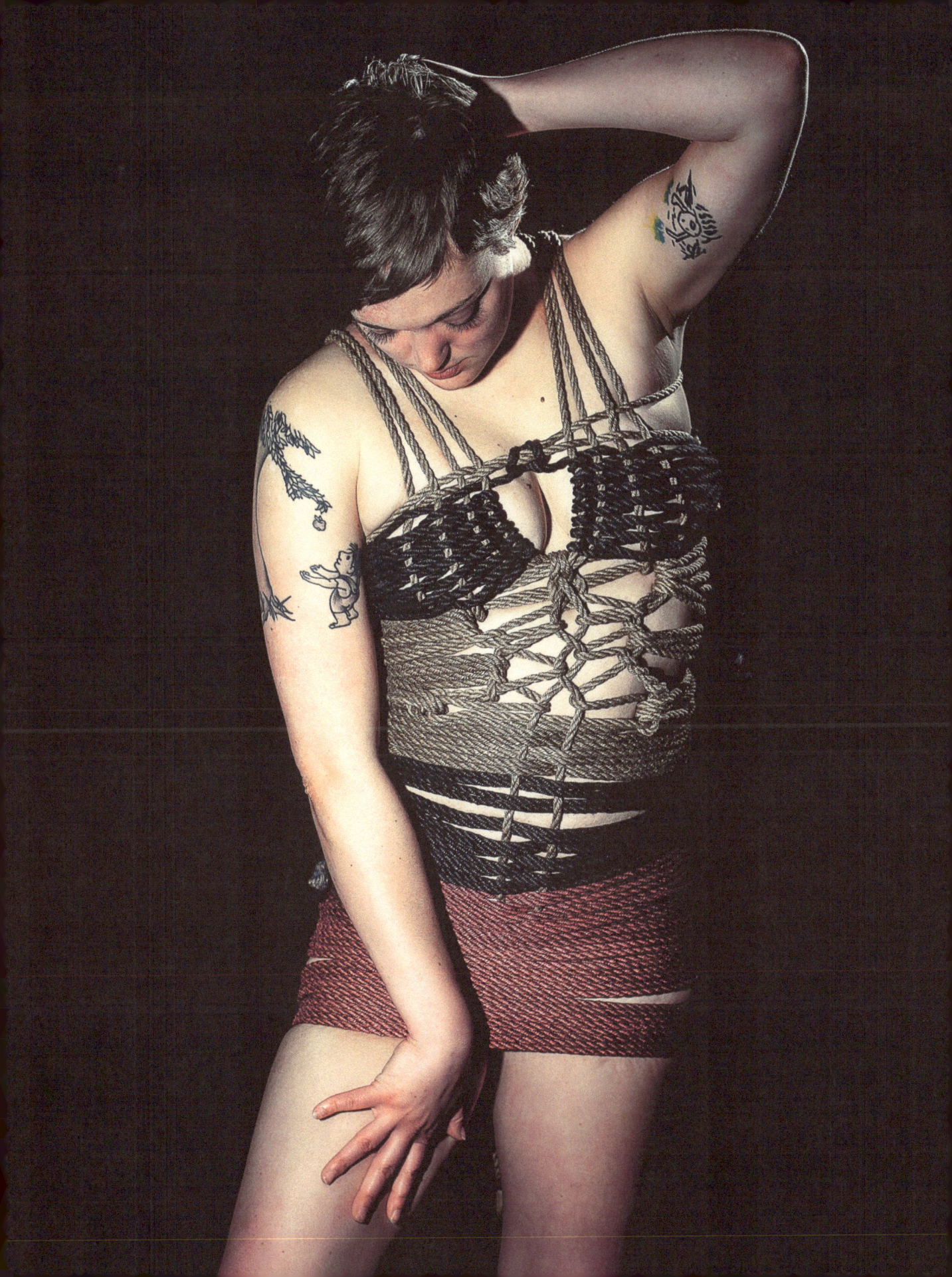

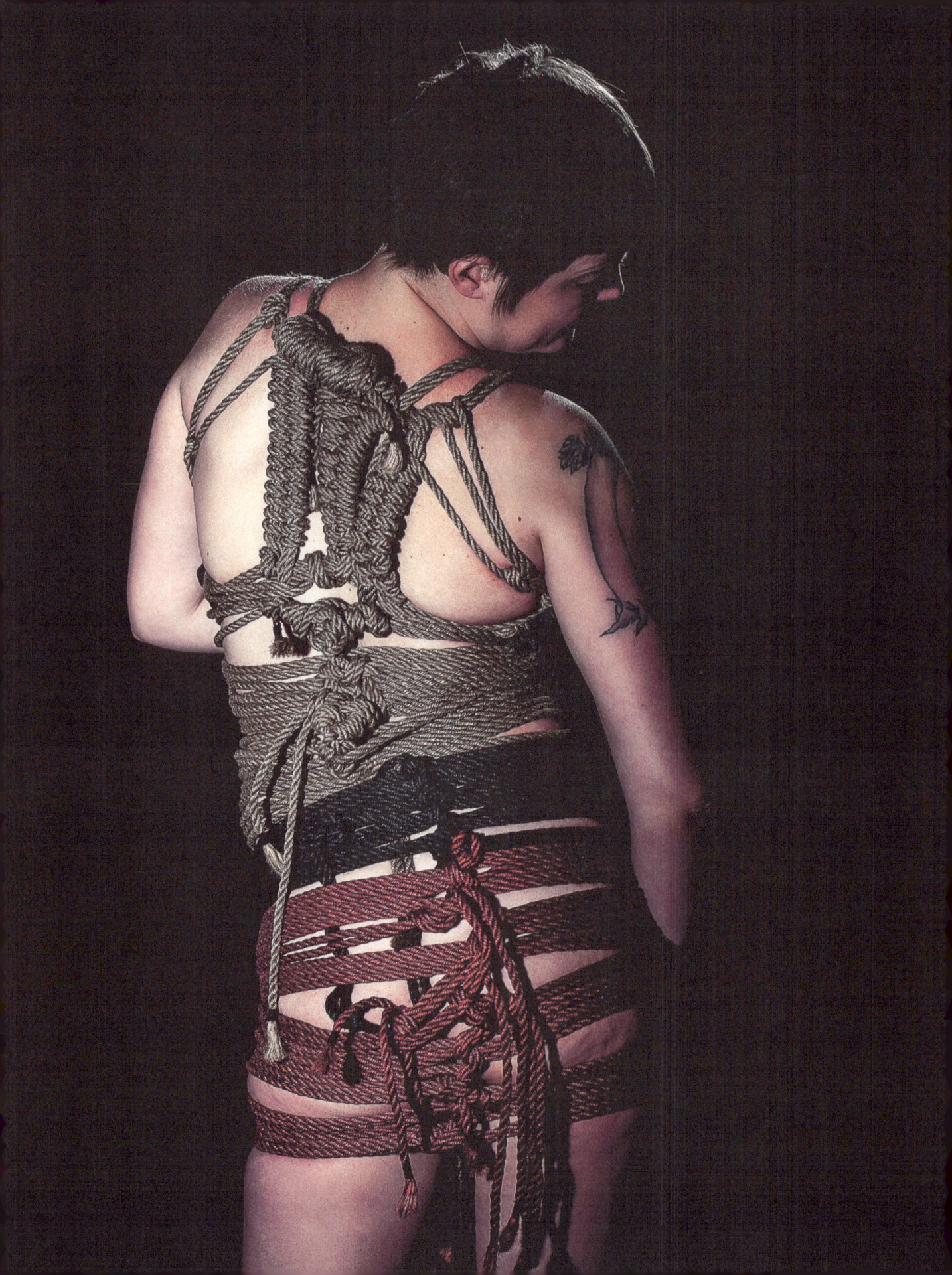

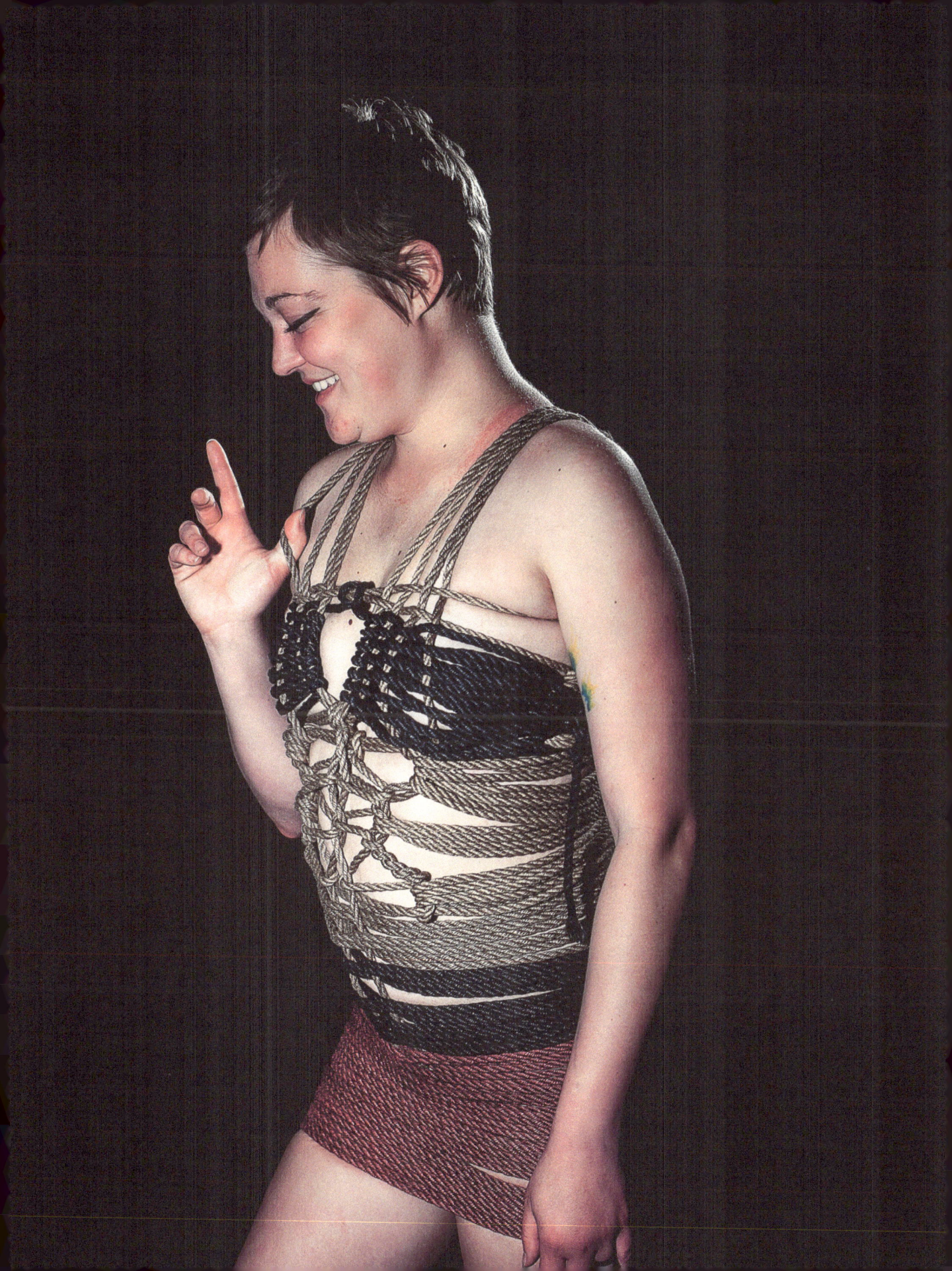

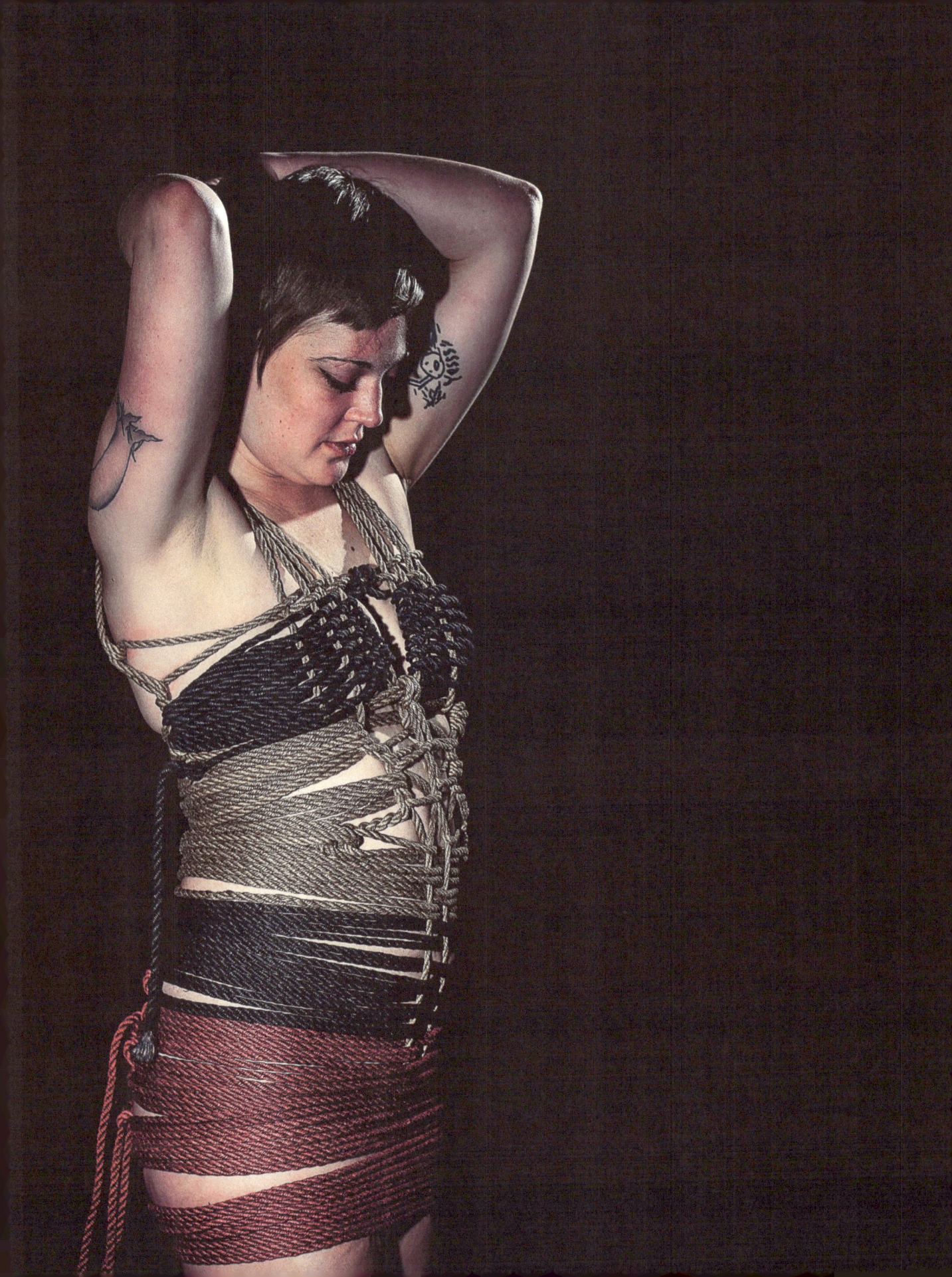

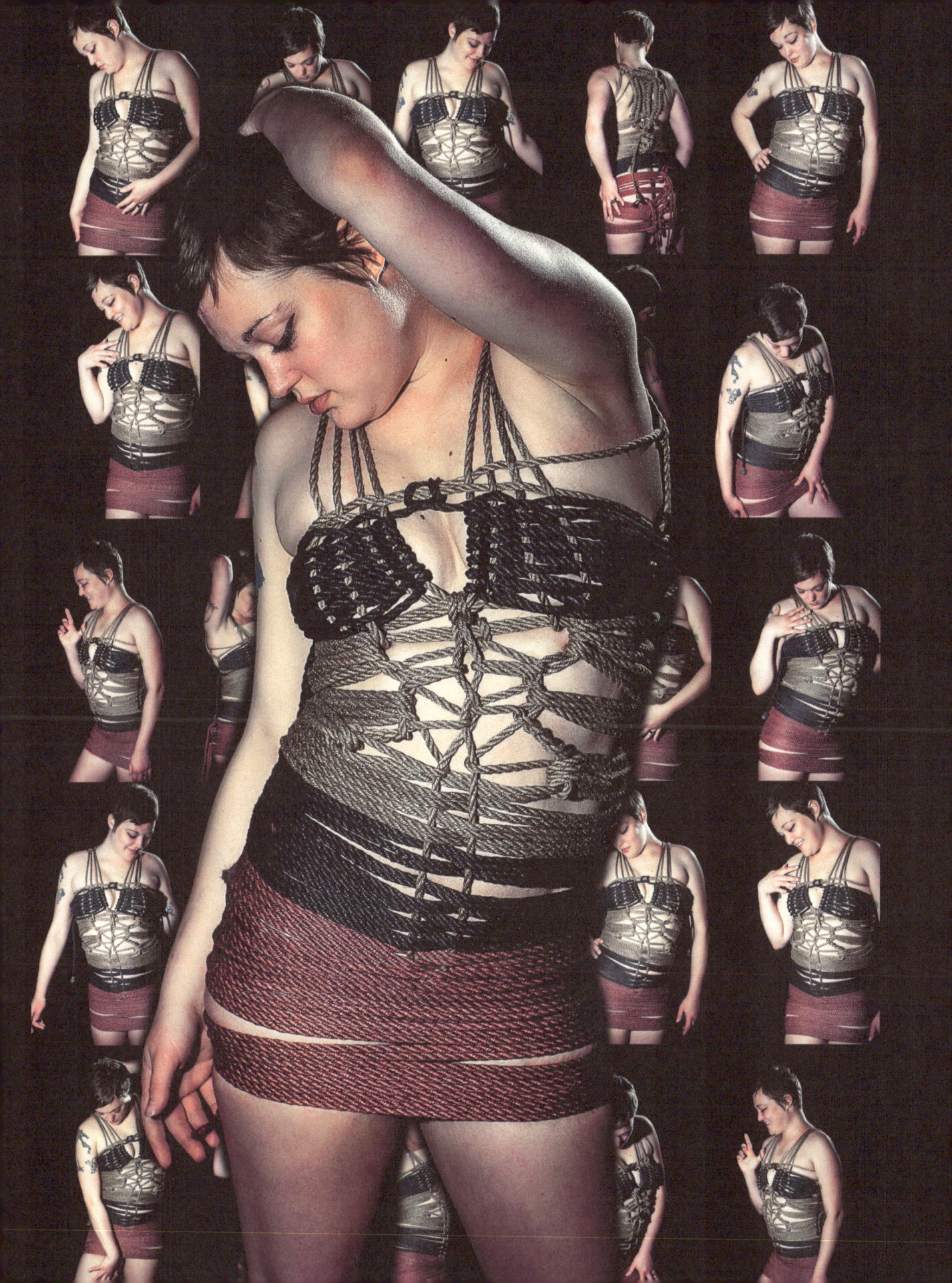

Delaney

There is always a first time for everything. Just because you've never done it before doesn't mean you should never do it.

Q: What was your experience with bondage before this?
A: Nothing. This was my first time.

Q: What did you think of this experience?
A: It was awesome and opened my eyes to the world.

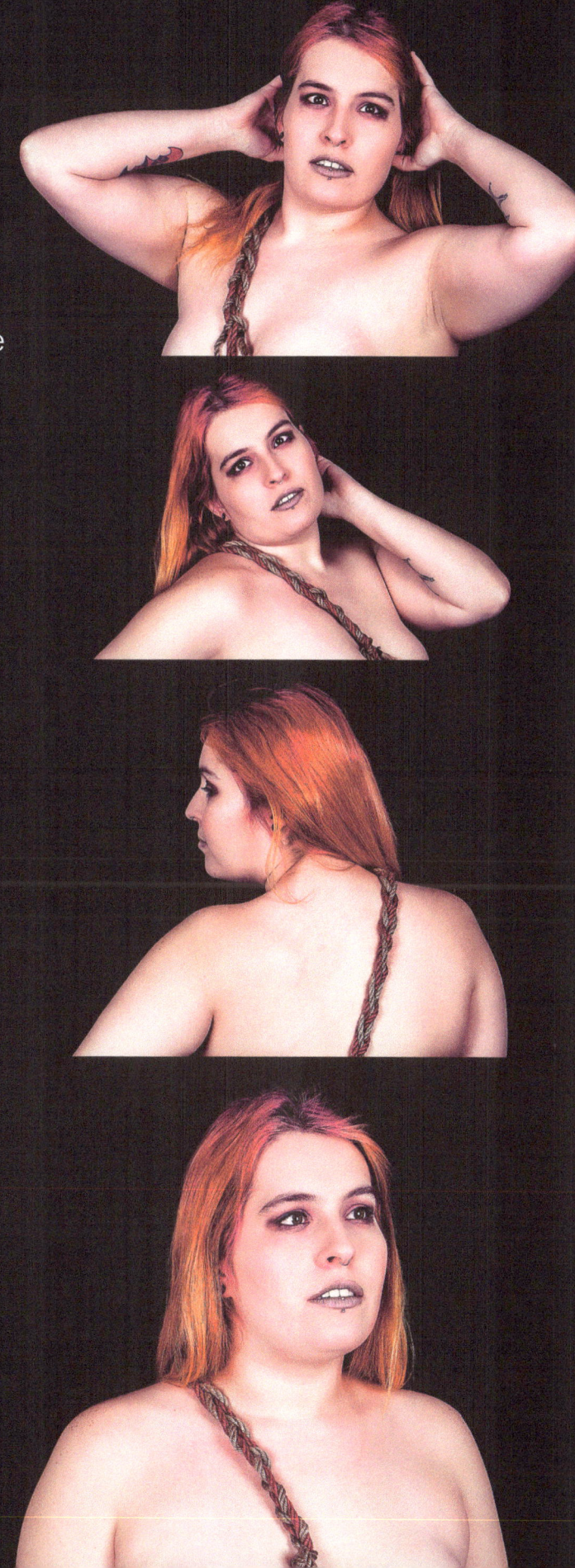

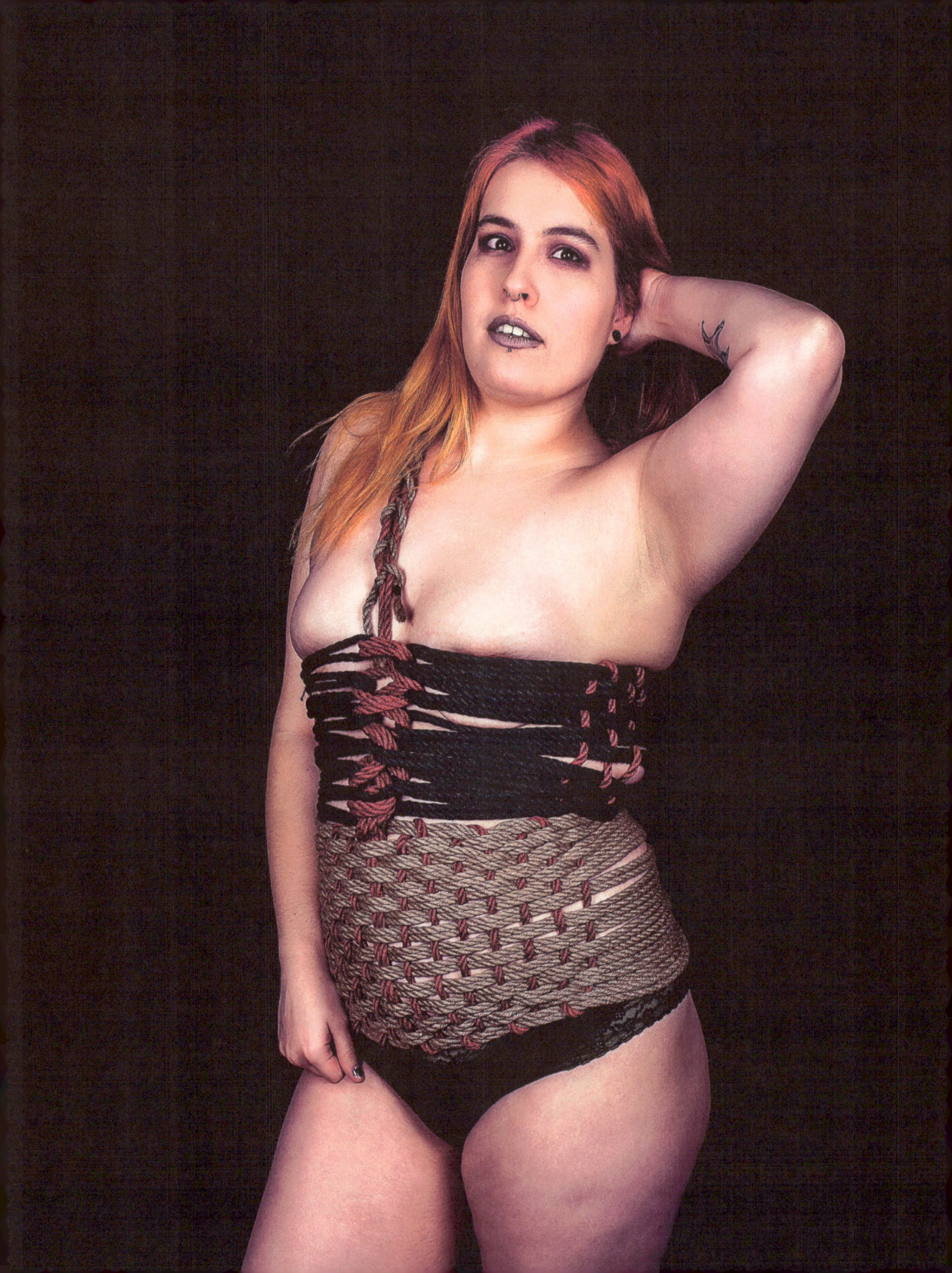

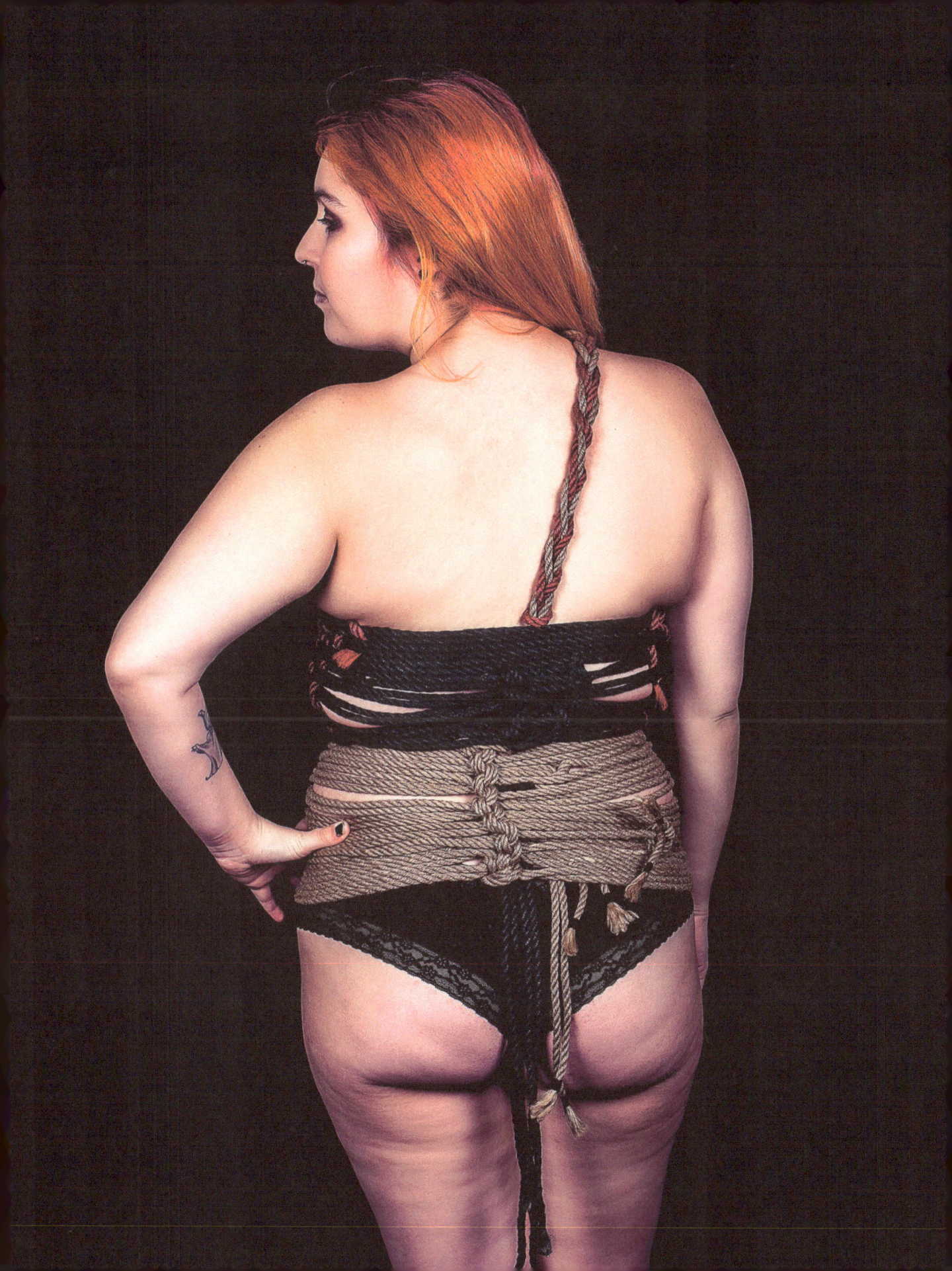

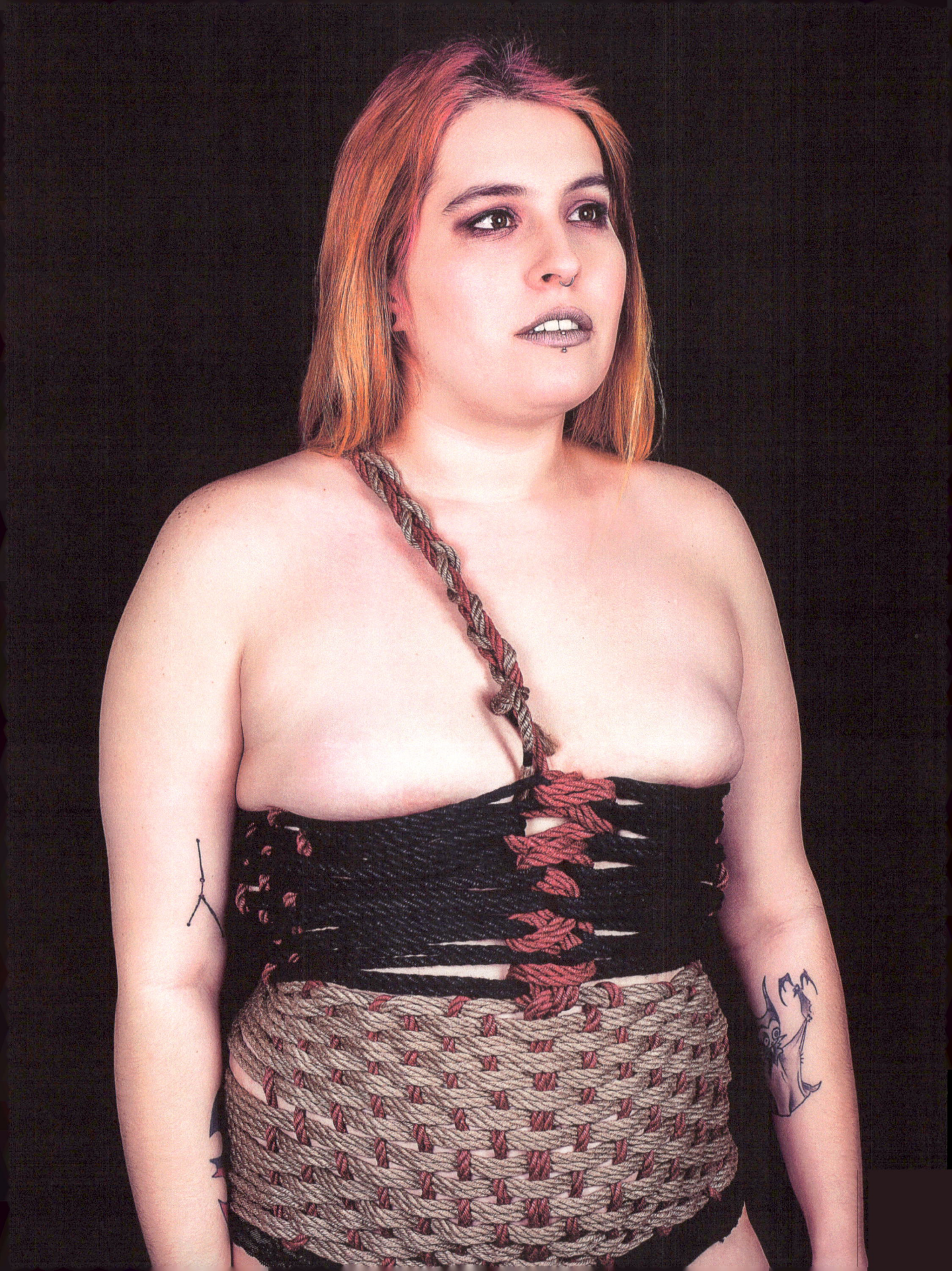

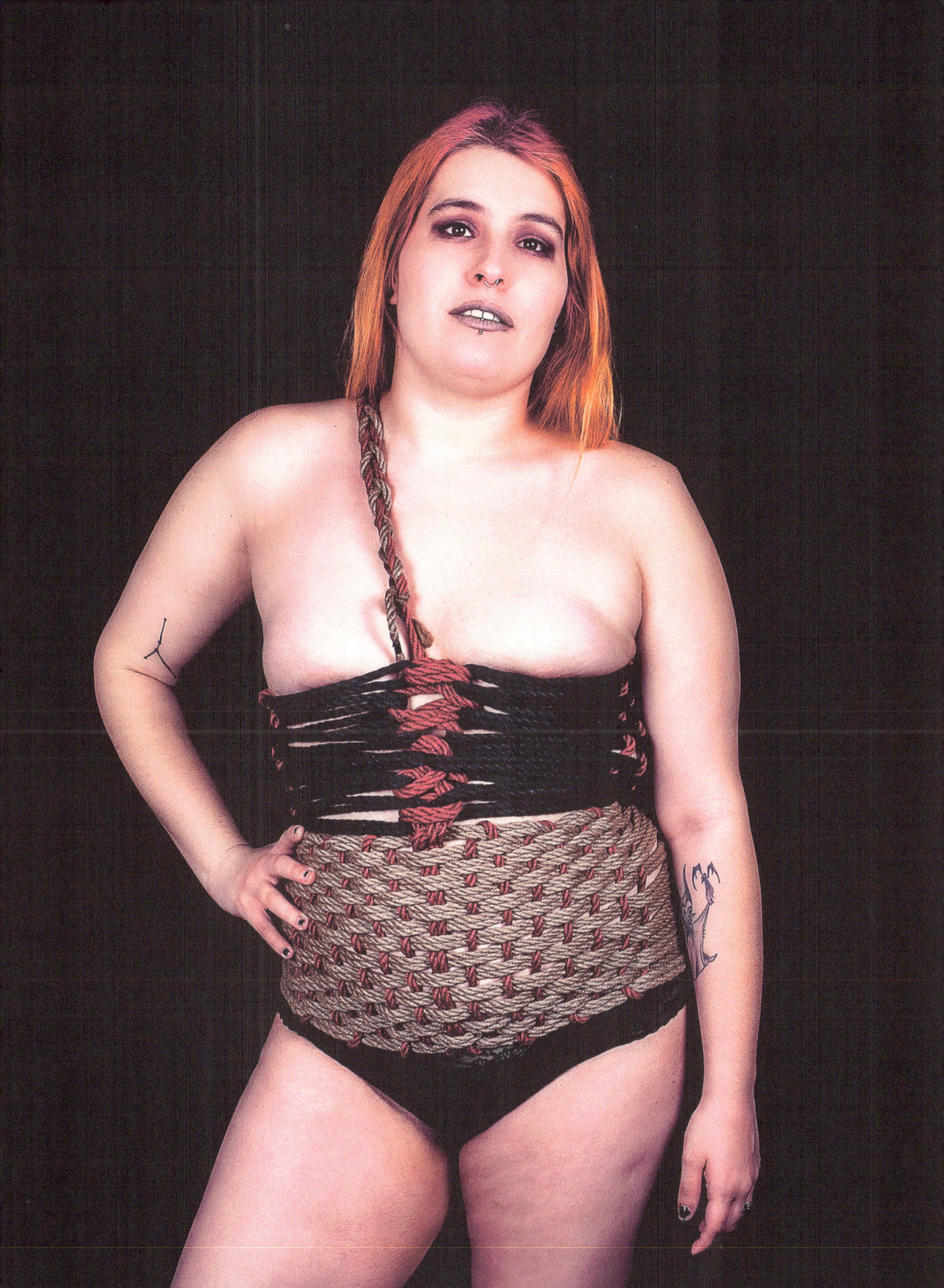

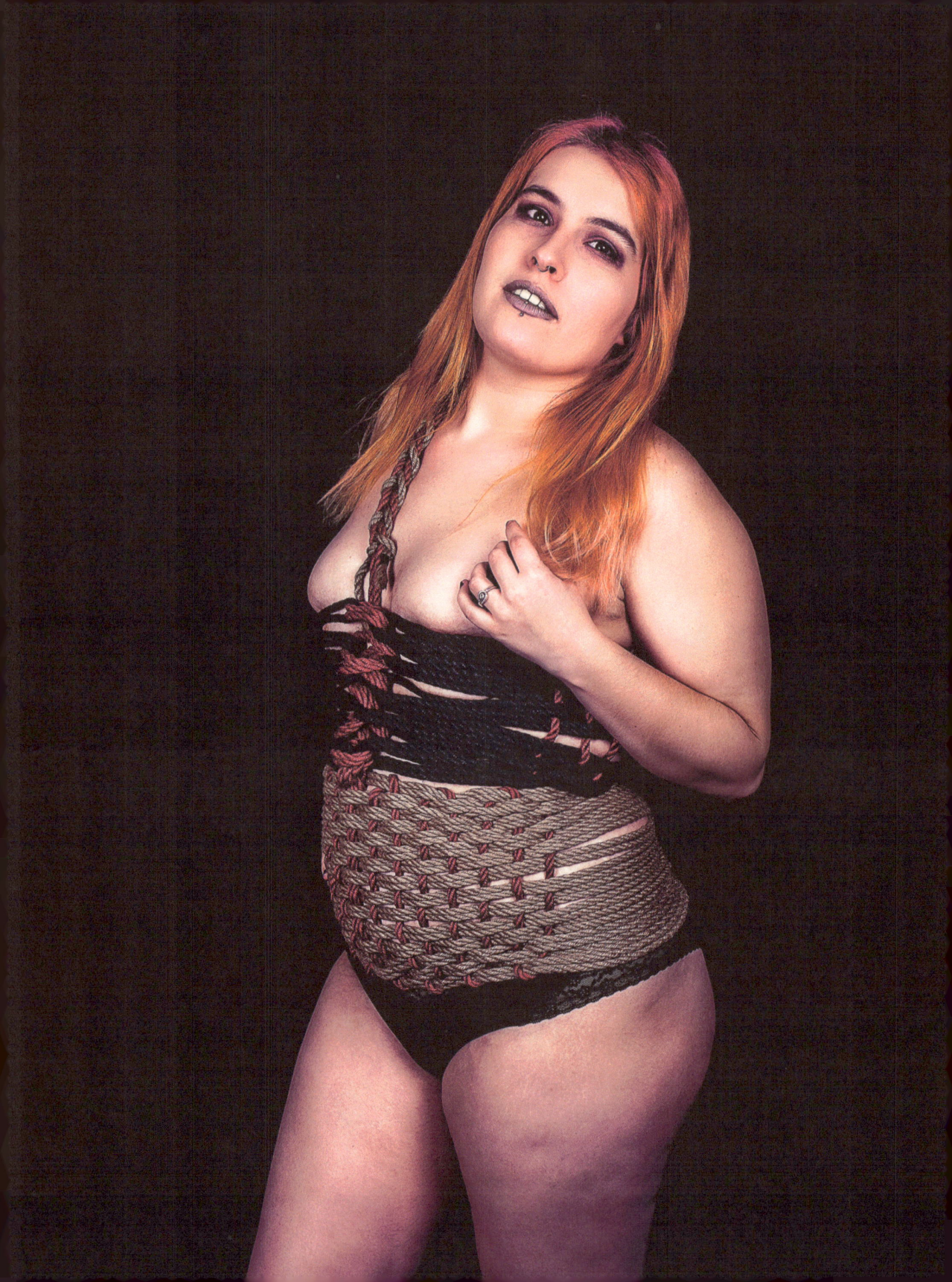

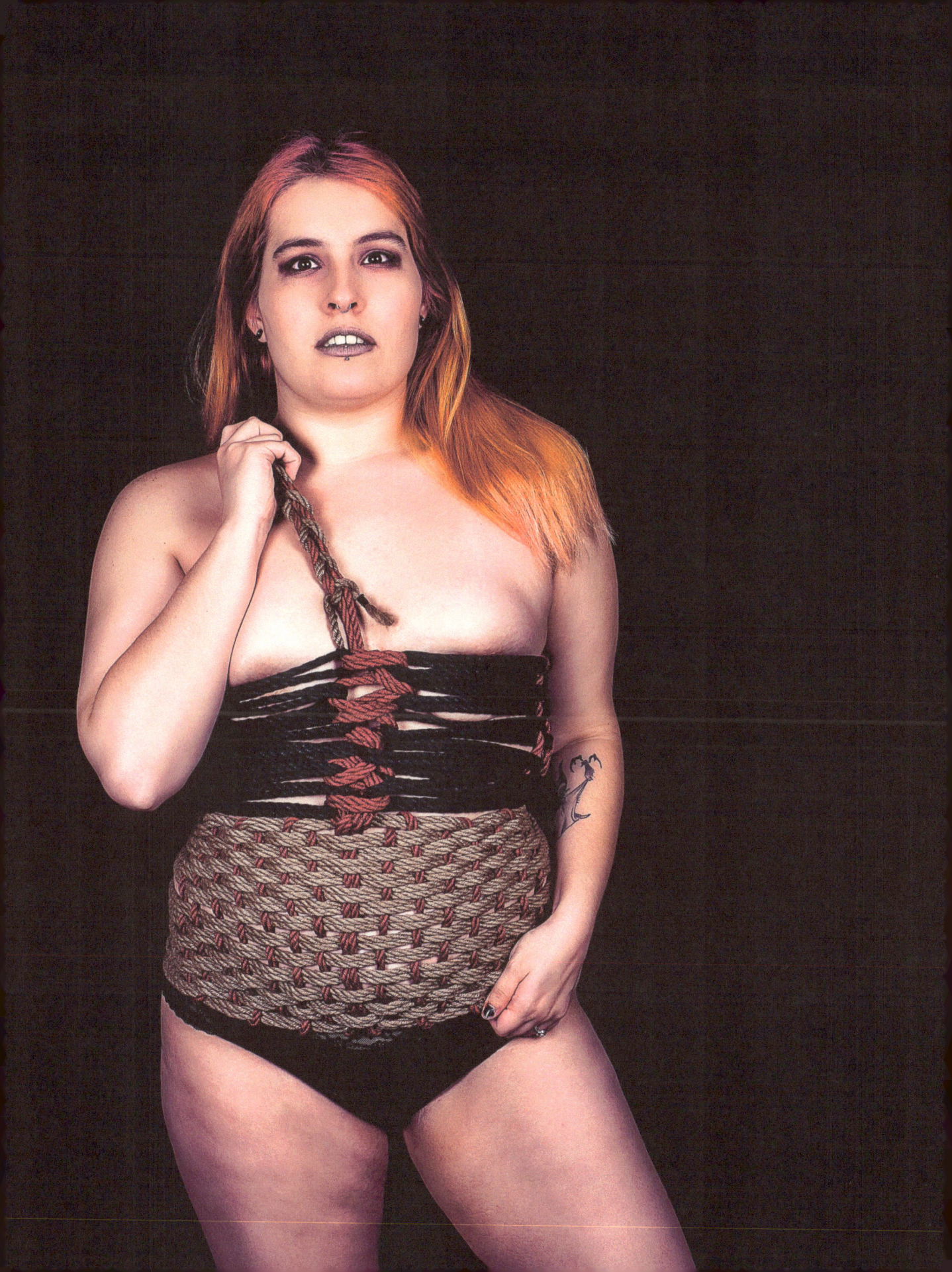

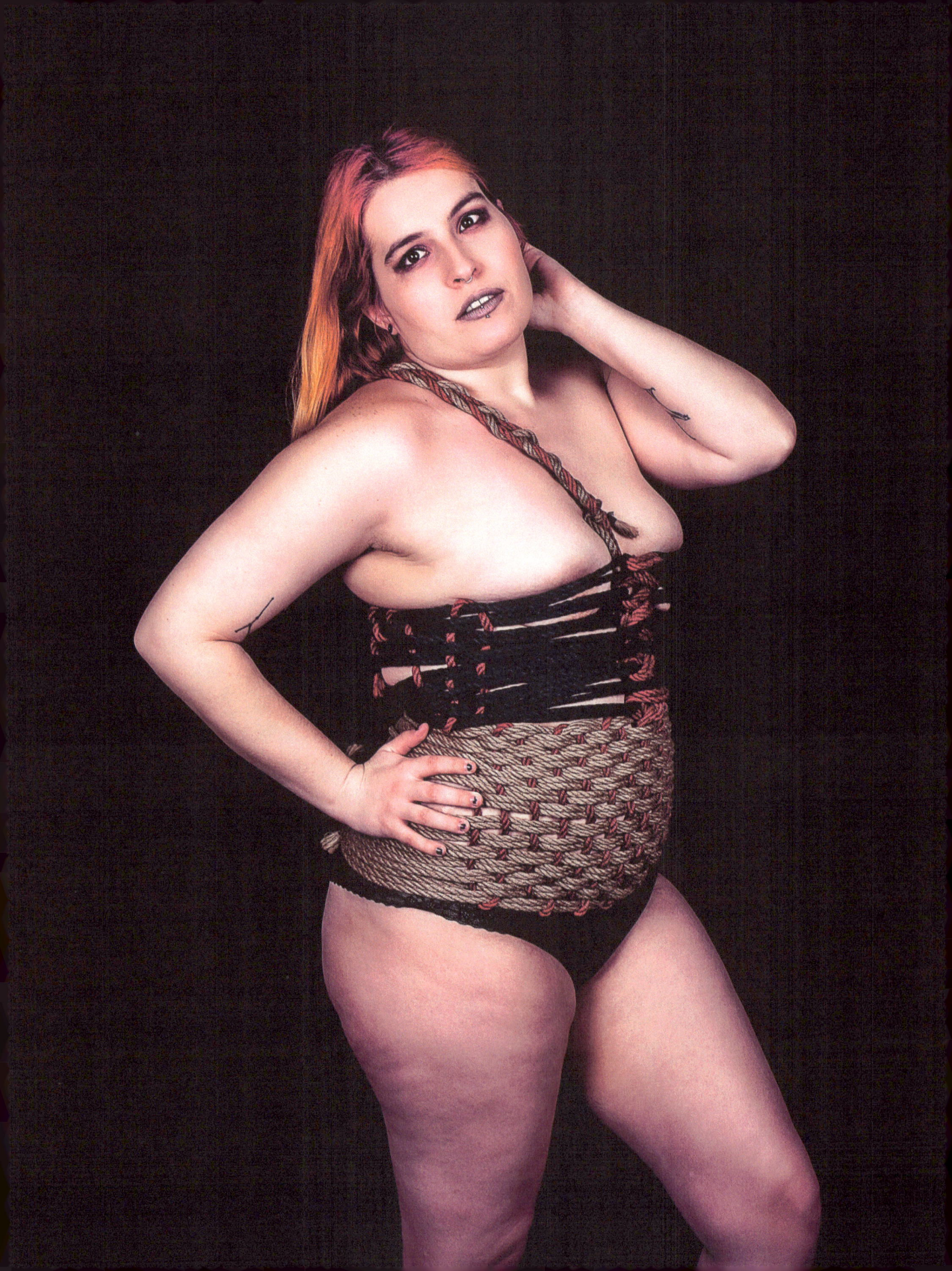

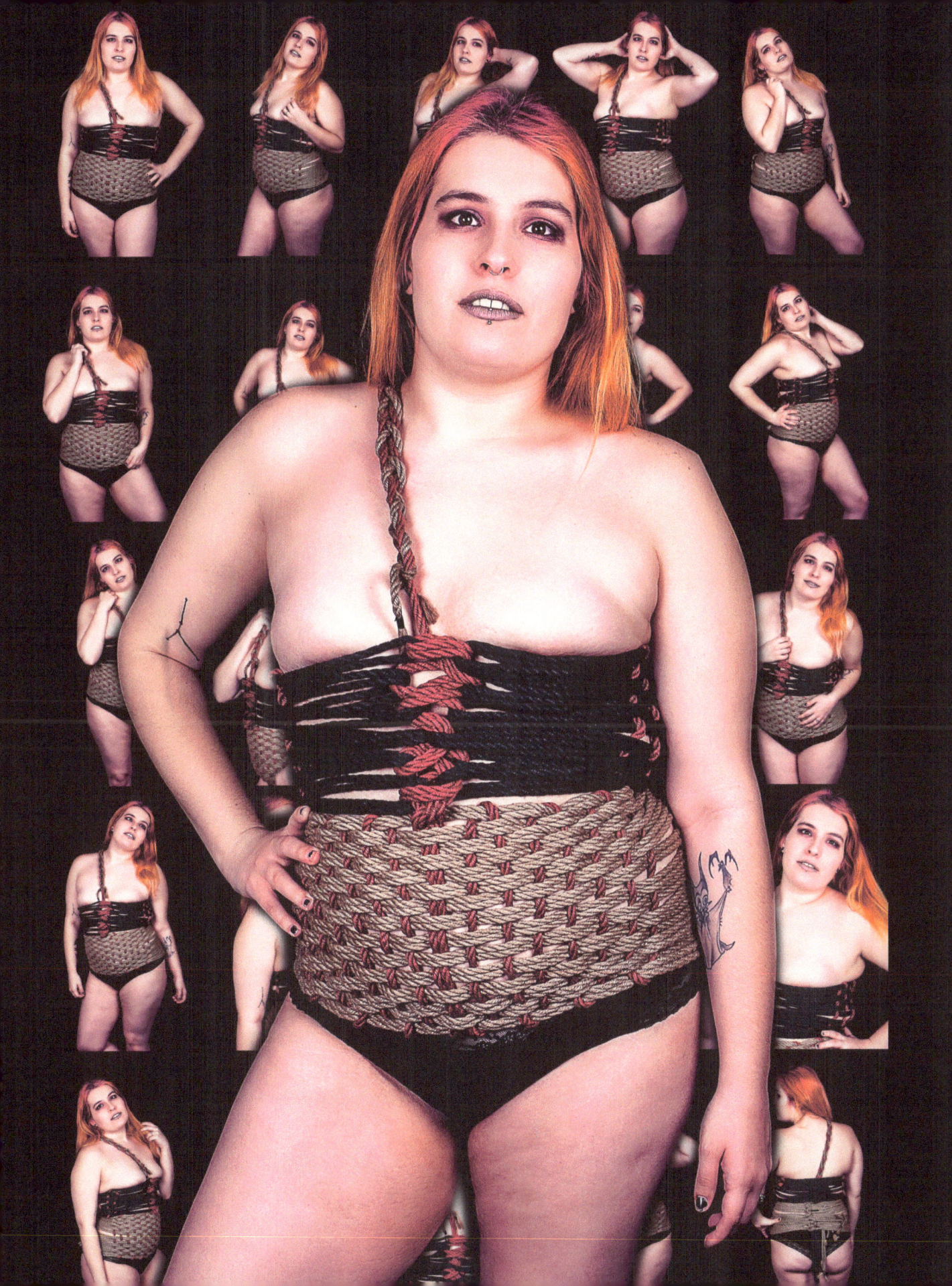

Naevia

When you make sure your bunny is comfortable and is having a good time they will most likely start experimenting with more advanced things all on their own.

Q: What was your experience with bondage before this?
A: Occasional participate.

Q: What did you think of this experience?
A: Fun!

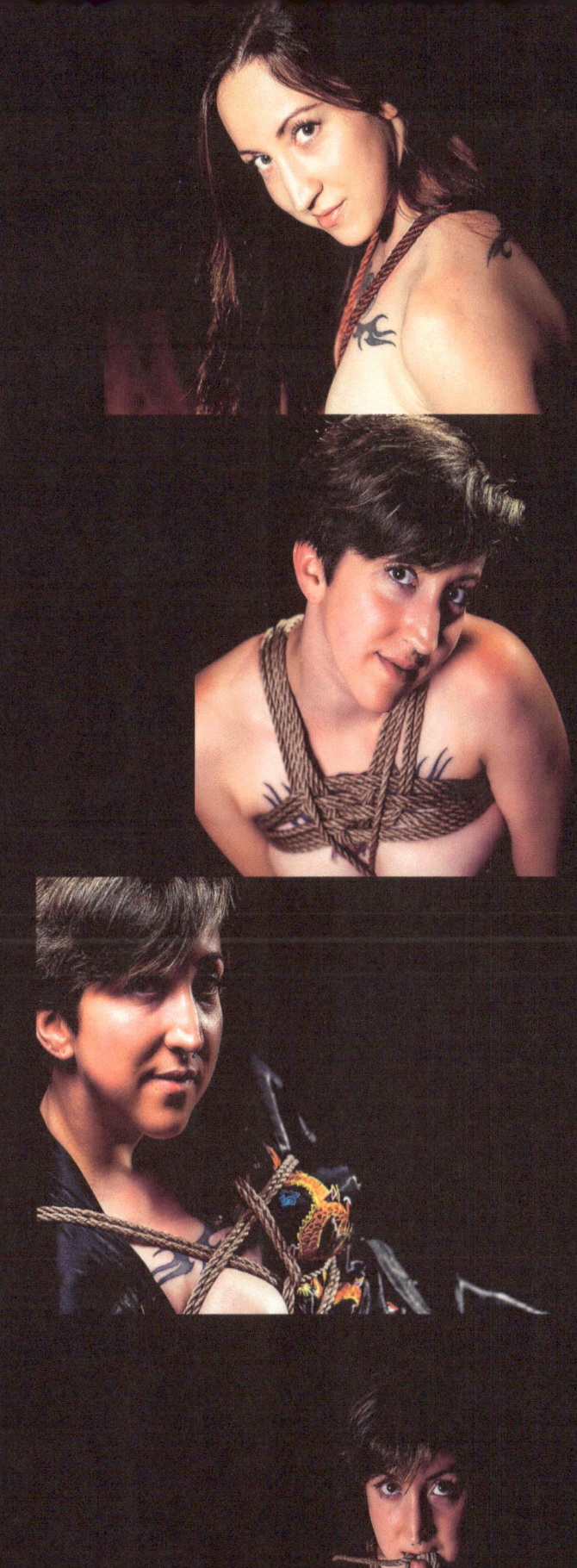

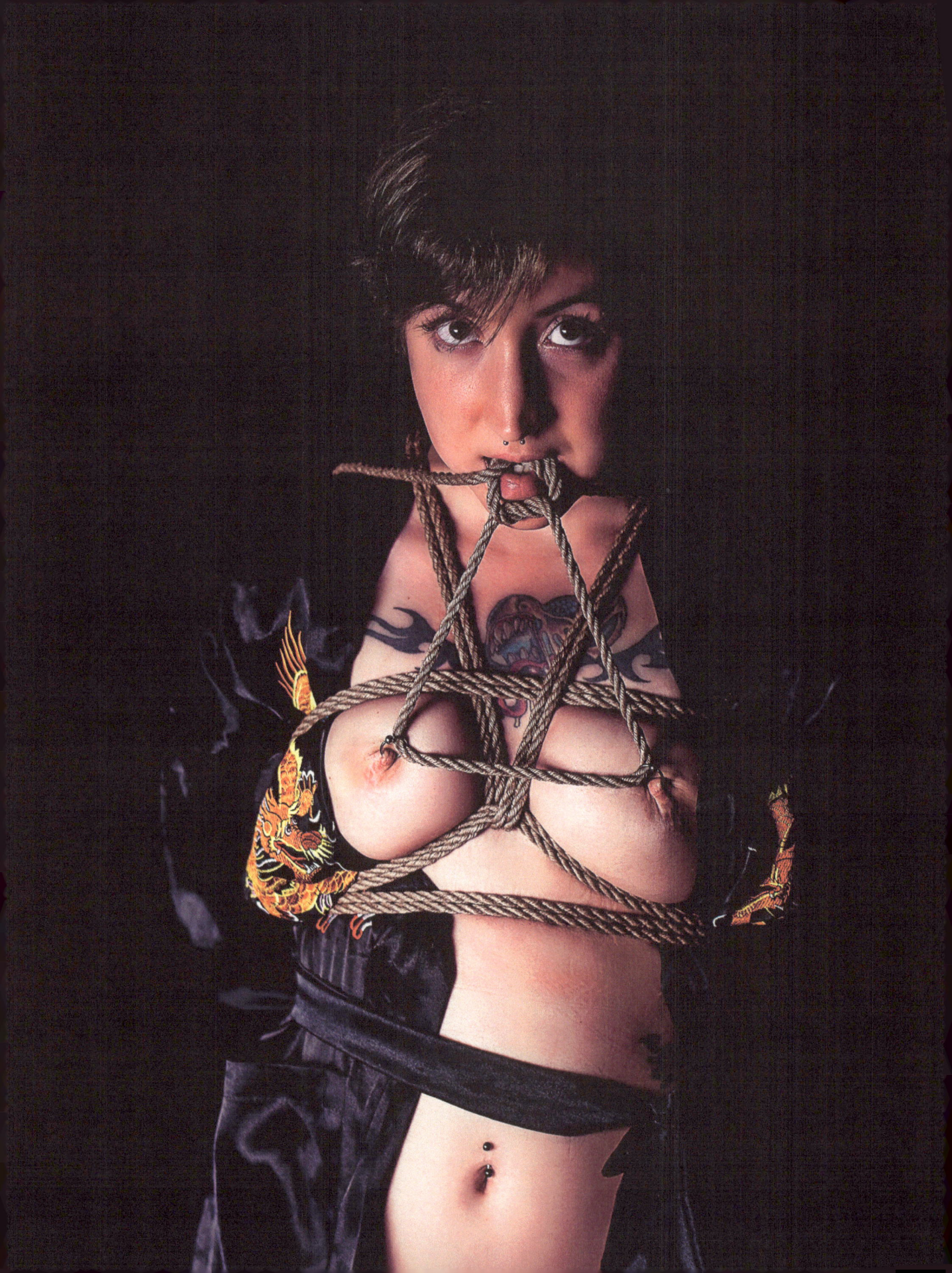

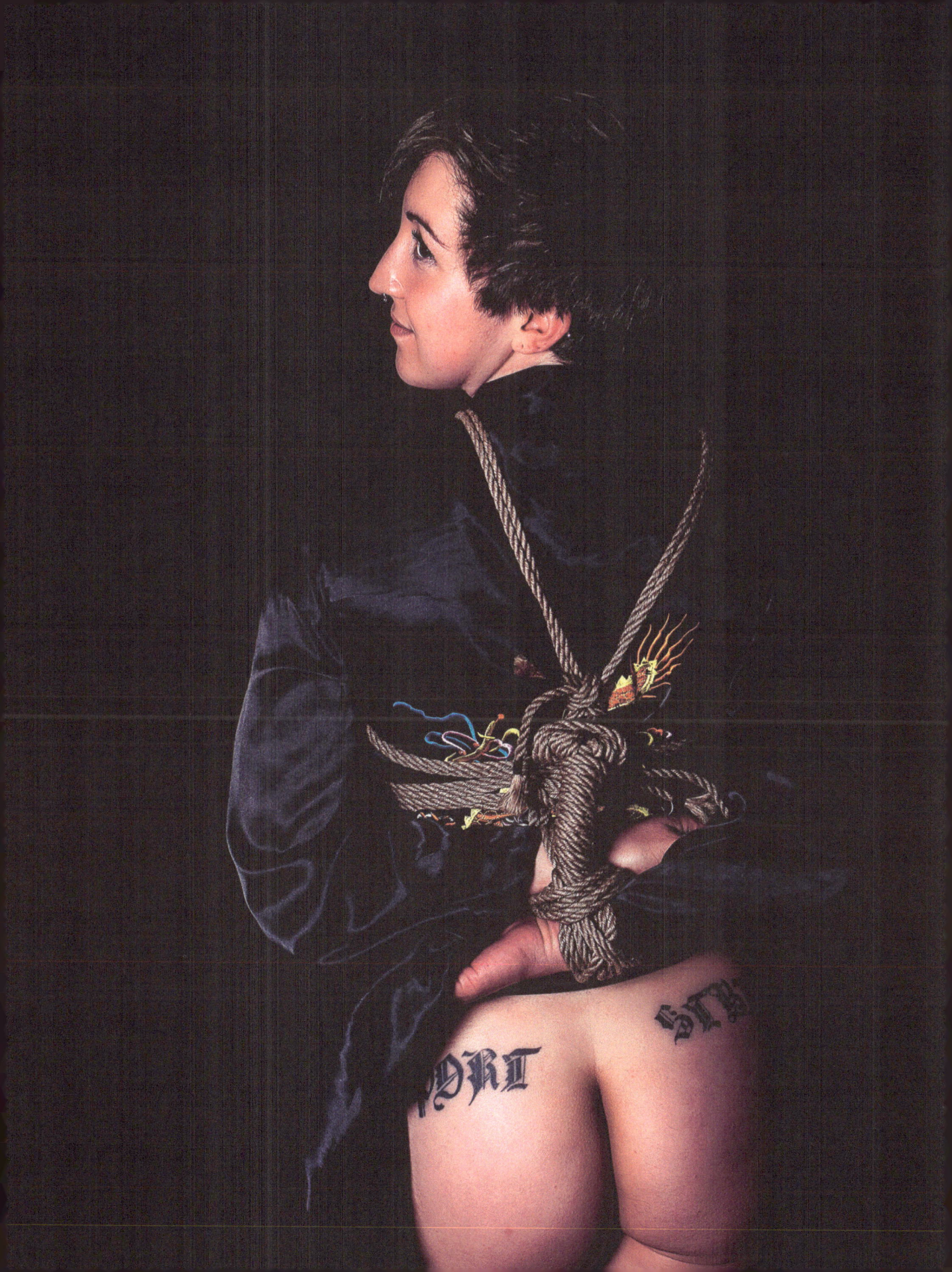

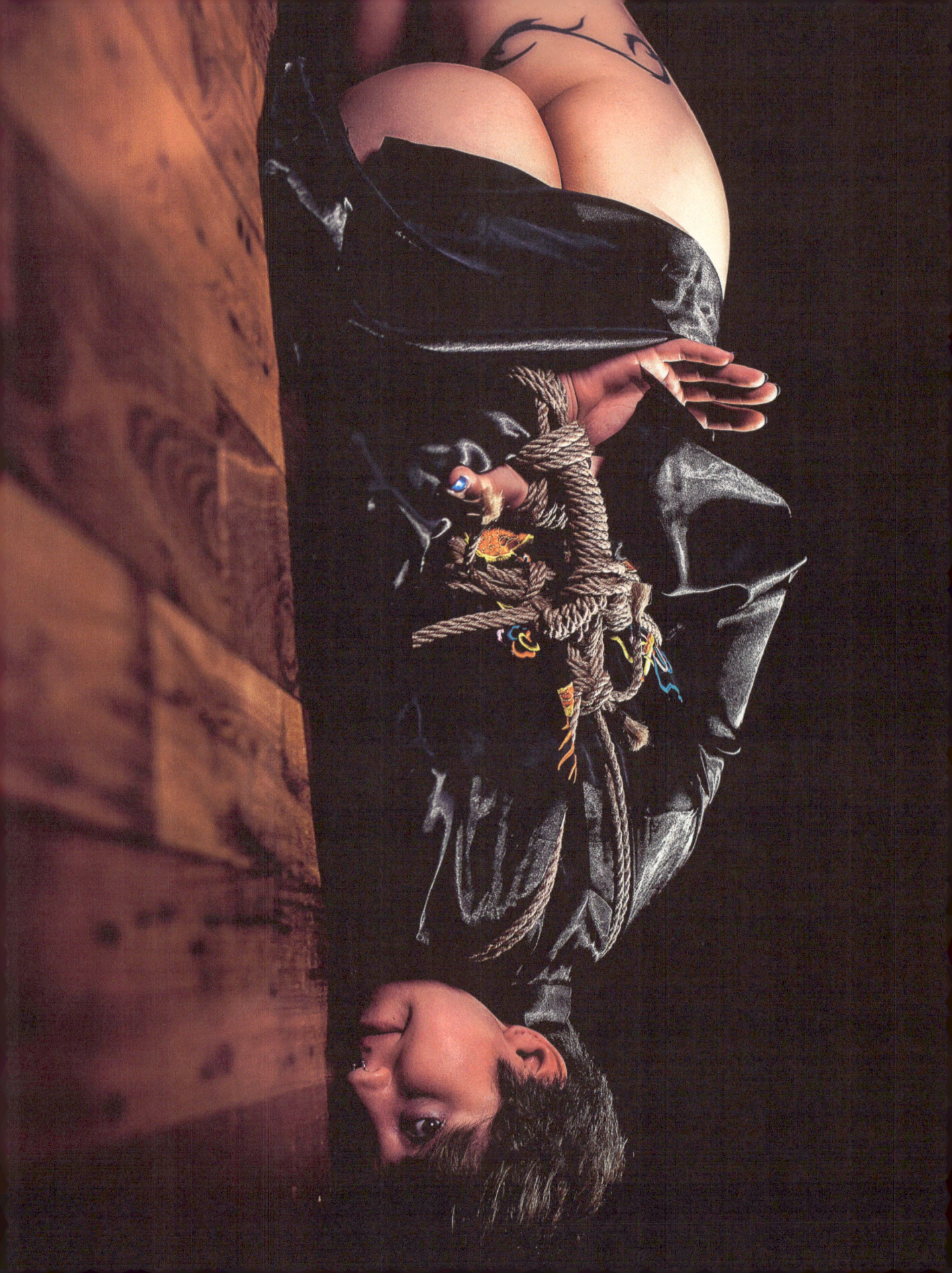

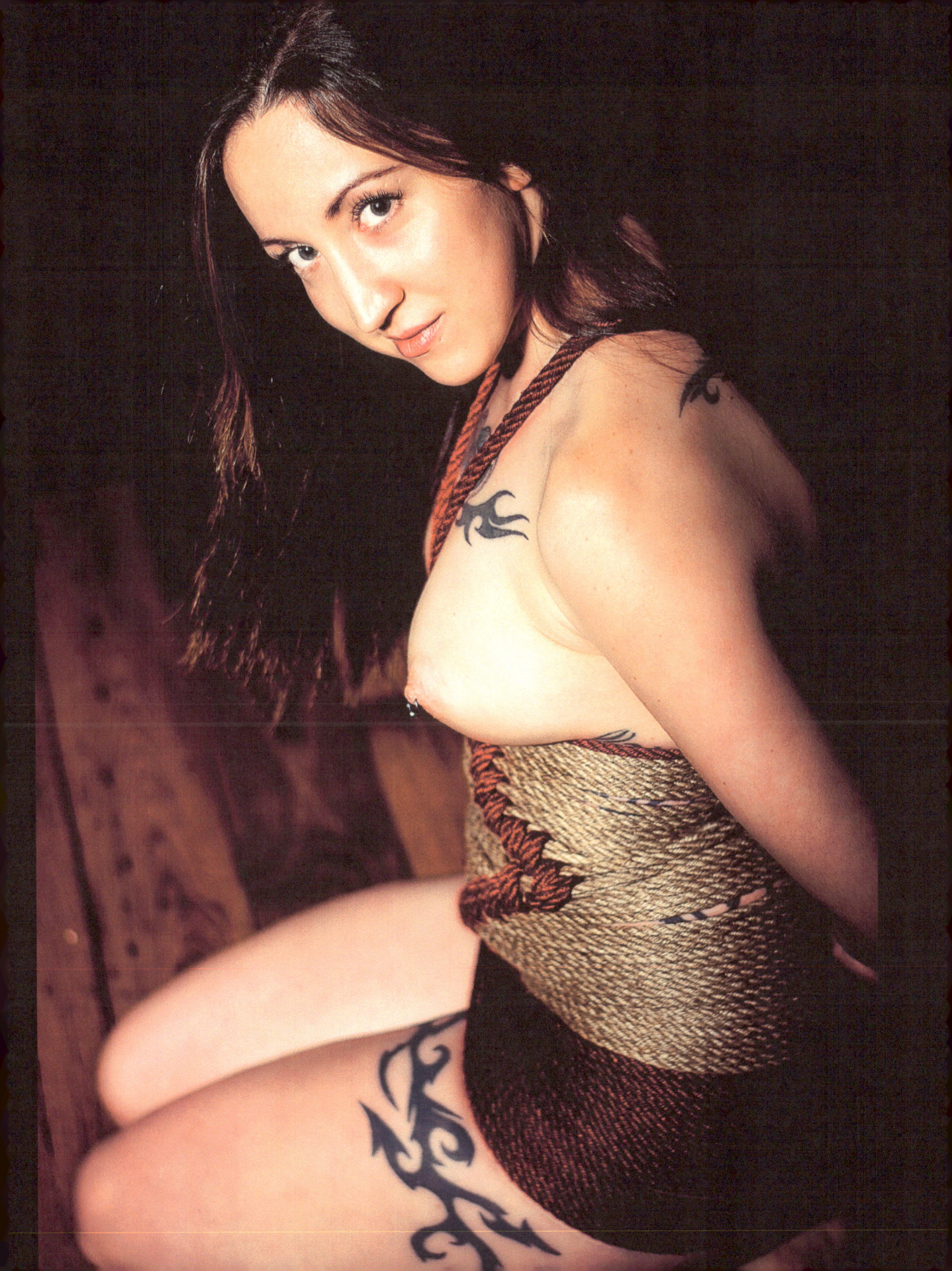

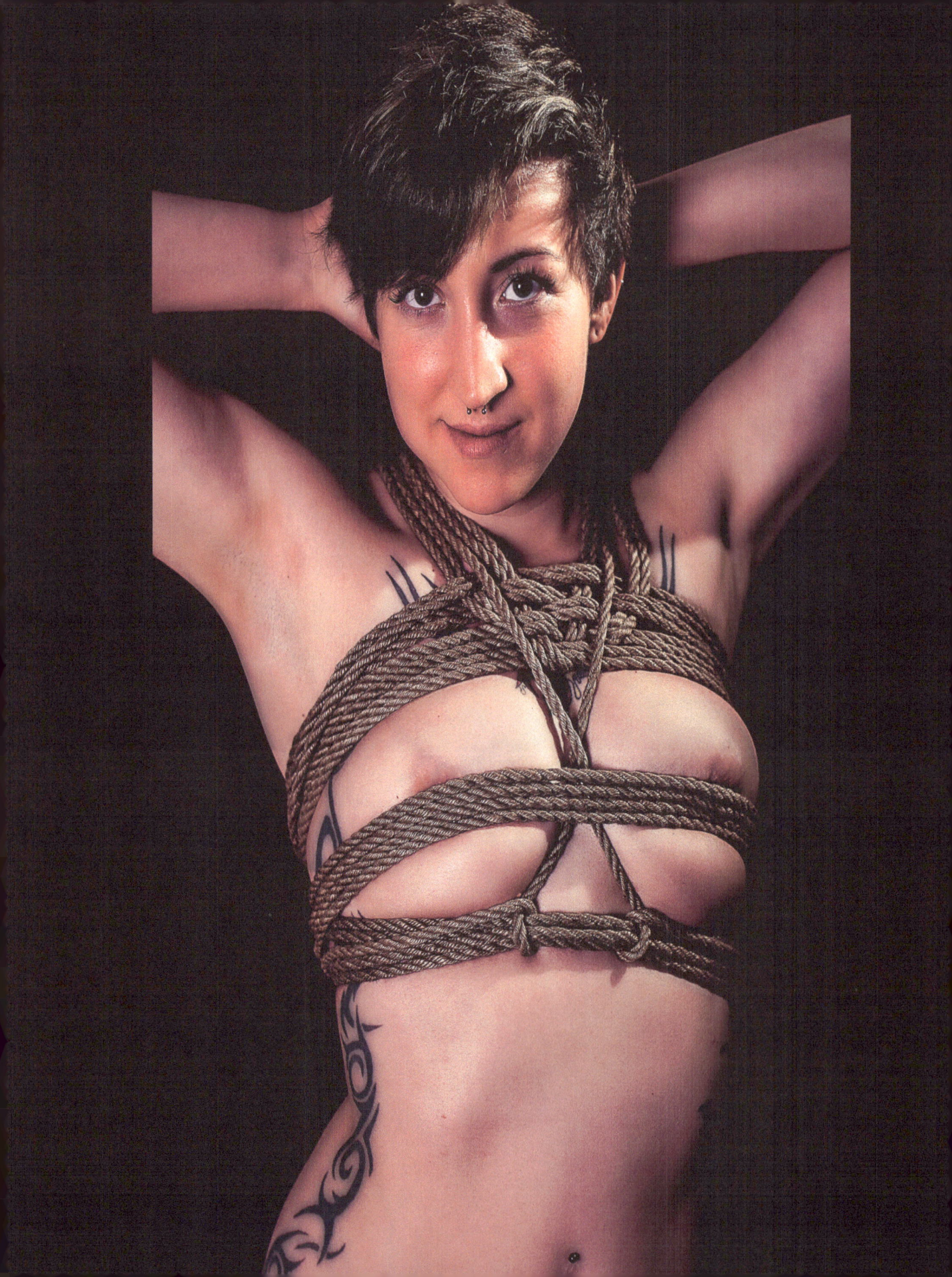

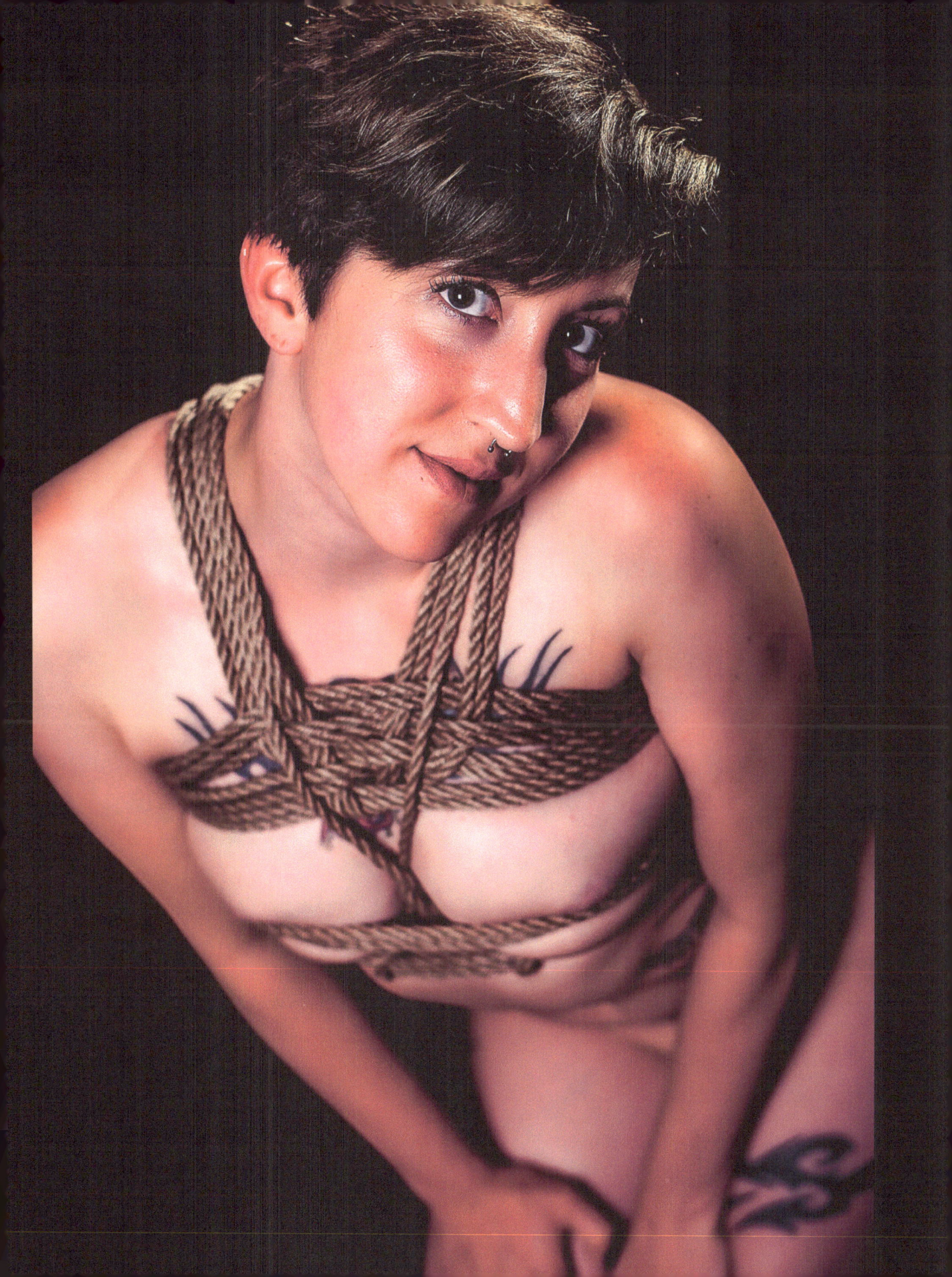

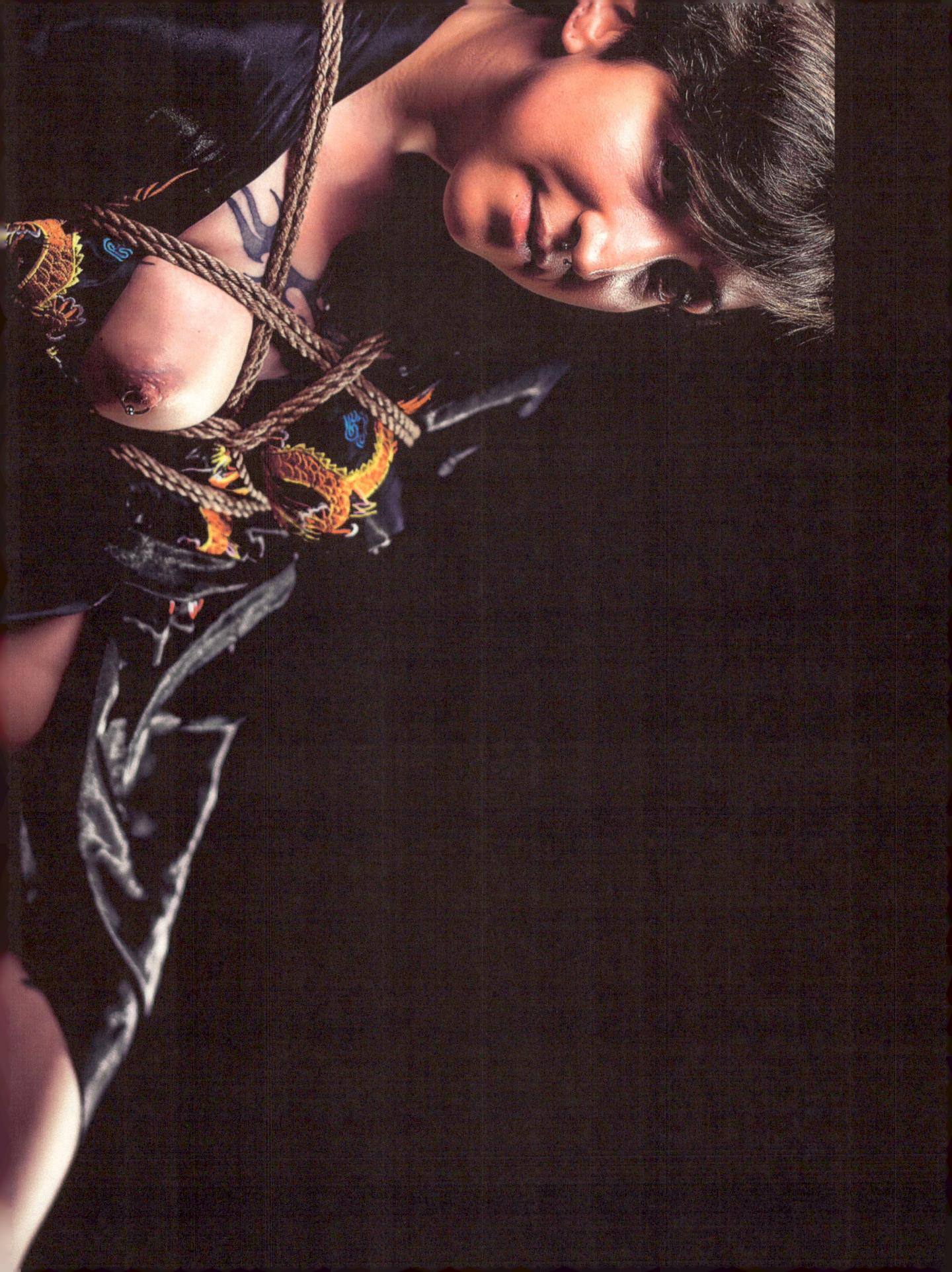

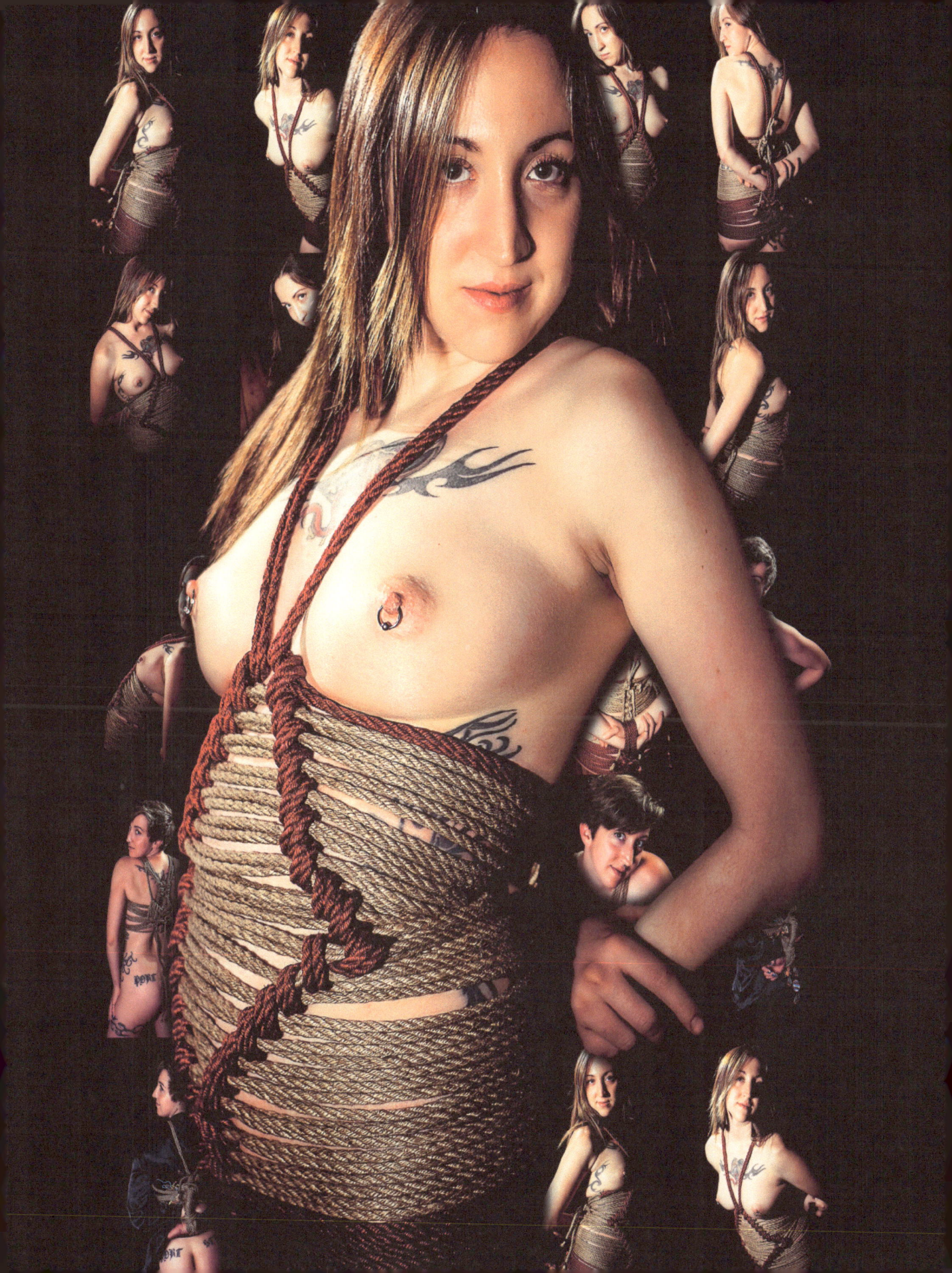

Sydney Mayhem

One of the things I enjoy most about what I do is all the different kinds of people I meet. All the time I get to meet people who have beautiful souls and I know they are something special.

Q: What was your experience with bondage before this?
A: I had little to no experience, other than a kind of inexperience playing around with handcuffs and I don't really count that.

Q: What did you think of the experience?
A: It was fun and exciting! I learned quite a bit. Everything was so professional.

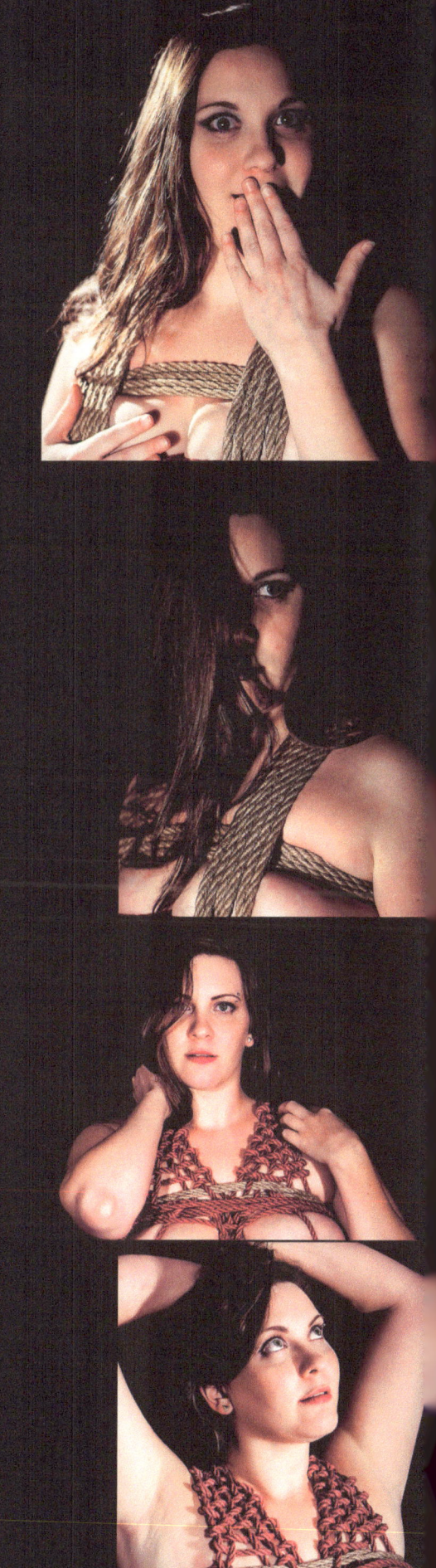

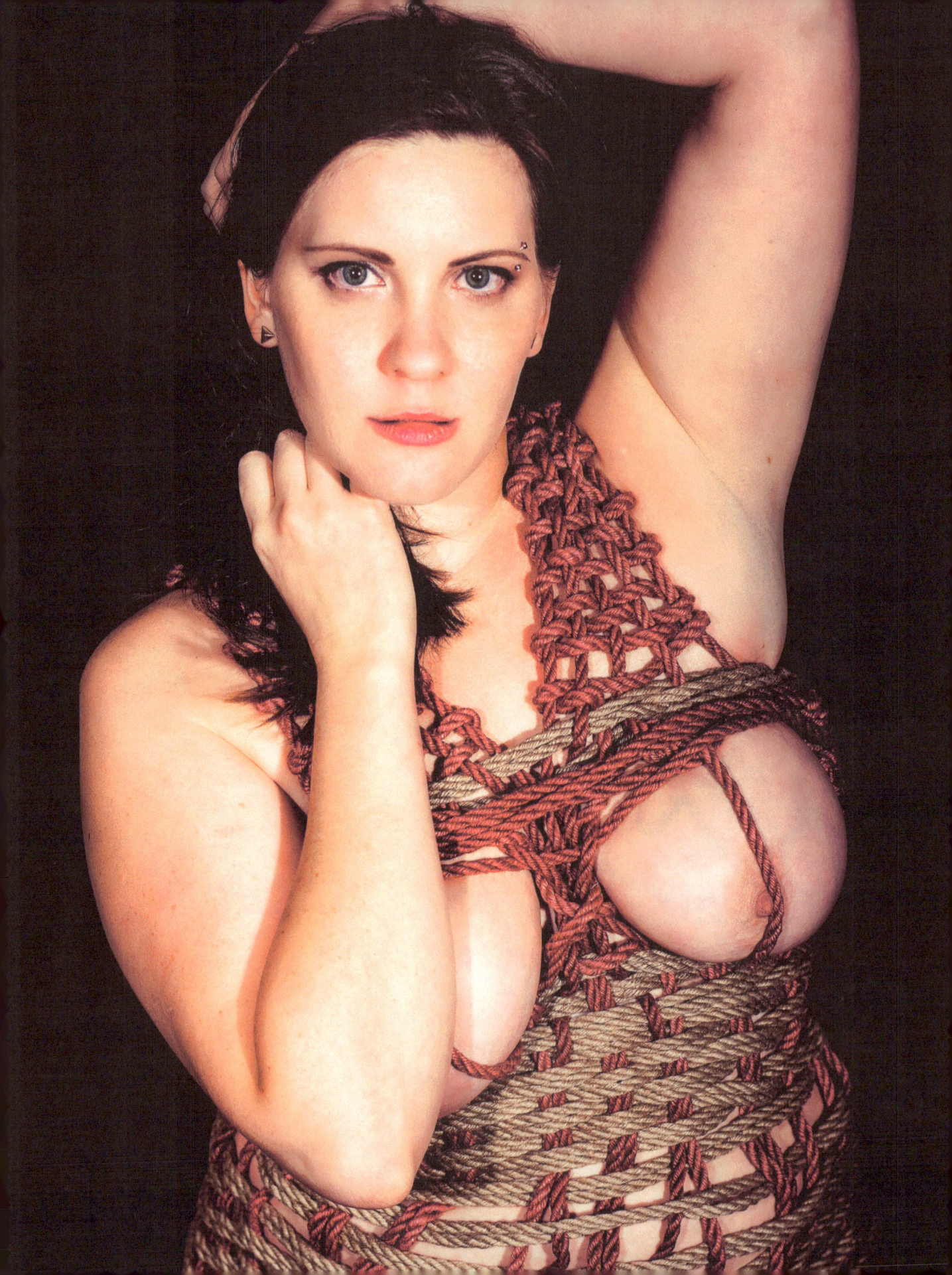

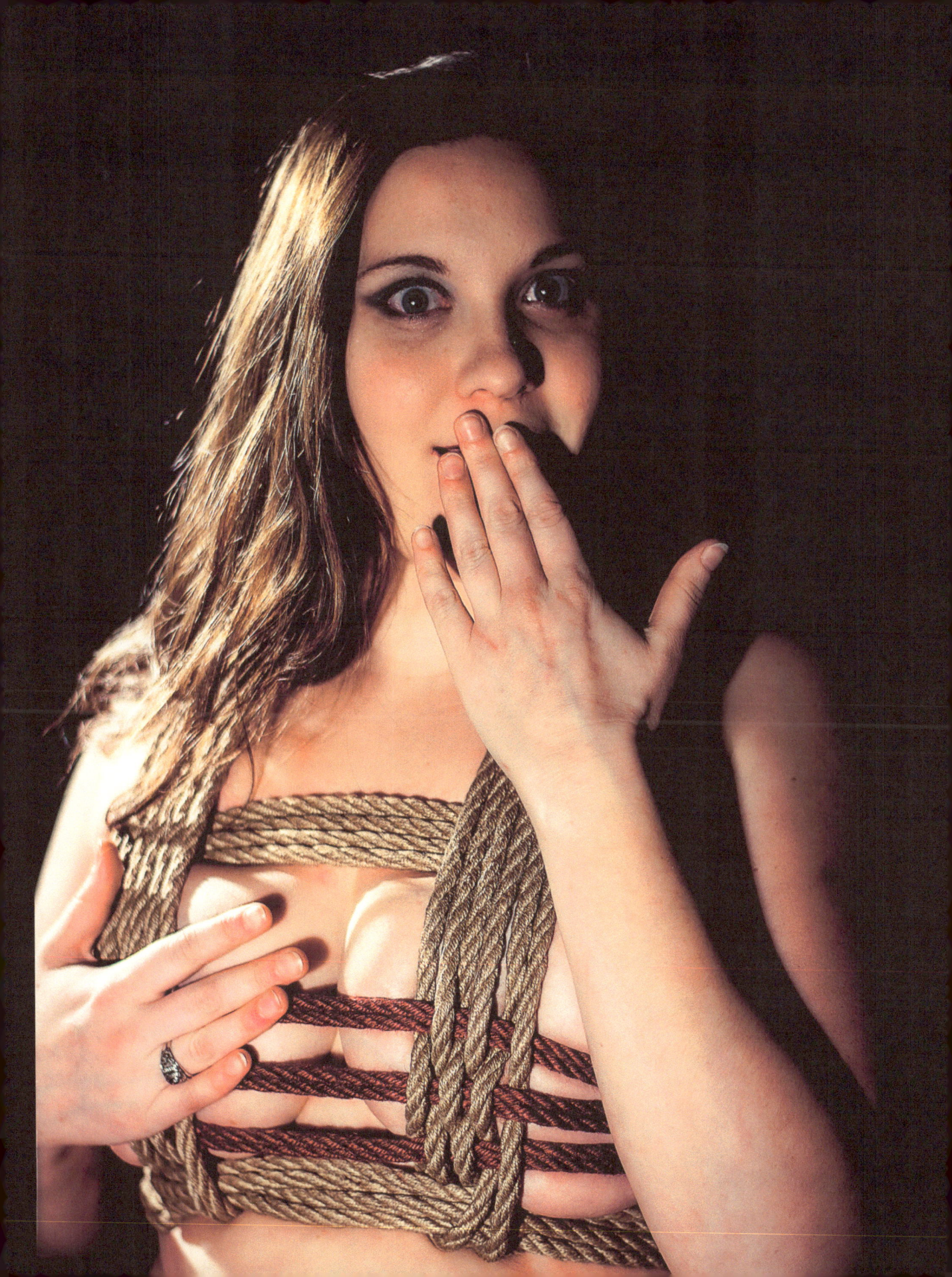

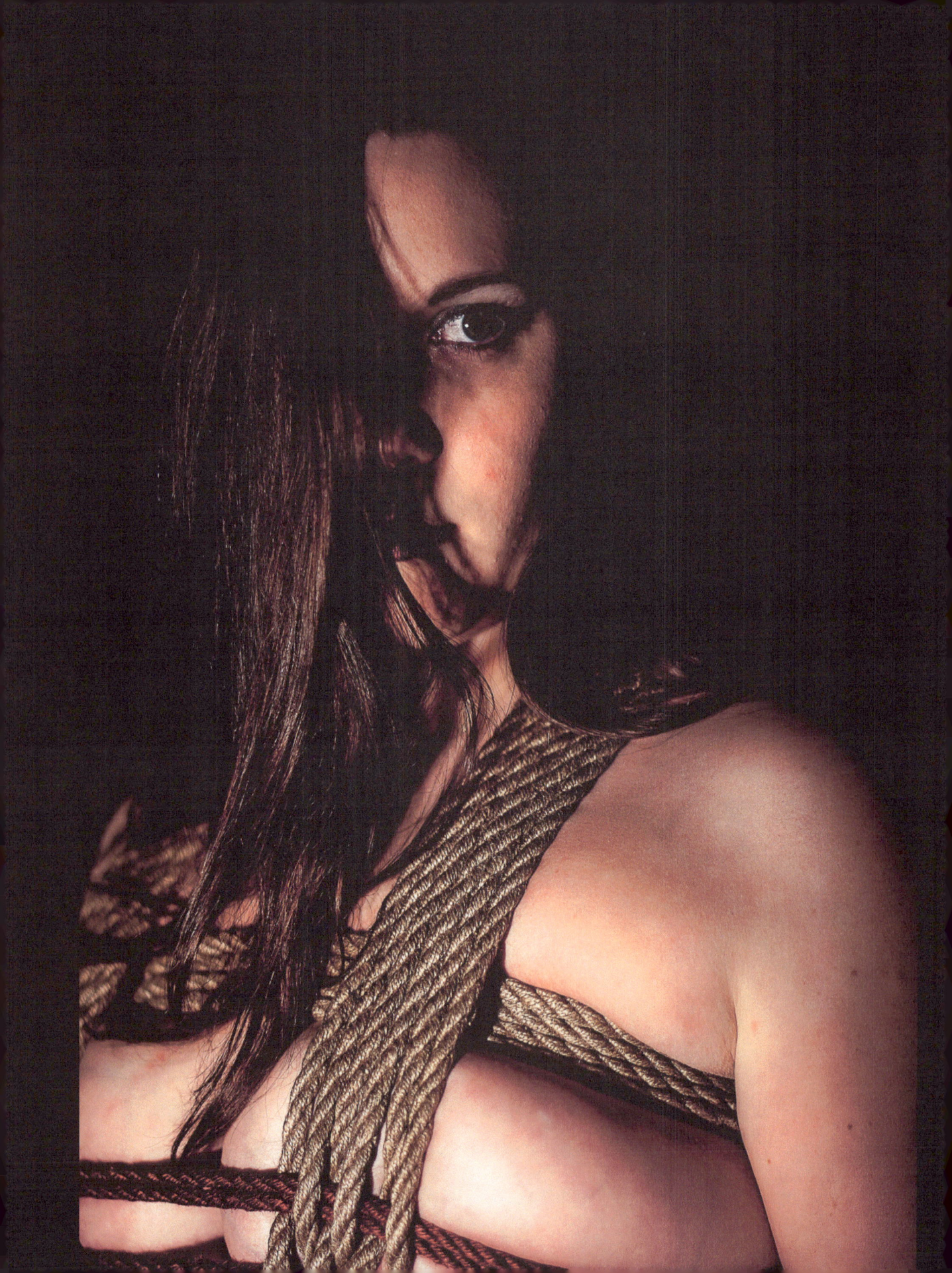

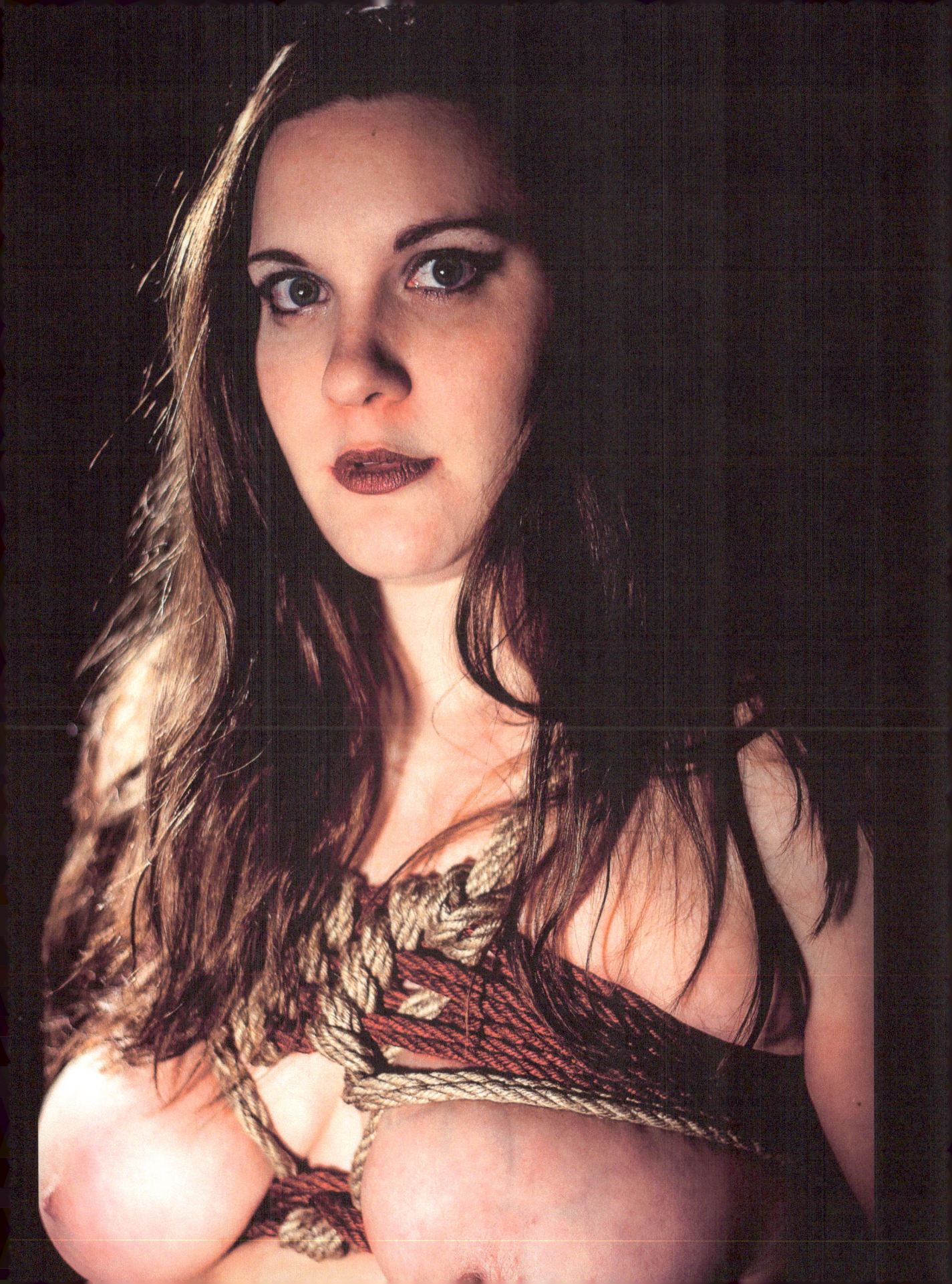

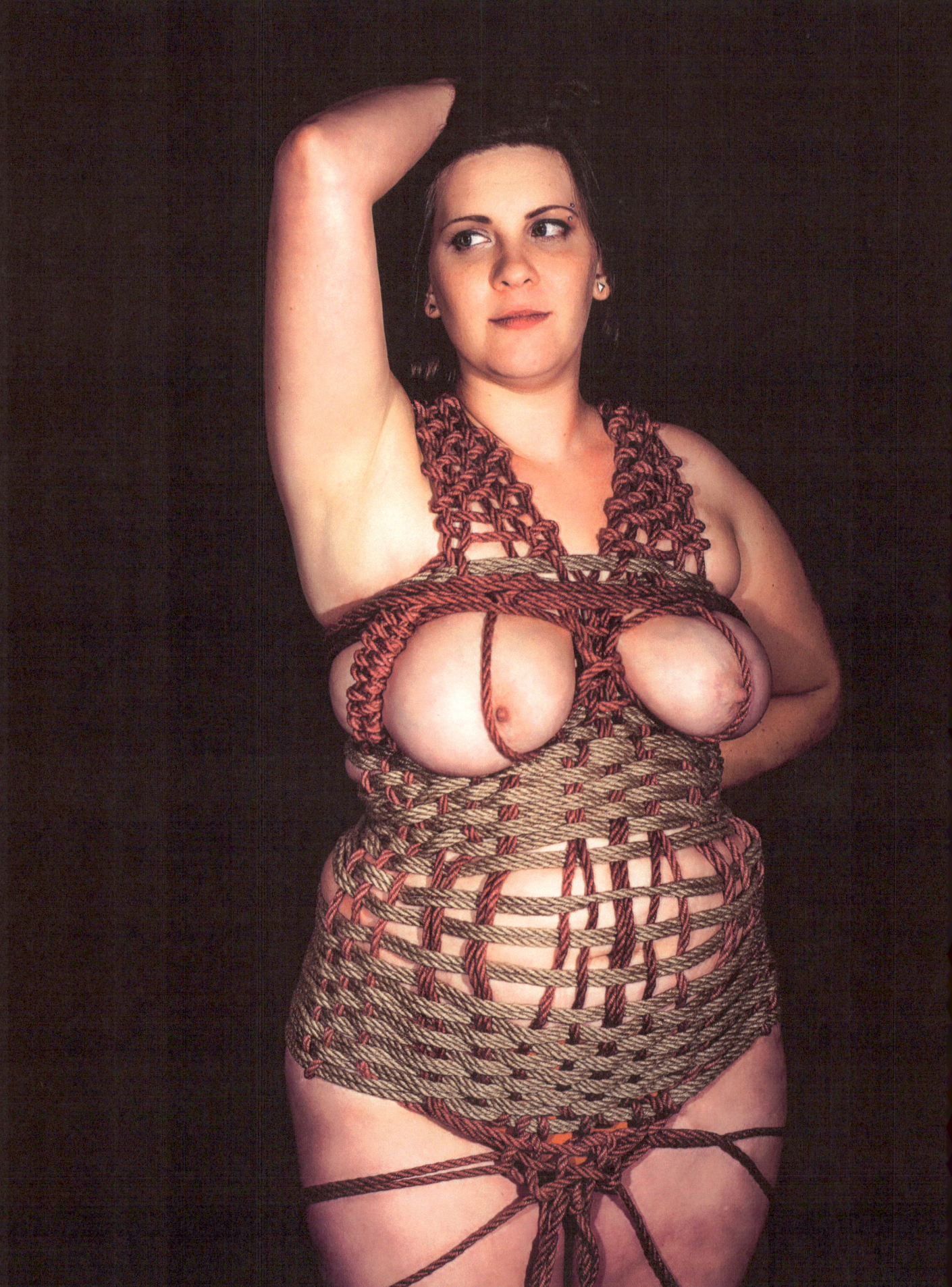

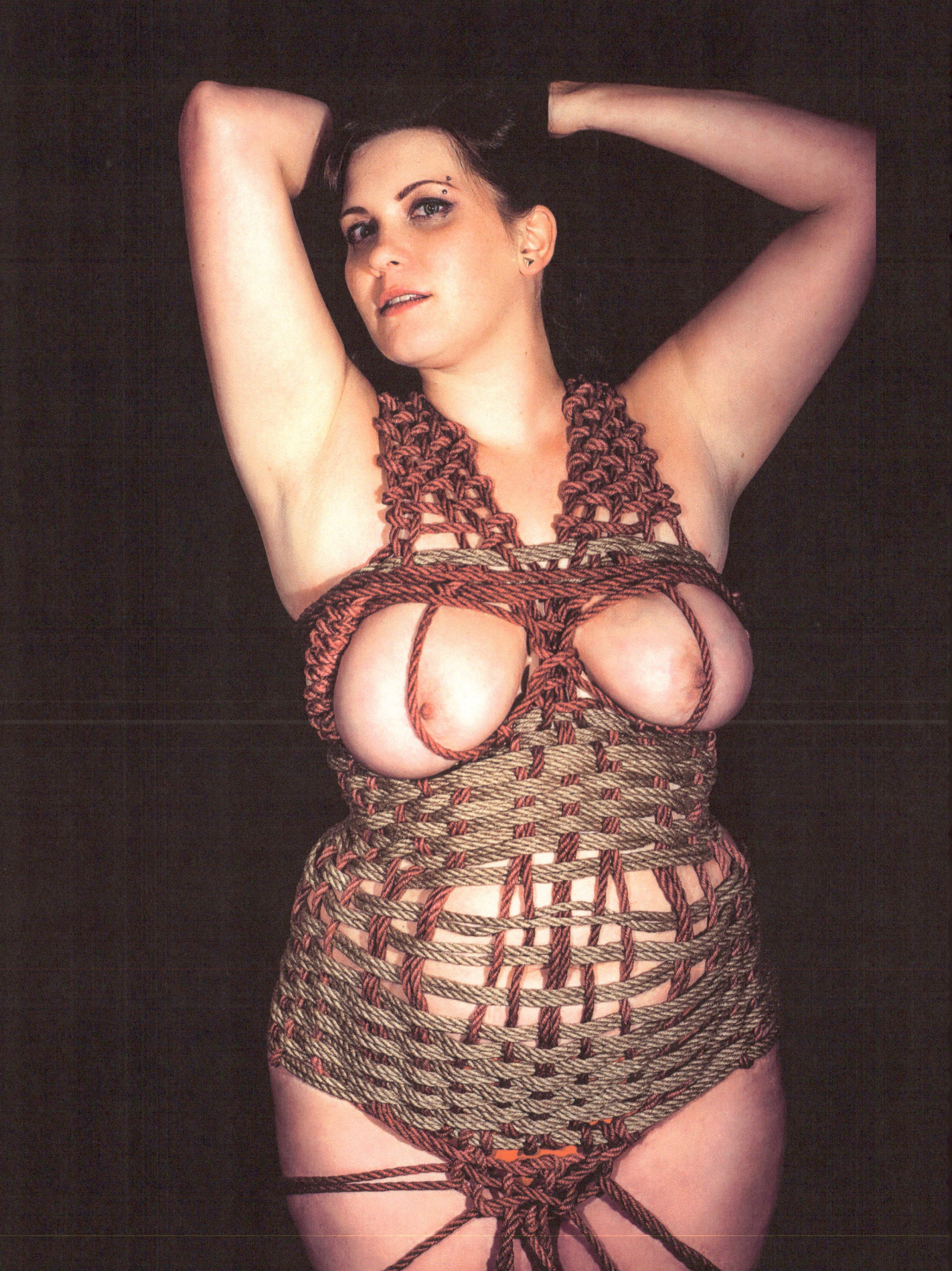

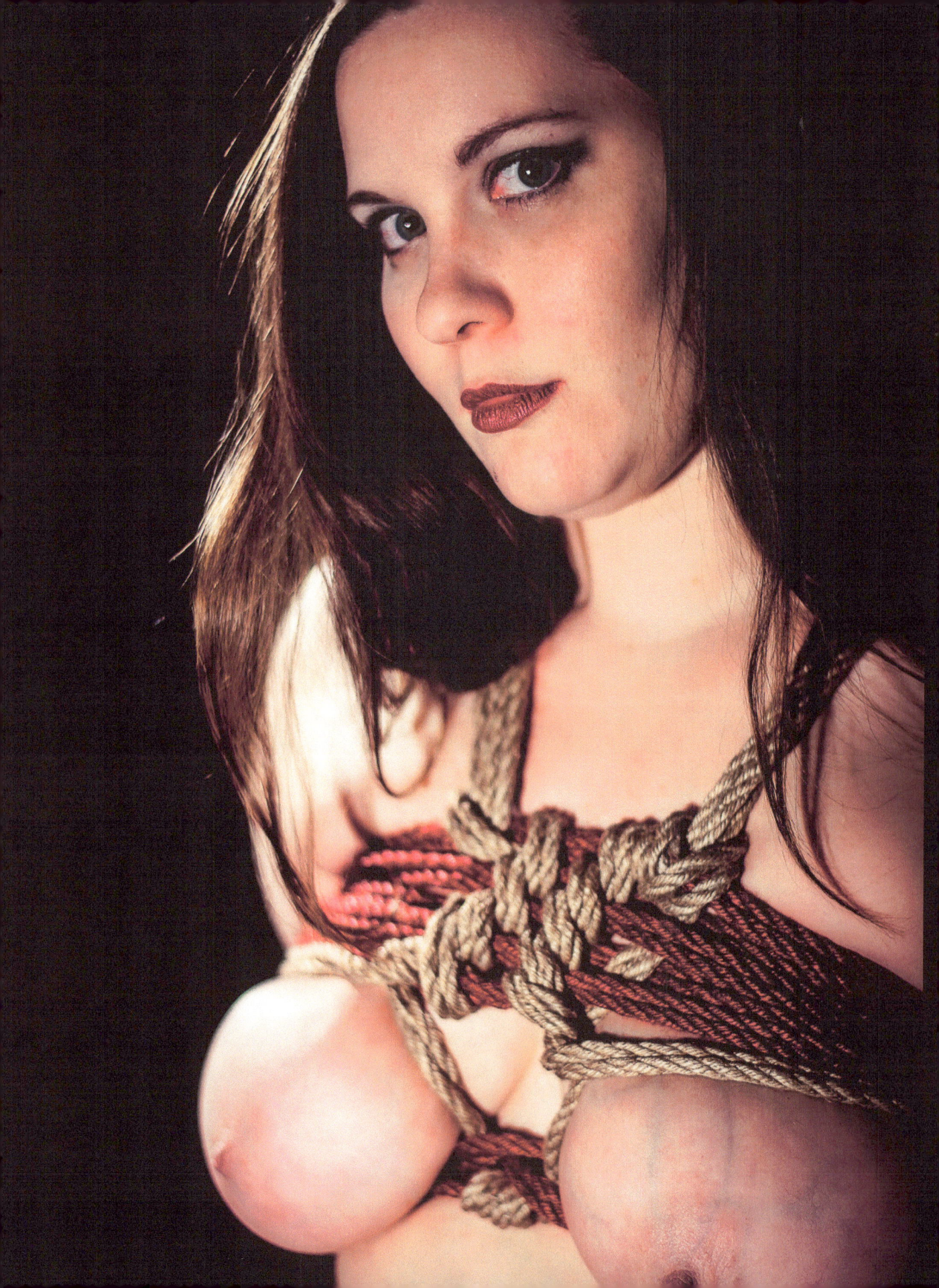

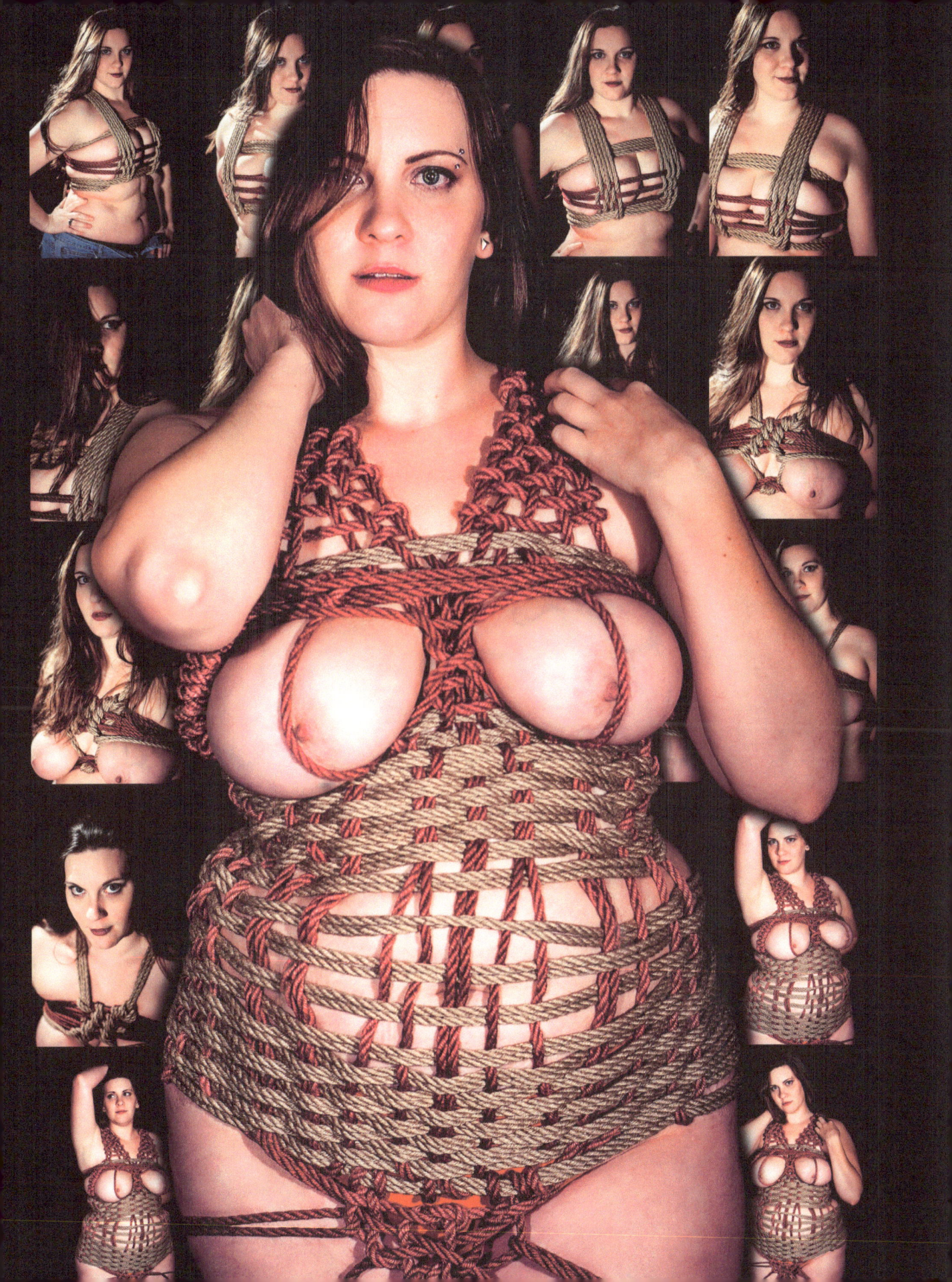

Thessaly Jane

I was preparing for a panel when the bunnies I had arranged for the panel all canceled last minute. So I asked some of the friends I knew if they could do this for me just this one time. During the panel I brought up that I was looking for people who wanted to be in this book. My friend, whom I thought was just doing this as a favor, made it very apparent that she wanted to do it. I've said it before, when it comes to fetish and kinks you can never assume someone isn't into it. You want know unless you ask.

Q: What was your experience with bondage before this?
A: None

Q: What did you think about this experience?
A: Fun!

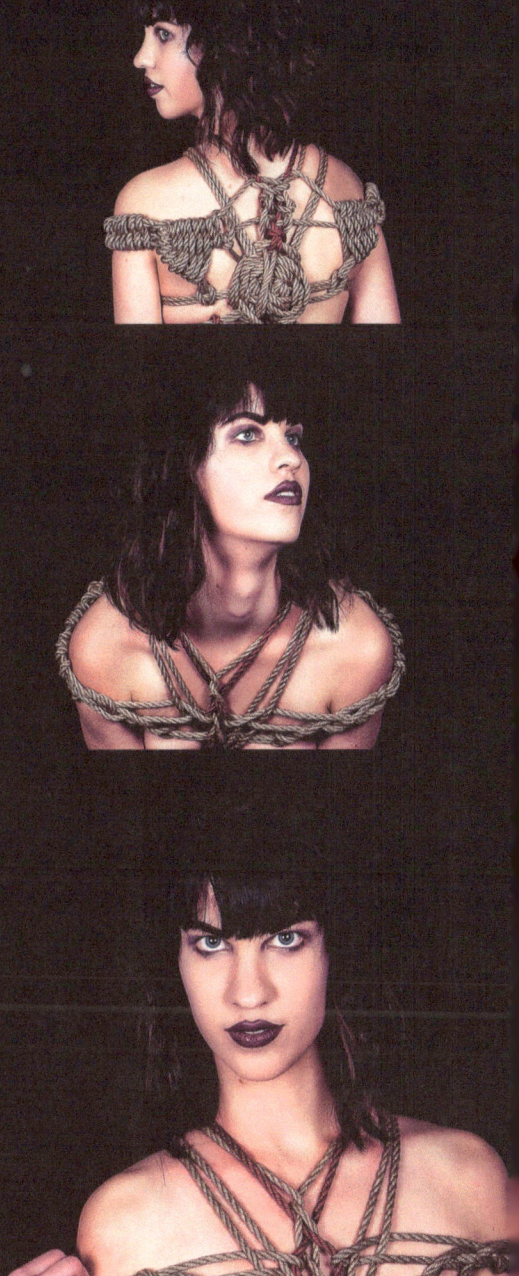

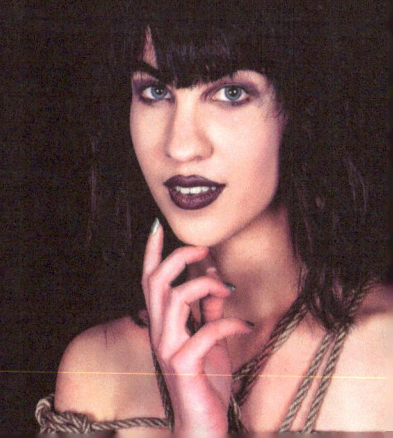

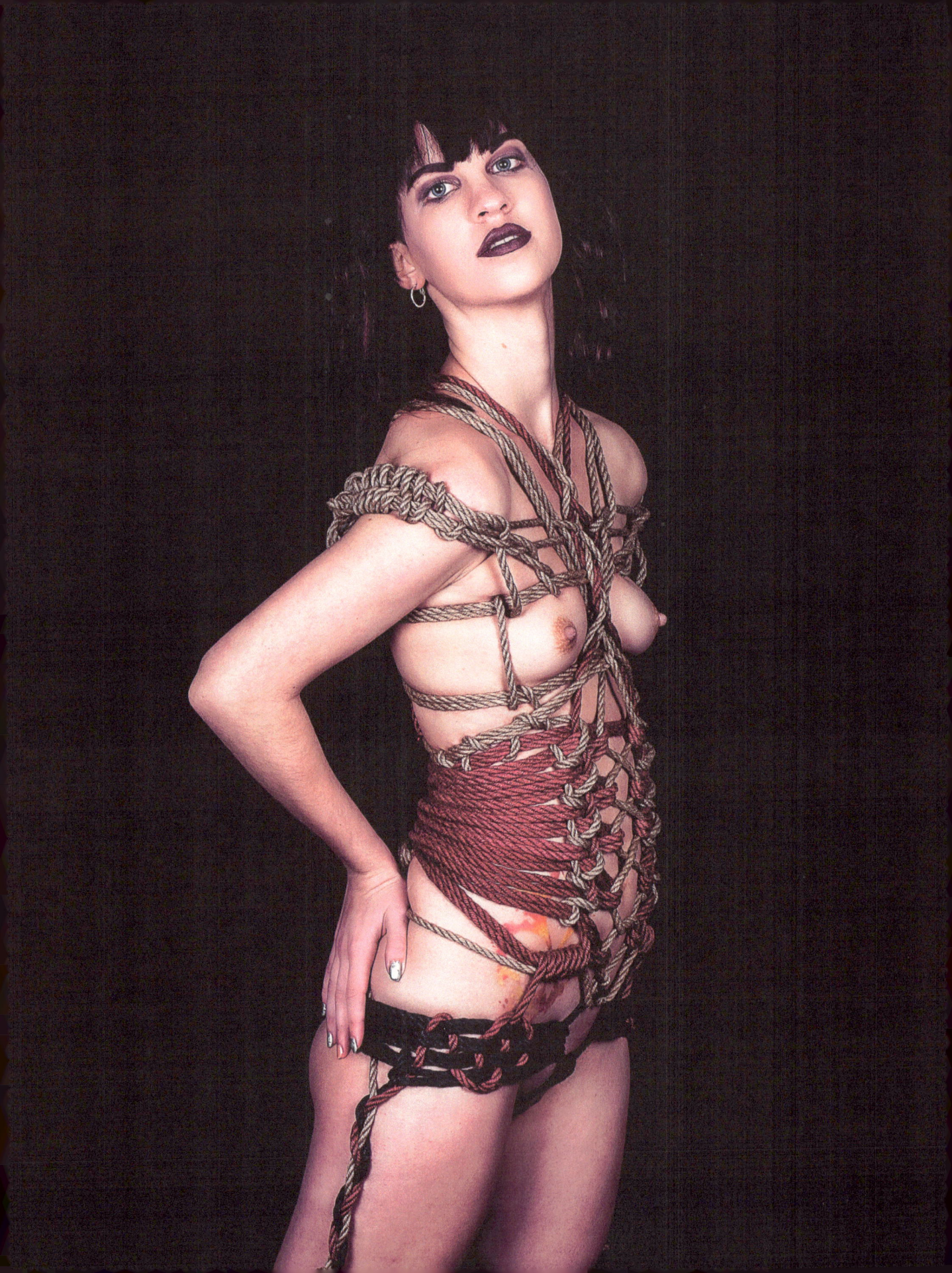

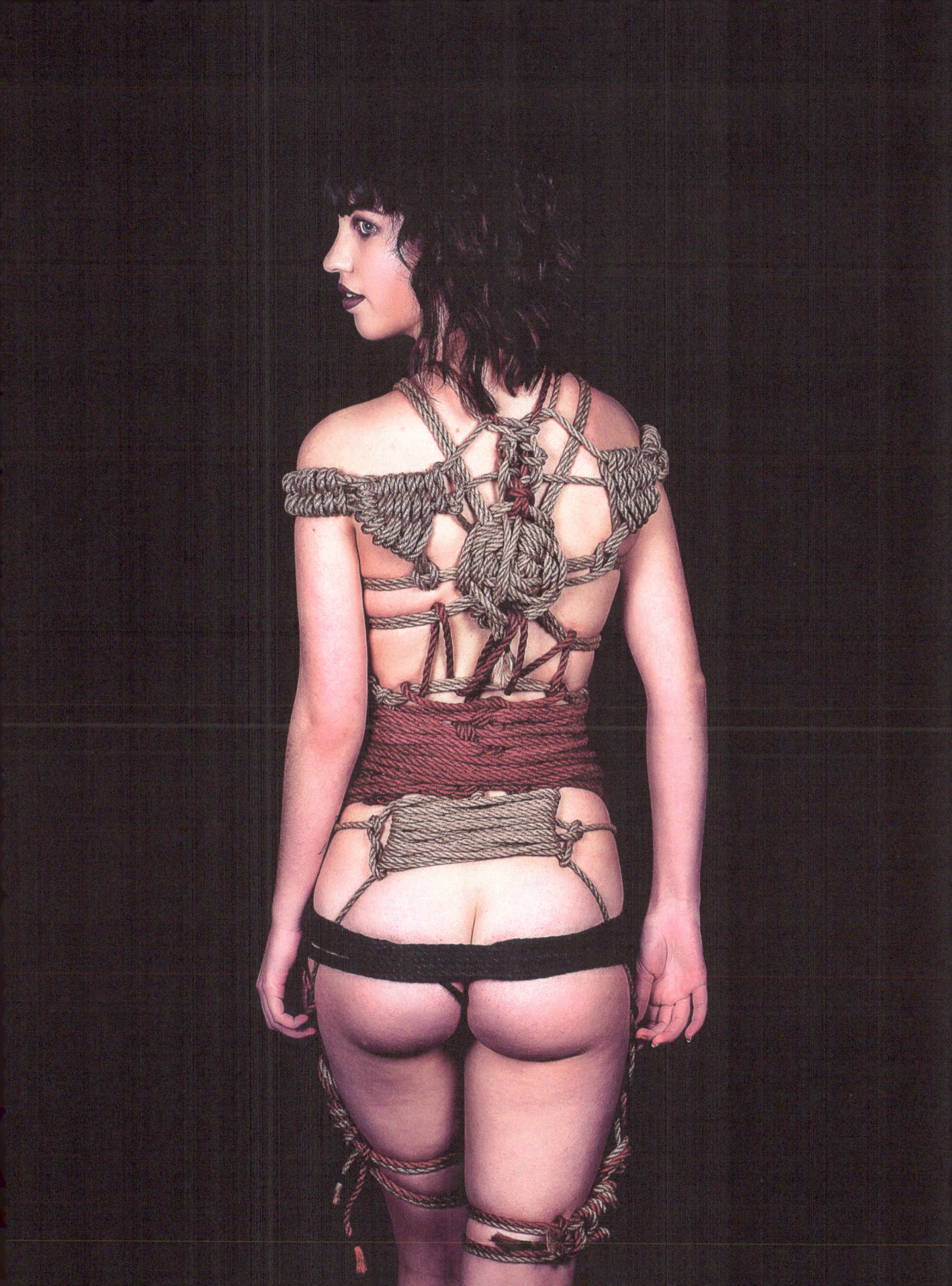

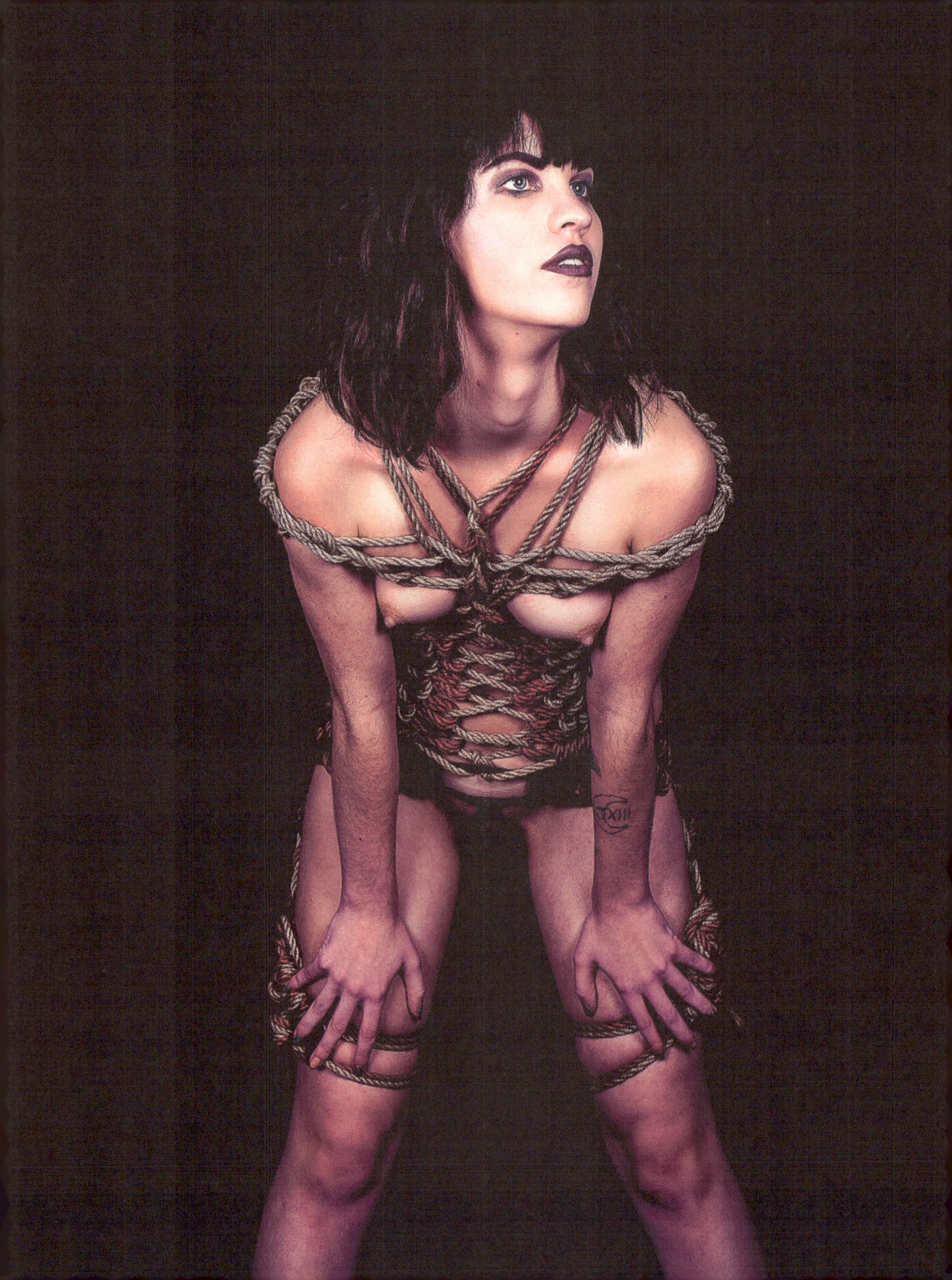

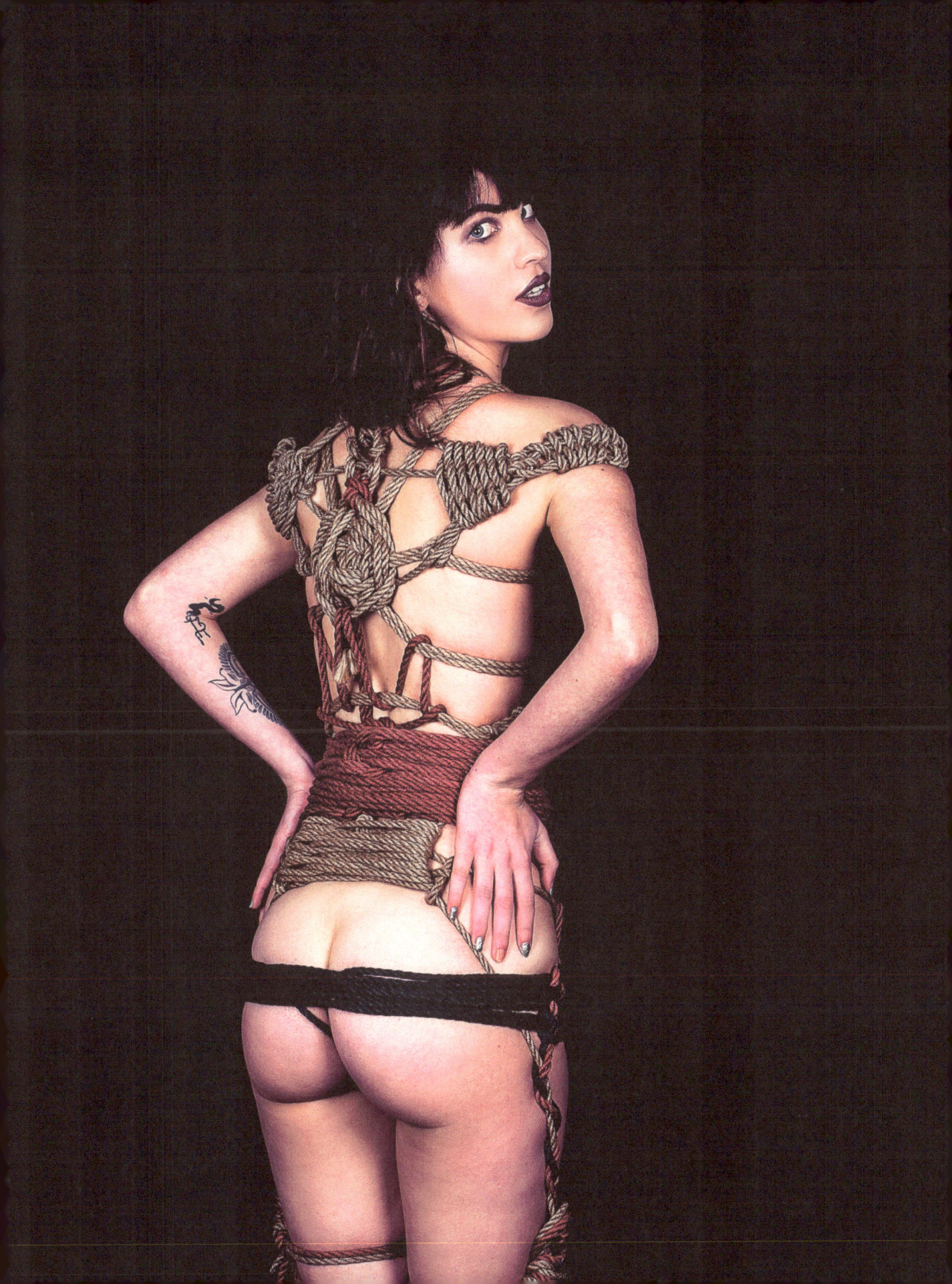

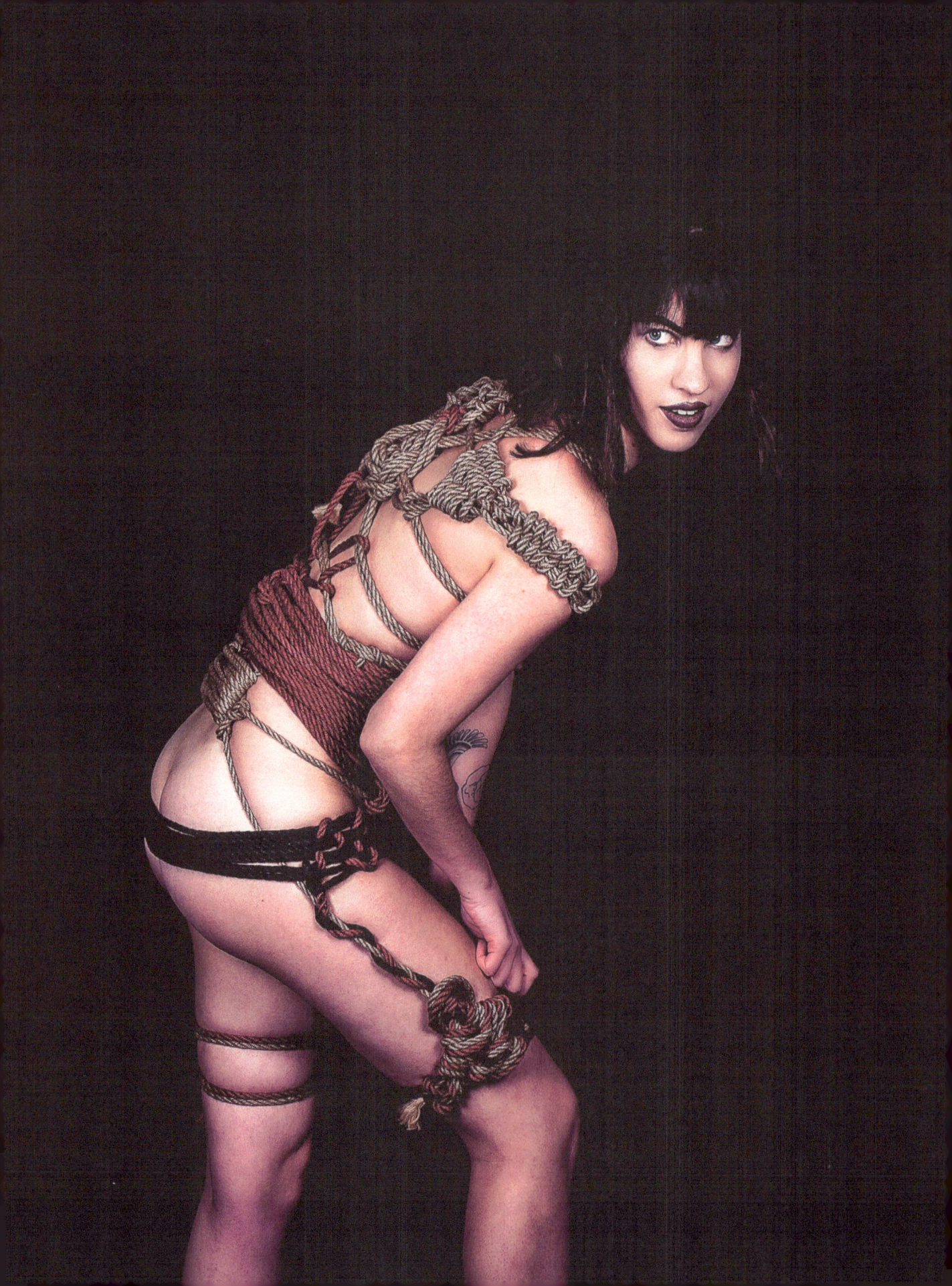

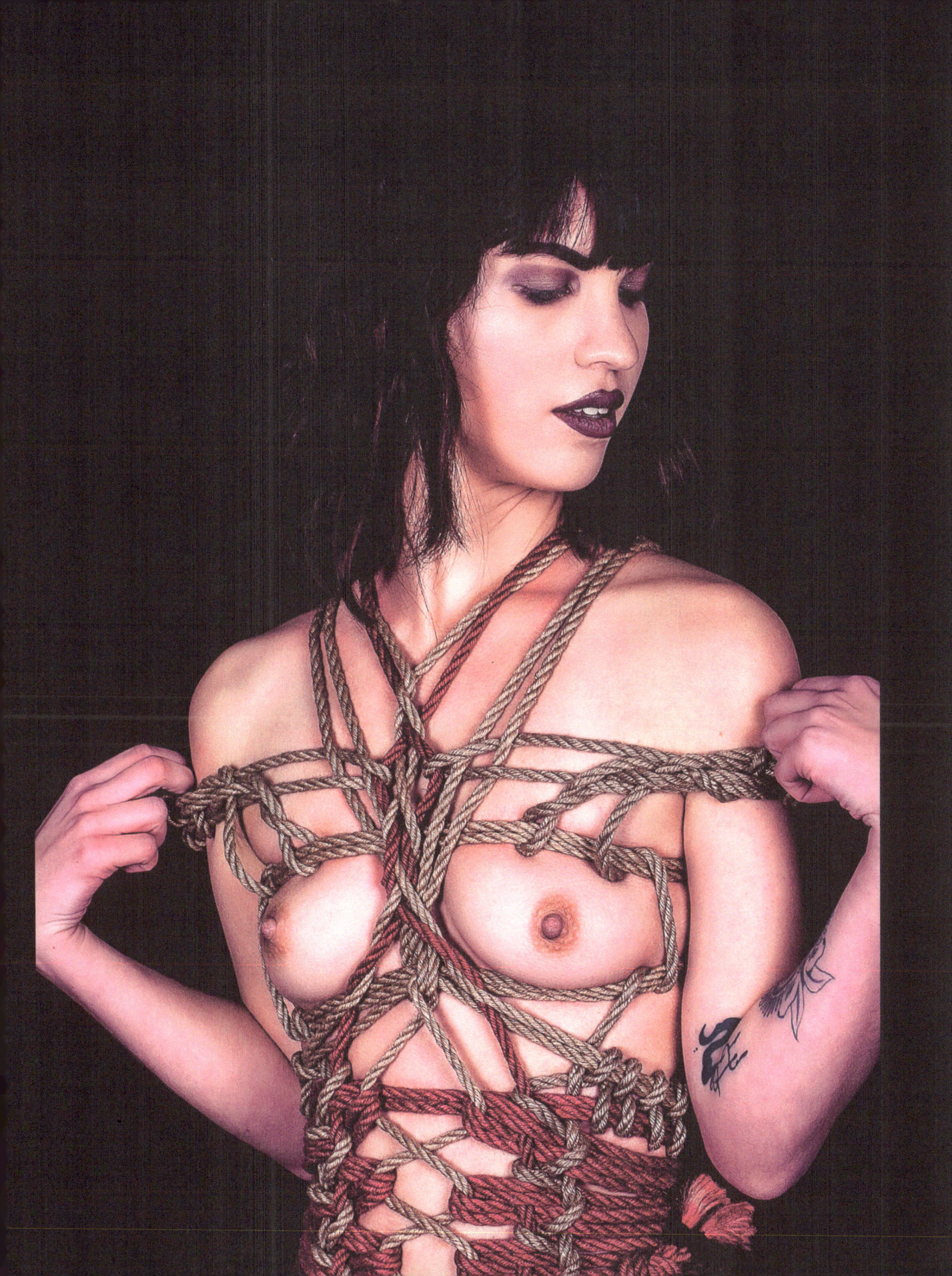

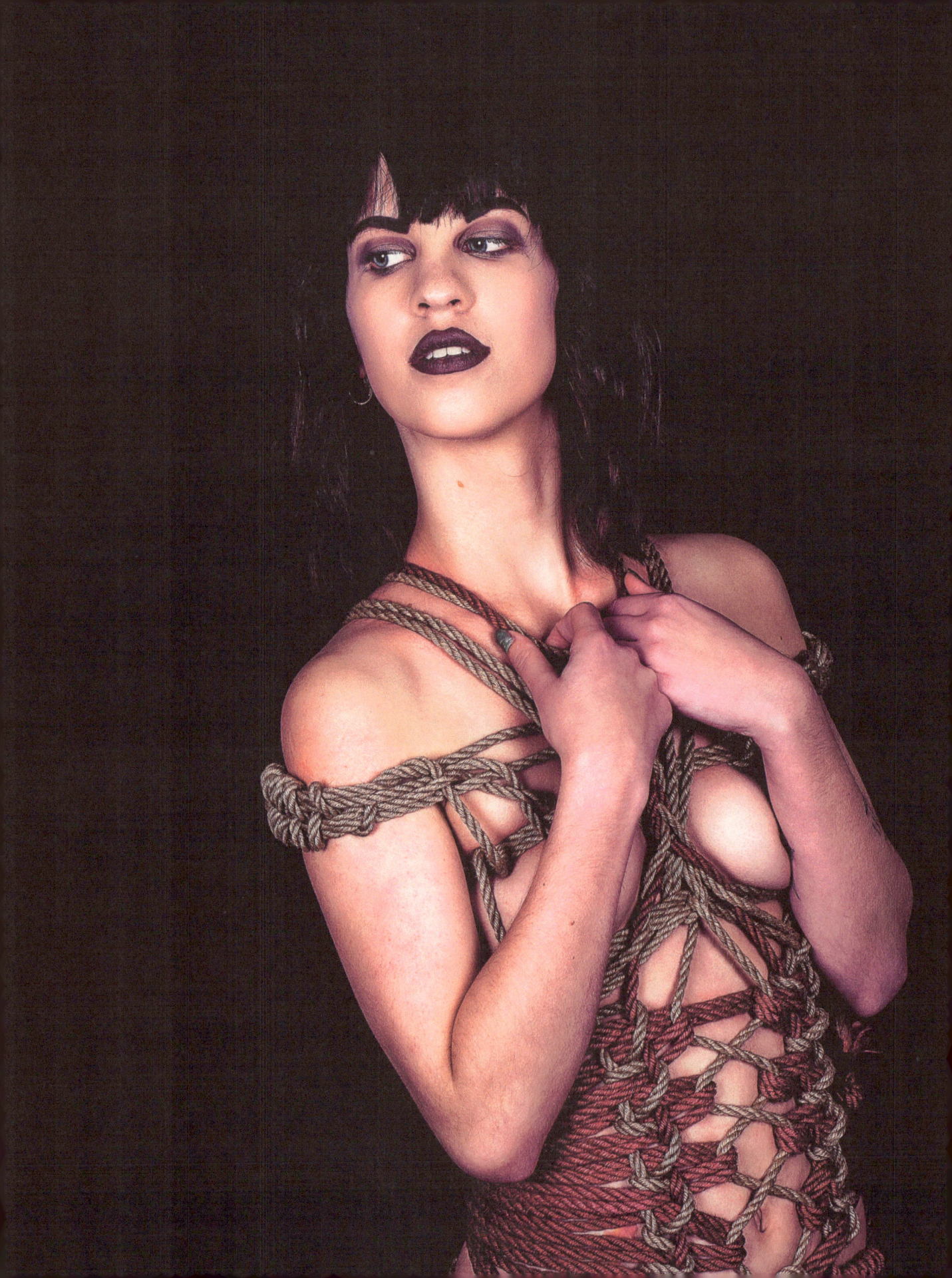

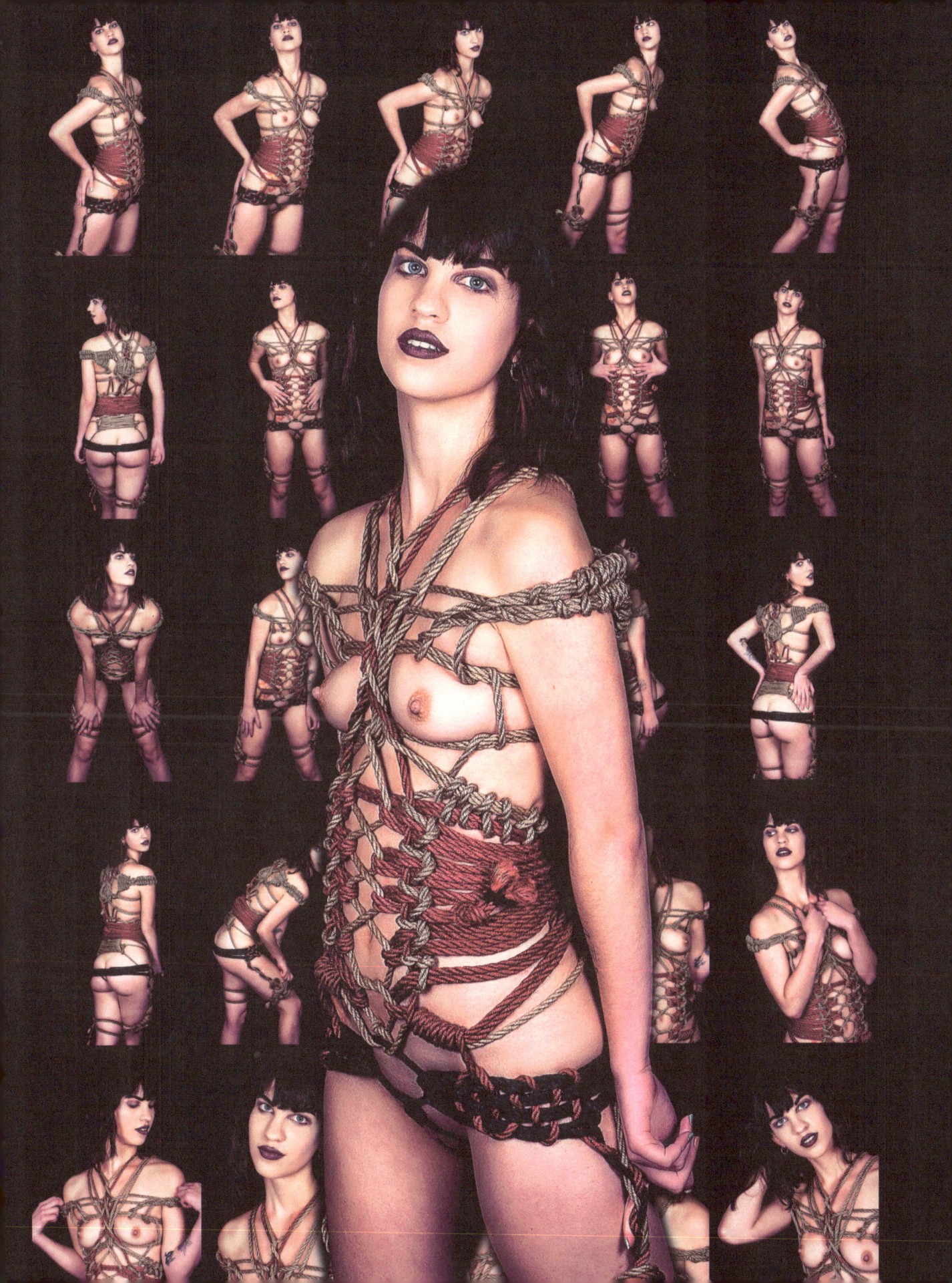

Miss Claws

I've been very lucky. Every person who
I have tied up has become good friends
of mine. I love each and everyone of
them.

Even when they forget to fill out the Q &
A section.

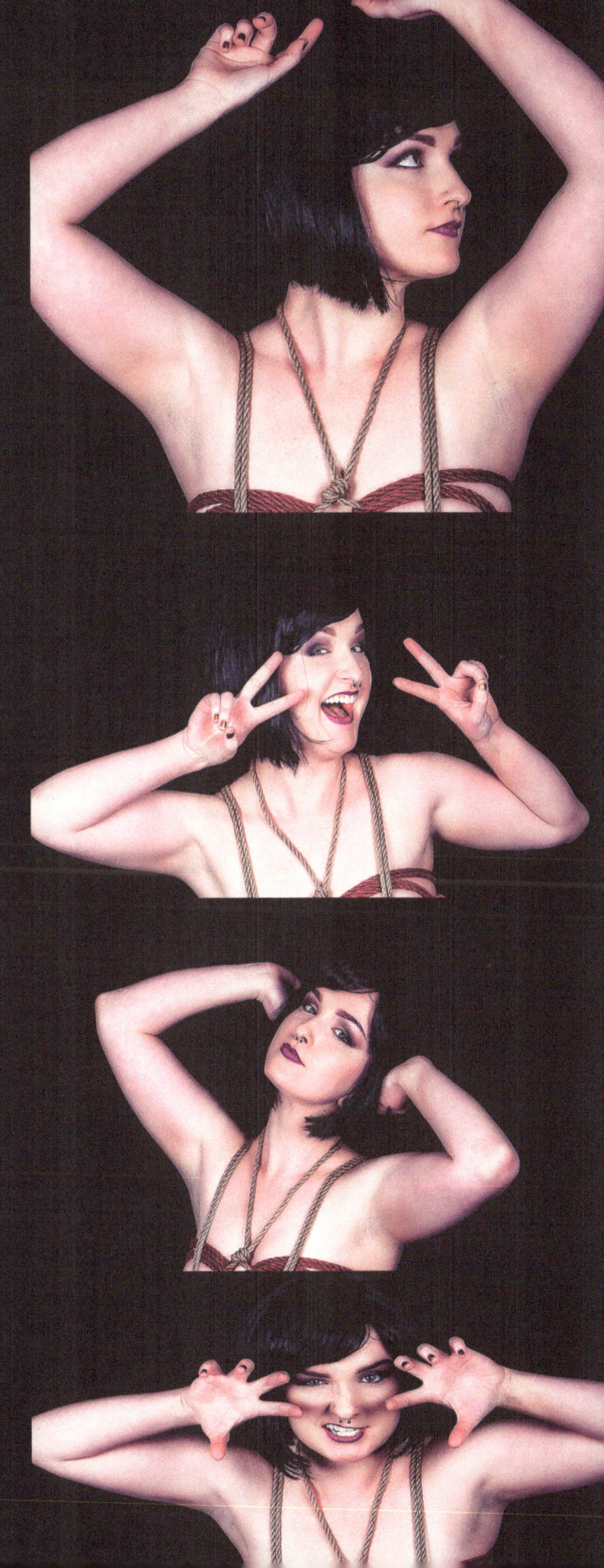

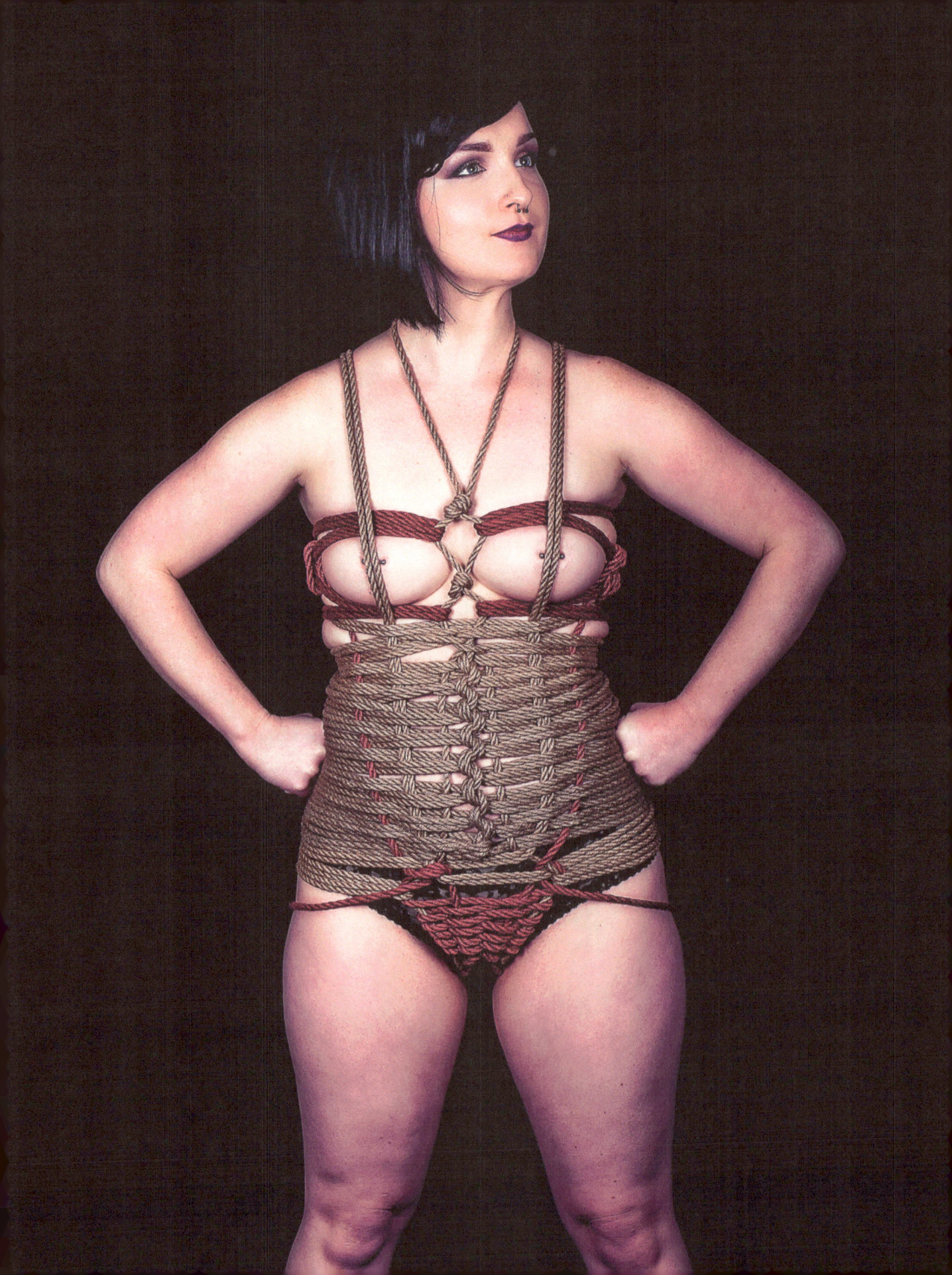

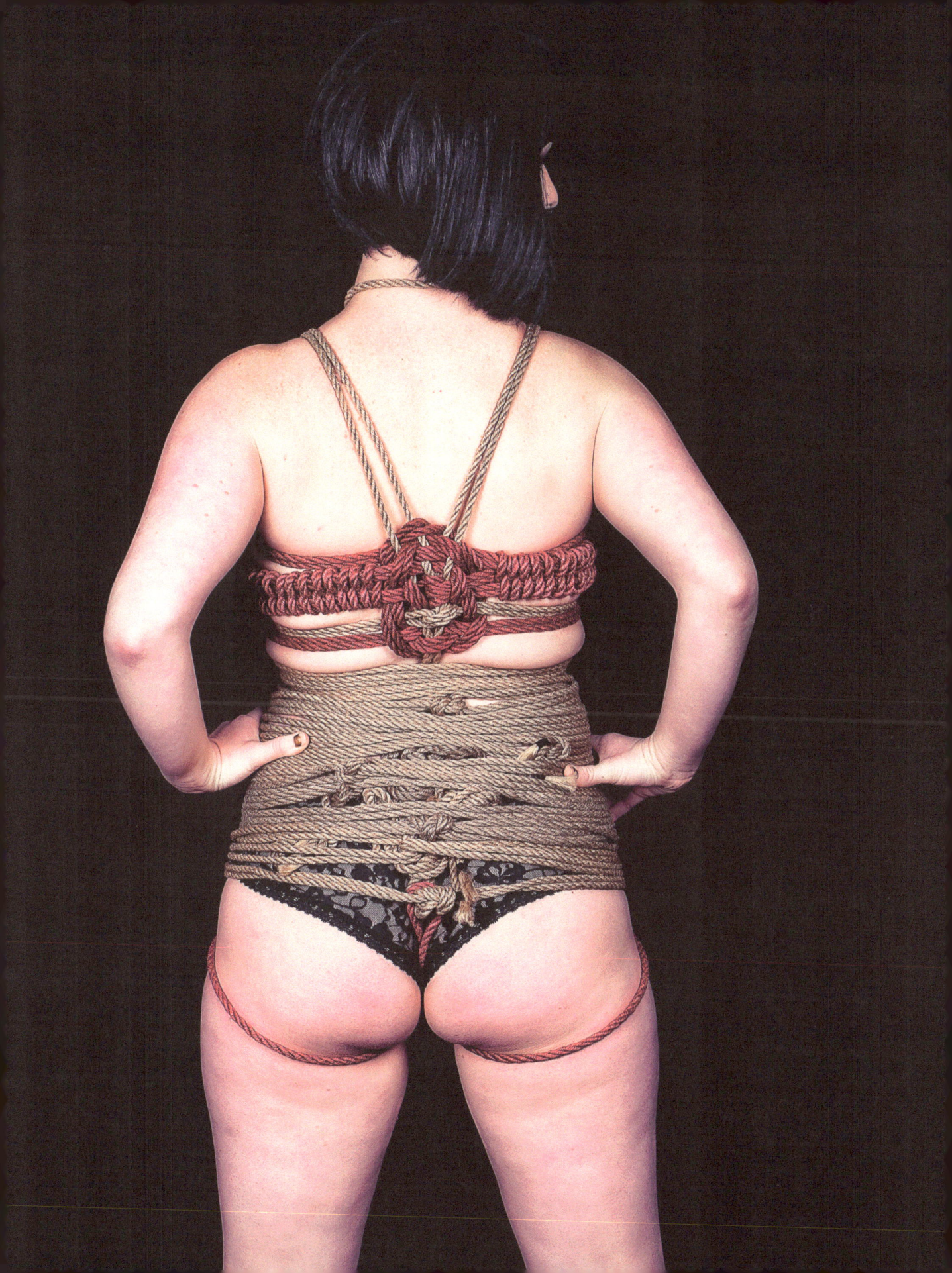

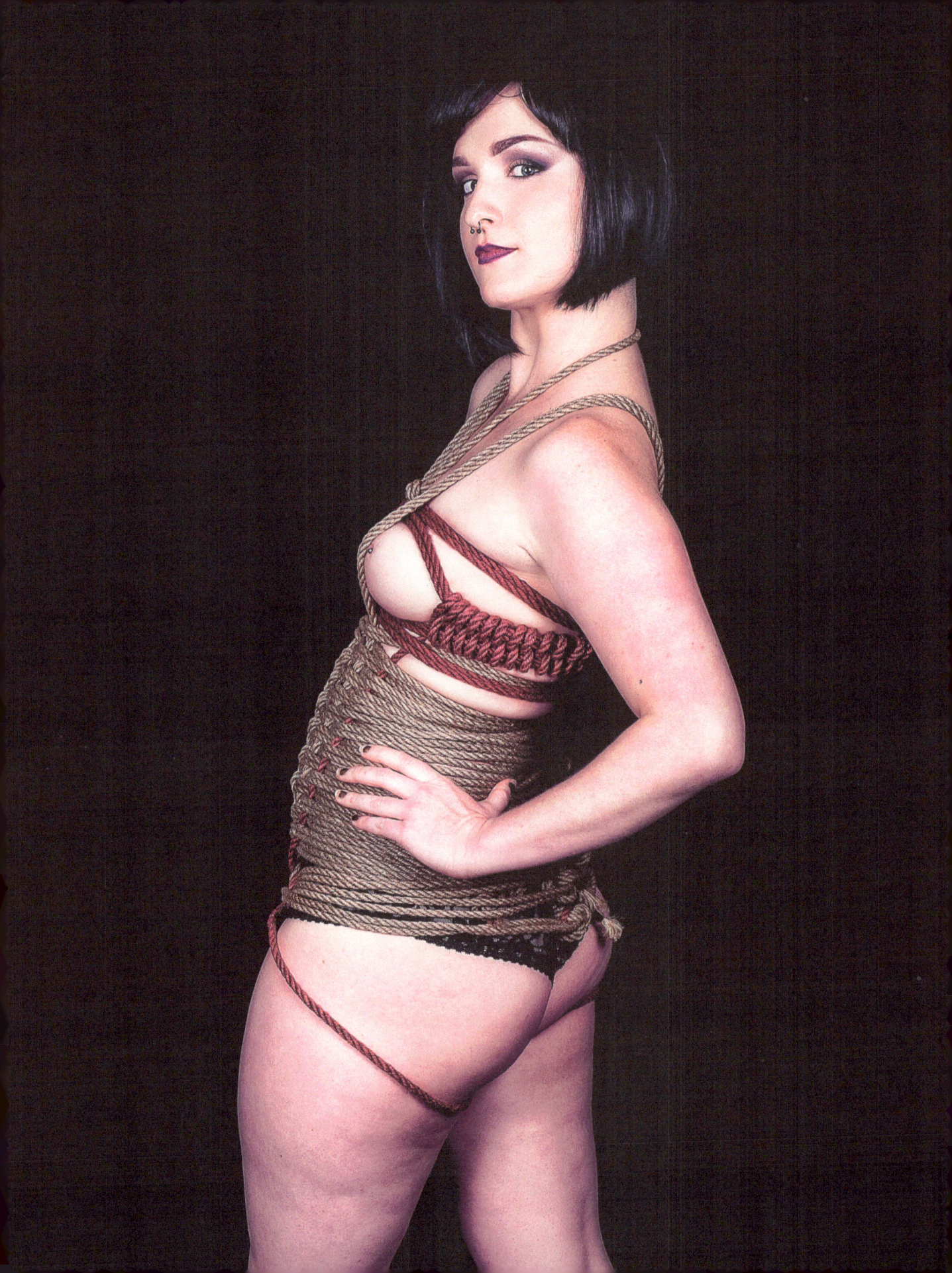

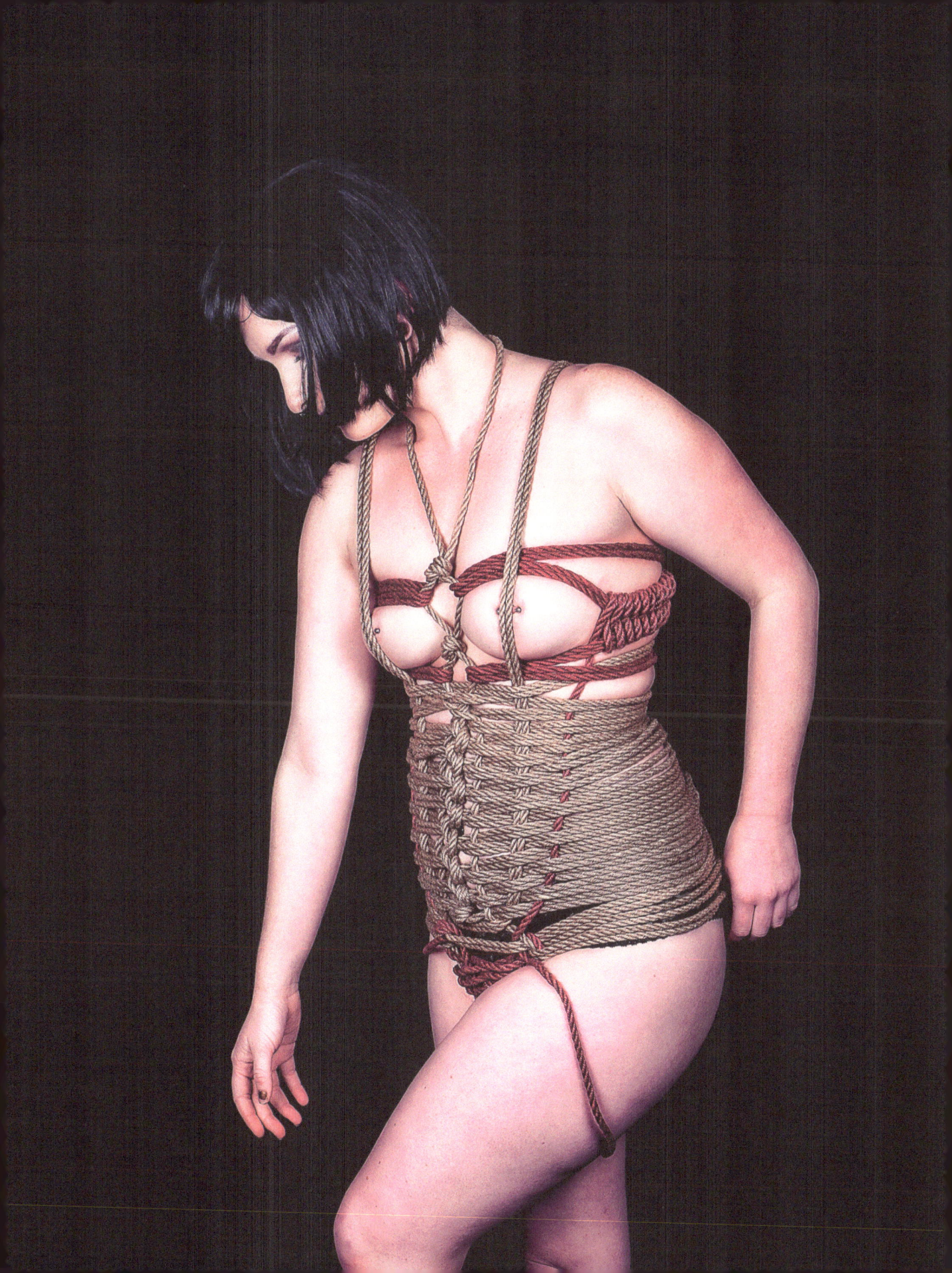

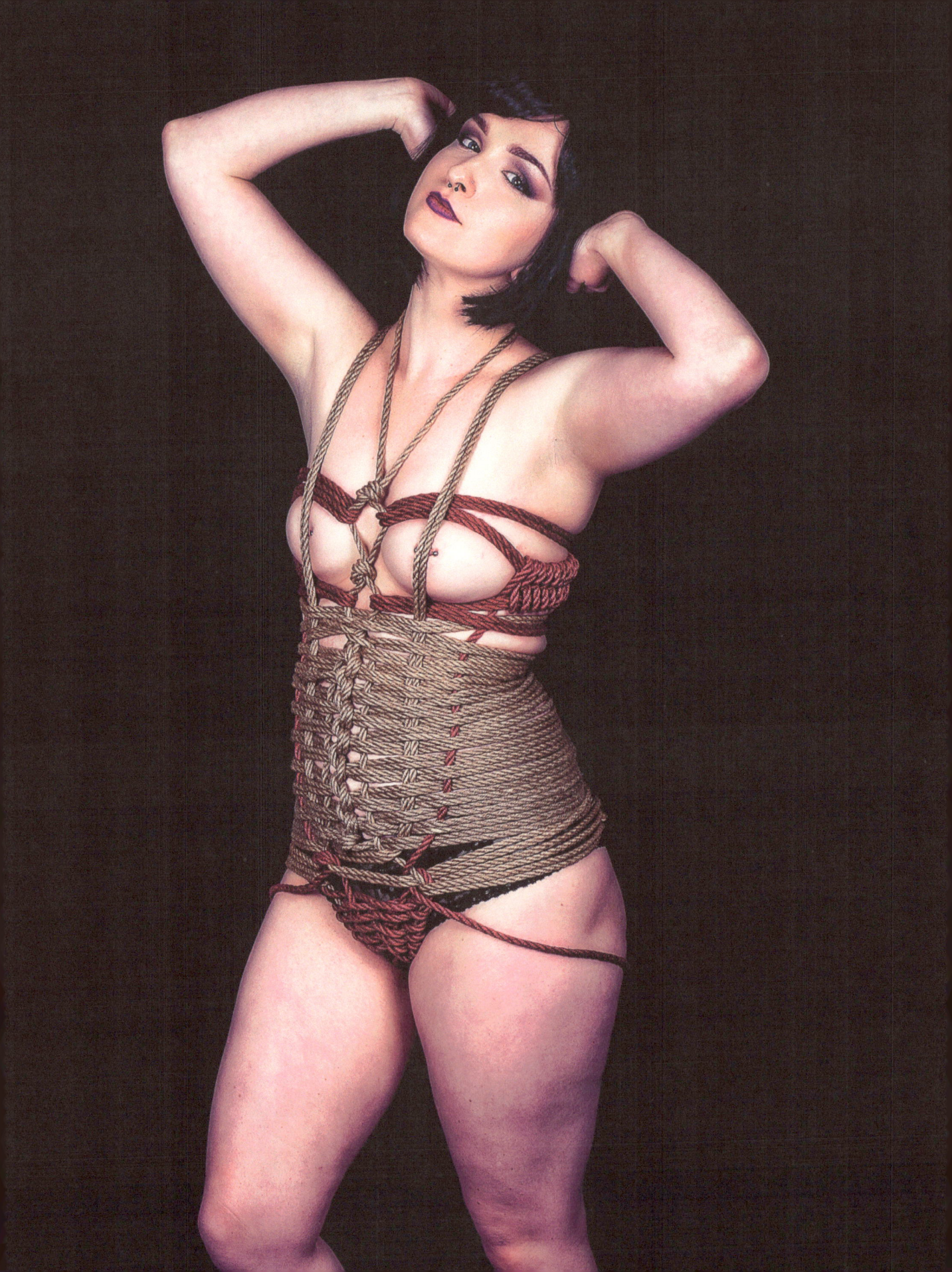

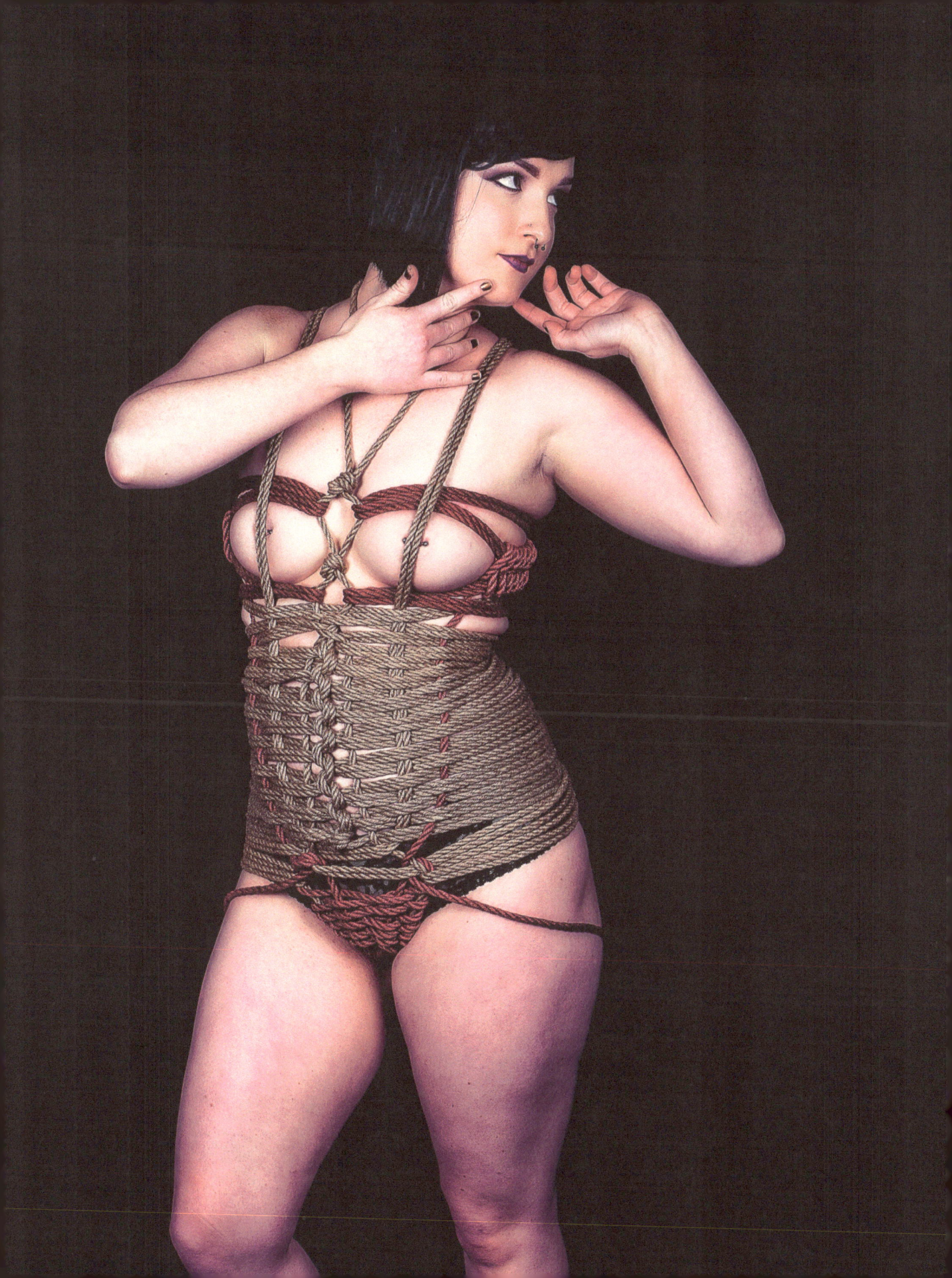

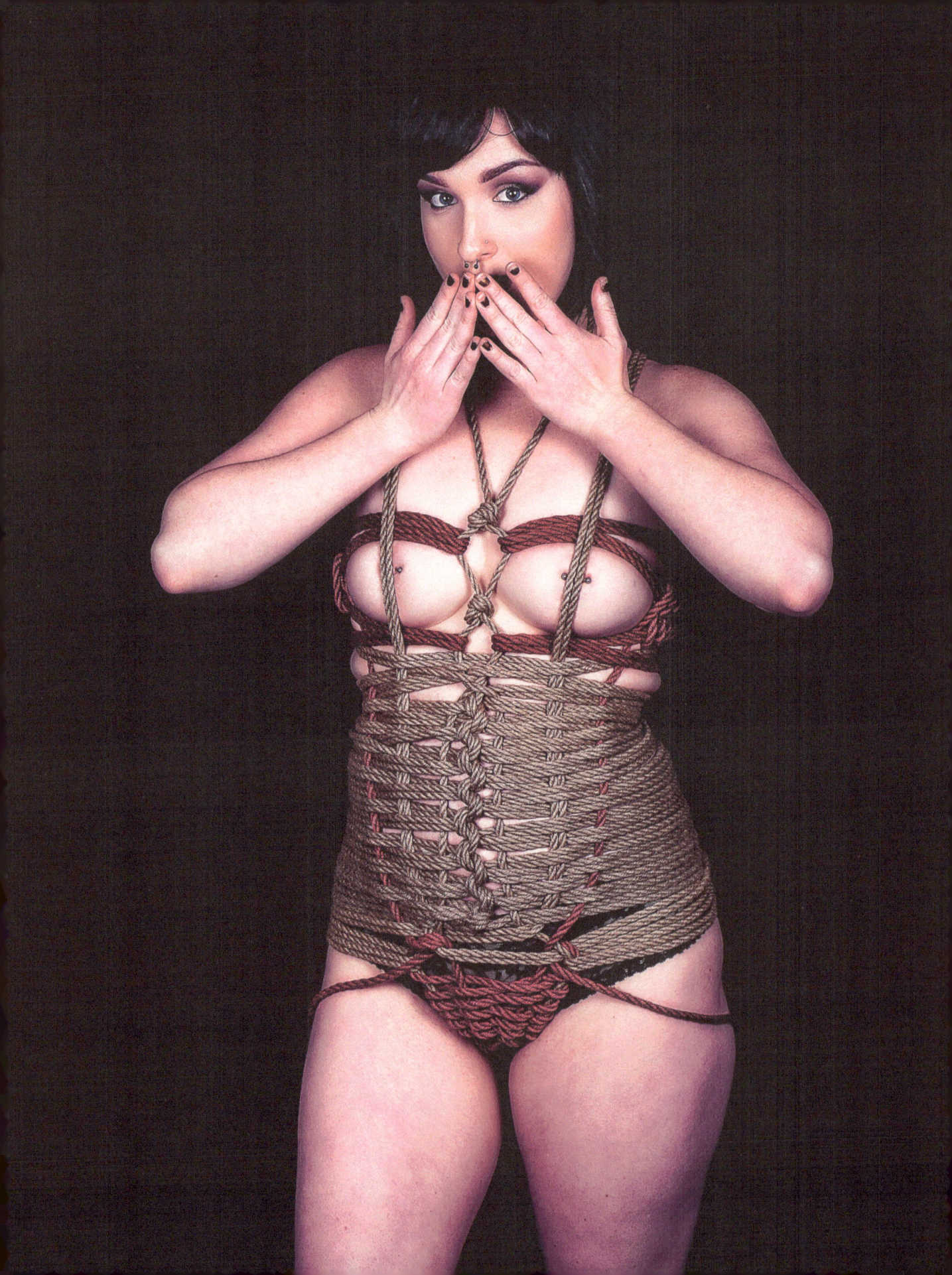

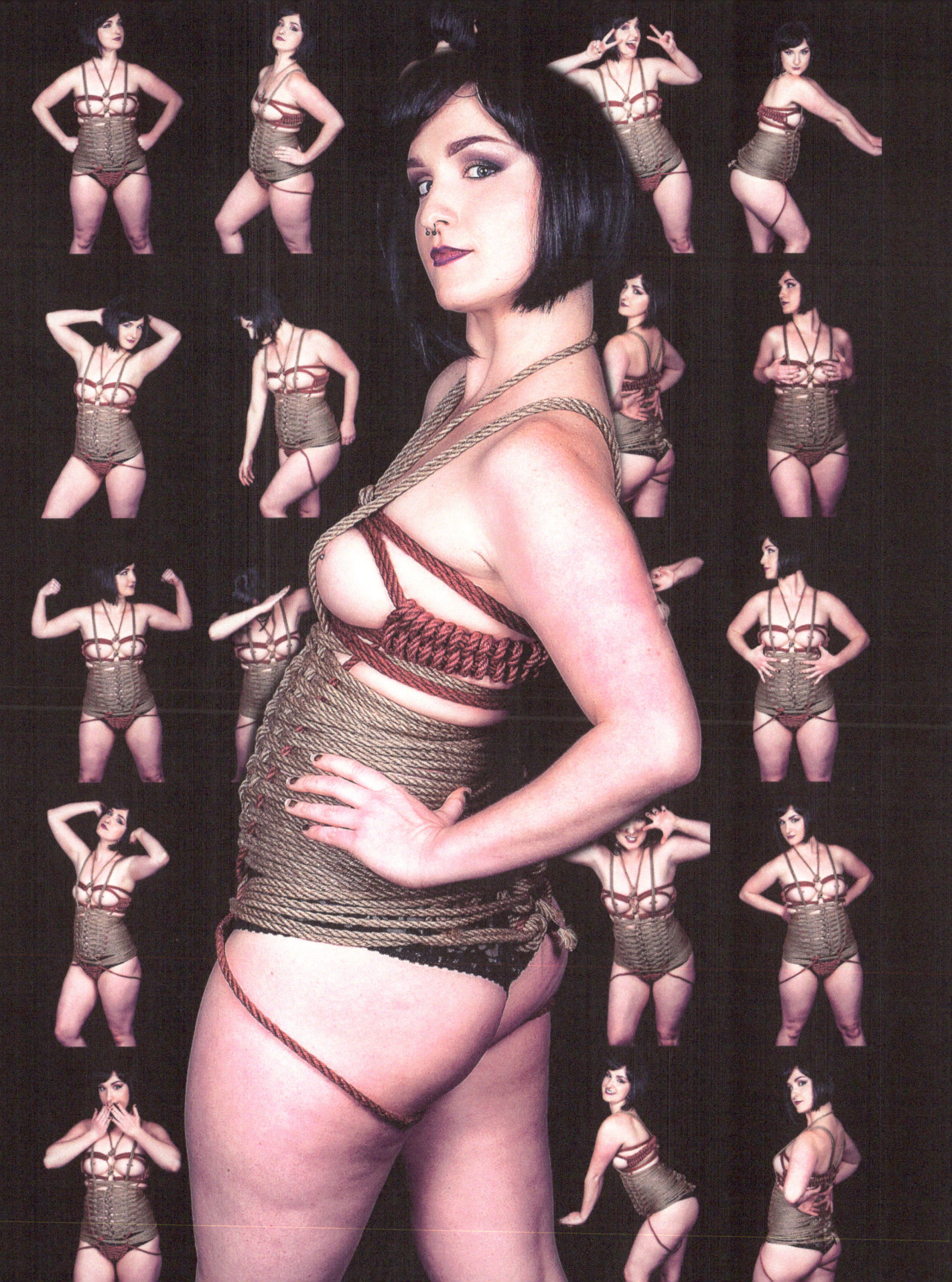

No How-to?

There are so many resources out there for learning how to do bondage. I may very well do a how-to book in the future myself. This book is more about inspiring creativity. Breaking the ice. My way of saying "Hi there!"

I hope everyone reading this book has seen at least one thing that they want to try. I'd love to see what you can do! You'll find my email address in the resources section of this book so please feel free to contact me. Remember: Be safe and have fun!

About the Author

Mr. Richards has been in involved in the BDSM community since the early 2000's. While versed in many different kinks and fetishes, He has always had a special connection with bondage. Not satisfied with just simply tying someone up he began researching different ways. Their histories and forms. Different ropes, accessories. Anything he could read or watch he did.

As almost a separate part of his life he took up photography back in 2011. Simple things mostly; landscape, portraits, model portfolios. One day he realized he could combine his love of photography and his love of bondage. So begins his journey into Art Bondage. It is an adventure he is well prepared for and willing to show others the way.

Based in the Nashville, TN area he teaches classes to groups and one-on-one. Married to a beautiful woman who has been in the BDSM community for even longer than he has. They have been together since 2006 and still going strong. Believe it or not, he is not a model himself.

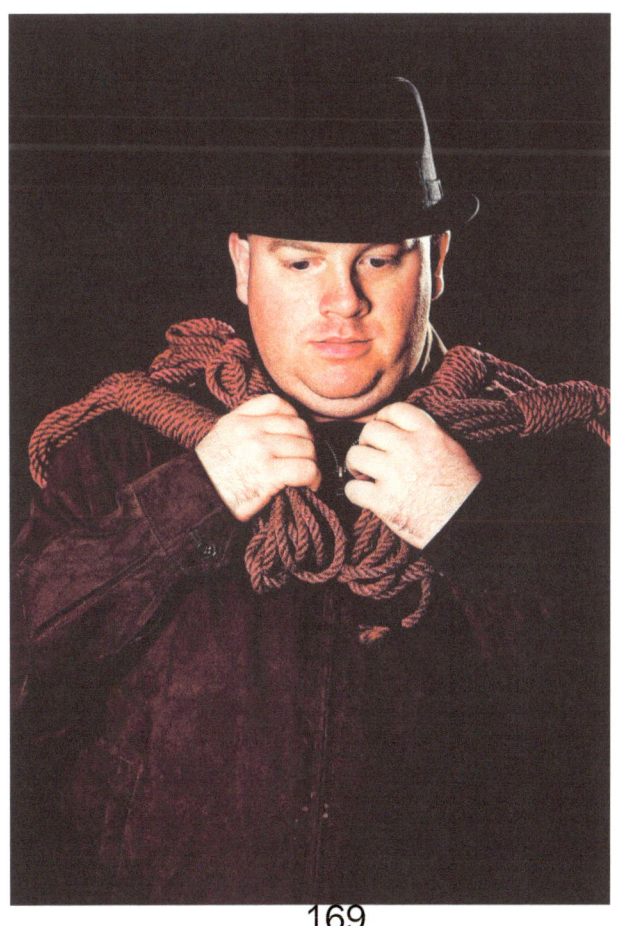

Resources

Online Resources

http://www.fetlife.com
An online community for kinksters. Sort of like Facebook but kinky.

Top 5 suppliers of bondage rope and accessories:
http://www.mynawashi.com/
https://www.twistedmonk.com/
http://www.jaderope.com/
http://www.omegajute.com/
https://www.knotandrope.com

Bondage Instruction:
http://www.knottyboys.com/
http://www.japaneseropeart.com/
(please research more past these two pages. This is intended as just a starting point.

Other Books

These are great books to use. There are more out there, these are just my personal favorites.

- Complete Shibari series by Douglas Kent
- Shibari you can use by Lee Harrington
- Nawanano by Kinoko Hajime
- The Beauty of Kinbaku by Master "K"
- Decorative Fusion Knots by J.D. Lenzen
- The Seductive Art of Japanese Bondage by Midori
- Showing you the Ropes by Two Knotty Boys

Glossary of Terms

- Aftercare: Means to take care of the bottom after a scene. Every bottom is different and will require different kinds of aftercare. For bondage in particular this could mean warming up a bottom that got too cold, applying lotion, cleaning off fibers, making sure the bottom is stable before letting them stand on their own.
- Anal Hook: A metal hook shaped device inserted anally to give a different anchor point for bondage. Can have different sizes and shapes.
- Bad Pain: A term to mean any injury or pain that was not intended or consented to.
- Bakushi: A shorten form of Kibakushi commonly used to refer to a Bondage Master.
- BDSM: As an acronym is means "Bondage and Discipline, Sadism and Masochism" but is used to mean most any of the various forms of sexual activity that falls beyond the scope of vanilla activity.
- Bight: Technically the center of a bend in a rope. Most commonly used to mean the center of a length of rope when folded in half.
- Bondage: Restraining a person. Could be by rope, chain, handcuffs, scarves, etc.
- Bottom: The person "receiving" in an activity. For bondage this would be the person being tied up.
- Breast Bondage: The act of tying the breasts in a way that restricts them or causes them to bulge out. Typically used to restrict the blood flow to increase sensation.
- Bunny: The person being tied up. Not necessarily a person belonging to the BDSM community.
- Consent: Permission to do something.
- Dom: A person who identifies as the Dominant member of a D/s relationship
- Domme: Although "Dom" is technically correct to mean both male and female it is typically used to mean male, so Domme is used to mean a female Dom.
- EMT Shears: Scissors used in the emergency medical fields. Will cut through just about anything.
- Fetish: Sexual desire that is linked to a particular object, body part, action, etc.
- Good Pain: Pain that is consensual and serves a purpose.
- Hemp: A natural fiber from the cannabis plant.
- Hojojutsu: The traditional Japanese art of restraining a person using cord or rope.

174

- Japanese Silk: Raw silk harvested in Japan.
- Jojoba Oil: An oil extracted from the seeds of a shrub found in America.
- Jute: Rough fiber from the stems of a tropical plant.
- Kinbaku: Literally "Tight Binding". Japanese erotic bondage.
- Kinbakushi: Bondage Master
- Kink: Sexual preference that may be considered unusual.
- Lashing: In this context a way to secure the loose fibers at the end of a rope my wrapping them in a string or cord.
- Ligature Mark: The marks left behind by the rope after being bound.
- Safe Word: I pre-agreed upon word that signals the end of the scene or encounter. In media it is often portrayed as being a word completely out of context however "Red" is a fairly universally known Safe Word.
- Safe, sane and consensual: A phrase often used in the BDSM community as a credo to what BDSM is all about. It means that no matter what you are doing, even the more edgy kinks, you should always make sure it is done as safe as possible, that everyone involved is in their right mind and not under the influence of anything and that everyone involved not only has consented but has been given all the needed info for them to properly consent to.
- Scene: This typically means any BDSM related activity, sexual or not, that is performed in front of others. Scenes can have their own set of rules but the most important one to remember is that unless you've been told otherwise you should not assume you are invited to participate.
- Shibari: Literally "to tie".
- Sub(missive): A person who identifies as the submissive party in a D/s relationship.
- Suspension: Bondage involving suspending a person from a point above them so that they are suspended in the air.
- Switch: A person who feels they are both dominant and submissive and can switch between the two depending on the situation.
- Top: The person who is "giving" in a scene or other BDSM related situation. Often a Dom but not always.
- Whipping: In this context it is another way to bind together the loose strands at the end of a rope.

Connecting with the Author

Feel free to contact and connect with me. I would love to hear about your journey into the wonderful world of bondage. I look forward to hearing from you!

Email:
dragonseyeimages@gmail.com

Website:
http://www.dragonseyeimages.com

Fetlife:
https://fetlife.com/users/2167609

www.ingramcontent.com/pod-product-compliance
Lightning Source LLC
Chambersburg PA
CBHW050712180526
45159CB00003B/1011